Praise for The End of Conflict

"IT IS FINISHED! Or is it? We may be 'OK with God,' but not with our neighbor. Or boss. Or spouse. Or sibling. Or child. Yet, if the Gospel is about conflict serving redemption—and it is—then the pardon of the resurrection should result in the power for reconciliation here and now. With clarity, charity, and concision, Andy Johnson wrestles with and pins down 'how then shall we live' in the redeemed world so that love, forgiveness, and reconciliation become more than slogans; they become the substance of our very lives. And, that is the life worth living here and now."

Jeffery J. Ventrella, JD, PhD, Senior Counsel,
Senior Vice-President, Alliance Defending Freedom

"Andy Johnson's book is a compendium of teachings on the topic of conflict resolution. He draws from thinkers in philosophy, psychology, and theology. In addition to offering insights from his own life experience and thoughtful Bible study, Andy cares about people, and he wants to see people unified in truth and love. My prayer is for this book to help make that happen."

Sarah Sumner, PhD, Former Dean of A. W. Tozer Theological
Seminary and Author of *Leadership above the Line*

"This is the best book I have ever read about conflict and the associated issues. Andy has done a brilliant job sharing new insights through the scriptures, his own experience, and the resonance of a 'fictional' story that is weaved throughout. Comprehensive, creative, and enlightening. My understanding of 'the end of conflict' is forever changed."

Ron Price, Internationally recognized business advisor, speaker, and author

"*The End of Conflict* is a deftly written and much-needed theology of conflict. For those leaders who hope to squarely address the widespread condition of brokenness in our churches, *The End of Conflict* will go a long way to help them ready themselves for the battle."

Max Edwards, North American Conference Superintendent, Evangelical Methodist Church

"As a Superintendent of fifty-eight churches, I am recommending Andy and his material to pastors and leaders in the Pacific Conference. I'm looking forward to making his book, *The End of Conflict* available to each of our pastors. I know God has chosen to inspire and employ Andy for such a purpose as this."

Chris Nielson, Pacific Conference Superintendent, Evangelical Church

The End of Conflict

Resisting False Utopia in Hope of True Restoration

Andy Johnson

The End of Conflict: Resisting False Utopia in Hope of True Restoration
By Andy Johnson

For further information about speaking engagements, professional consultation, special bulk pricing, or other related inquiries, see the author's website at
www.restoration-consulting.com.

Cover Design: Cari Campbell, Cari Campbell Design
Interior Design: Shiloh Schroeder, Fusion Creative Works
Primary Editor: Kim Foster

Print ISBN: 978-0-9893390-0-1

Library of Congress Control Number: 2013908125

First Printing
Printed in the United States of America
Published by Restoration Publishing

Dedication

This book is dedicated to all those who are or have been neglected, oppressed, mistreated or abused, for whom this subject is anything but academic.

The Spirit of the Lord GOD is upon me,
because the LORD has anointed me
to bring good news to the poor;
he has sent me to bind up the brokenhearted,
to proclaim liberty to the captives,
and the opening of the prison to those who are bound;
to proclaim the year of the LORD's favor,
and the day of vengeance of our God;
to comfort all who mourn;
to grant to those who mourn in Zion—
to give them a beautiful headdress instead of ashes,
the oil of gladness instead of mourning,
the garment of praise instead of a faint spirit;
that they may be called oaks of righteousness,
the planting of the LORD, that he may be glorified.
(Isaiah 61:1–3)

Acknowledgments

There are no self-made men. I could not have written this book without the encouragement and support of the following:

First and foremost, I want to thank the Trinity for providing not only the basis of restored relationship for me in the cross, but also the means of drawing me back into a relationship with Them. Thank you Abba for being a perfect Father whose love for me makes all the difference. Thank you Jesus for your incarnation, suffering, and sacrifice for me. Thank you Holy Spirit for remaining with me even when I have broken Your heart. Thank You for uniting me to Christ and in Him to You for all eternity!

Sherri, you've been with me through thick and thin. When nearly all others forsook me, you remained my most faithful friend and support. I truly don't know where or what I would be without you. Your love and acceptance have meant the world to me. Jordyn, Meaghan, and Abbie, you have been a joy to parent. You all remind me of how much God loves us as His children, something I desperately need to understand. You have made our lives so meaningful. I hope that the principles in this book will someday help you move the ball forward in the next generation. Jen, you've been my constant companion since childhood. Together, we have been able to navigate, though imperfectly, through many difficult waters in this life. I'm so grateful to God for giving you to me.

Pastor David Rosales, you challenged me twenty-five years ago to live this Christian life, and showed me that lordship was not only possible, but also required for following Christ. Thanks to those of you who took the time to read the original manuscript and provide me with good feedback.

Ron, Howard, Carris, Jim, Phil, Sarah, Max, and Jeff, you have all given valuable feedback on the original manuscript.

Thank you, Maryanna Young and your team, for helping me realize this dream. Special thanks to Kim Foster for your effort to help me say what I wanted to say and say it well. Thanks to Cari Campbell for a cover design that connects so well with this theme. Thanks to Shiloh Schroeder for a great interior design.

To those who have made the contents of this book necessary for the maintenance of my own sanity, according to God's ability to bring good out of distress, I say thank you. Without the pain that I have experienced, I fear I would never have been able to empathize as deeply as I often do with those who weep. What you did not consciously mean for evil, God most certainly meant for good. My prayers and thoughts remain with you: that God would someday restore things this side of glory.

Contents

Prologue

The Contemporary Crisis in Evangelicalism

Christianity, at the beginning of the twenty-first century, has the following troubling tendencies that are pertinent to the topic of conflict and conflict resolution:[1]

Low View of Scripture and Biblical Illiteracy

The contemporary evangelical church, in many segments, is in no less than a crisis related to biblical truth. Many believers have had their confidence in Scripture seriously undermined by so-called Christian scholarship. Many students at Christian colleges have experienced an erosion of the faith they once held dear at the hands of trusted professors and the overall influence of academia. The foundational place of the Word of God as the sole ground of faith and practice is being shaken in our day. With the removal of the authoritative place of Holy Scripture, we are left as easy marks for the philosophy of the day.

In addition to the low view of Scriptural authority and a less-than-adequate ability on the part of the average evangelical to rightly interpret

1. For further understanding of current challenges, see Stott, *The Radical Disciple: Some Neglected Aspects of Our Calling*. Stott, in his final book before his death, prophetically expressed his concern over the presence of four challenges to the evangelical church. He identified pluralism, materialism, ethical relativism, and narcissism as the biggest challenges facing the church in the future.

the Bible, there is a looming problem of biblical illiteracy. "Simply put, most professing Christians do not possess a sound and coherent understanding of the Bible, beginning with sound doctrine and general Biblical history."[2] "Researchers George Gallup and Jim Castelli put the problem squarely: 'Americans revere the Bible—but, by and large, they don't read it. And because they don't read it, they have become a nation of biblical illiterates.' How bad is it? Researchers tell us that it's worse than most could imagine."[3]

Naturalism (Antisupernaturalism)

We live in a world of naturalistic explanations. The existence of things beyond our five senses is highly questioned. We have exchanged our Christian worldview, which is inherently supernatural, for the supposed certainty of science. Though there is no conflict between honest science and the revelation of God in creation and Holy Scripture, scientism is another story. Scientism exalts the fallible practice of science to an infallible place as the sole determiner of truth among us. Especially in the West, we seek doctors, not healing; we invest money in our retirement accounts, not in the kingdom; we trust in politics and not in the God we say we trust as printed on our currency.

In addition to this naturalistic bent in our culture, the church in many segments operates without the recognition of the need for the Holy Spirit. We have substituted the power of the Spirit through the proclamation of the Word and worship of God for a myriad of programs and strategies to create the same results.

There is no substitute, however, for a supernatural encounter with the living God. There is no human methodology that can bring about true transformation after the image of Christ. Nonetheless, we cling to our orthodox doctrines, divorced from life-changing power. All the while, the

---

2. Henry B. Smith, "Biblical Illiteracy," *Bible and Spade* (Winter, 2008), www.biblearchaeology.org /post /2008/09/ Biblical-illiteracy.aspx.

3. Albert Mohler, "The Scandal of Biblical Illiteracy: It's Our Problem" (June 29, 2004), www.albertmohler. com/2004/06/29/the-scandal-of-biblical-illiteracy-its-our-problem-2/.

world around us into which we are called perishes as we continue to be absorbed with our separation from it.

Overoptimistic Eschatology

It is imperative that we know where we are, historically speaking. God, who created all things, is outside of time. Nonetheless, He has created the world in which we live, a world that includes time. History is progressively unfolding in accordance with God's master plan. One of the issues that contributes to the misunderstanding of conflict is an overrealized eschatology. This problem confuses the "not yet" with the "now" and moves aspects of the kingdom to come into the present paradigm. D. A. Carson properly distinguished these two phases of redemptive history:

> Already the kingdom has dawned and the Messiah is reigning, already the crucial victory has been won, already the final resurrection of the dead has begun in the resurrection of Jesus, already the Holy Spirit has been poured out on the church as the down payment of the promised inheritance and the first fruits of the eschatological harvest of blessings. Nevertheless, the kingdom has not yet come in its consummated fullness, death still exercises formidable powers, sin must be overcome, and opposing powers of darkness war against us with savage ferocity. The new heaven and the new earth have not yet put in an appearance. Maintaining this balance is crucial to the church's maturity.[4]

So, the kingdom is *now* and *not yet.* With the first advent of Christ, the kingdom began to emerge. It will not be brought to consummation, however, apart from His second advent.

The early church misunderstood the nature of this *not yet* aspect of the kingdom. In fact, the temptation to suggest a premature realization of the perfection to come has been present in both the church and secular society for two millennia. In 1967, Thomas Molnar astutely referred to

4. D. A. Carson, *Showing the Spirit: A Theological Exposition of 1 Corinthians,* 12–14 (Grand Rapids, MI: Baker Academic, 1996), 16.

this inordinate desire for utopia as "the perennial heresy."[5] This supposed state is founded not on the truth of Scripture but on alternative supports, such as humanism, social engineering, and various political constructs. Utopian beliefs blind adherents to the reality of the present unrealized state of the created order. They overstate the positive aspects of the coming of the kingdom with the initial advent, death and resurrection of Christ. They fail to recognize the groaning of the creation for the full redemption to come.

Many contemporary theologies lack this tension. The *now* for many has become the venue by which *we* bring the kingdom into reality. Although a resurgence in understanding the need for social justice as an essential component to the fulfillment of the Great Commission is a welcome development, moving the mission of the church to be social justice only or even primarily is a concern. One writer commented,

> A good number of recent books have argued from these issues [related to the cultural mandate] to the conclusion that it is the mission of the church to provide health care, repair housing slums, plant trees, fund disease research, and clean streets—in short, to work toward the perfect, shalom-filled new heavens and new earth that God intends there to be at the end . . . understood within a certain way of thinking that makes perfect sense. But if you understand these issues in a different way—that God and not we will build the new heavens and new earth—well, that changes everything.[6]

We are citizens of the kingdom of heaven. We pray that His kingdom will come on earth as it is in heaven. We bring kingdom values to this present life and seek to make a difference in the world. However, thinking and acting as if we are able to bring heaven to earth is another story.

5. Thomas Molnar, *Utopia: The Perennial Heresy* (New York: Sheed and Ward, 1967).

6. Kevin DeYoung and Greg Gilbert, *What Is the Mission of the Church? Making Sense of Social Justice, Shalom, and the Great Commission* (Wheaton, IL: Crossway Books, 2011), 197.

Antinomianism (Cheap Grace, Cheap Forgiveness)

David Pawson wrote in the prologue to his book *Once Saved, Always Saved?* the following account of an interaction with a man on a train:

> While writing this book I took a train to London to visit my publisher. The last halt to pick up passengers was at Clapham Junction. A man boarded my carriage at the far end, sat down, stared at me for some minutes before walking down the aisle and taking a seat facing mine. As I recall, the conversation went like this:
>
> "I think I recognize you. Are you a preacher?"
>
> "Yes. Where would you have seen me?"
>
> "Fifteen years ago, someone brought me to Guildford to hear a preacher and I think it was you."
>
> "It almost certainly was. Are you a Christian?"
>
> "Yes. [pause] Can I ask you something?"
>
> "I can't guarantee an answer, but what's the question?"
>
> "Well, it's like this—I've left my wife and I'm now living with another woman."
>
> "Why did you leave your wife?"
>
> "Because I met this other woman and fell in love with her."
>
> "So what do you want to know?"
>
> "If I get properly divorced and marry this other woman, would that put it right in God's sight?"
>
> "No, I'm afraid it wouldn't."
>
> "Then what would?"
>
> "Leaving this woman and returning to your wife."

"I thought you'd say that."

"I believe it's what Jesus would say if you asked him."

This produced a silence between us. By now the train was slowing down for Waterloo and I realized I probably only had a minute or two more with him. I wanted to kindle the fear of the Lord that is the beginning of wisdom, so I reopened the conversation with:

"You have a difficult choice to make."

"What's that, then?"

"You can either live with this woman for the rest of this life or with Jesus for all the next, but you can't do both."

His eyes filled with tears but he jumped on to the platform and disappeared among the crowd. I felt a little of what Jesus must have felt when the rich young ruler left him. I prayed he would never be able to forget what I told him until he had repented.

But was I right to say what I did? Was I telling him the truth or trying to frighten him with a lie? What he really wanted was an assurance that his sin would not affect his salvation. That I could not give him.[7]

Antinomianism derives from the Greek word for law, *nomos*. An antinomian is someone who is against (anti) law, or in other words, lawless. This philosophy, albeit indirectly, teaches what we do doesn't matter. We are saved by grace alone, simply praying a one-time prayer to receive Christ. Following that, how we live, whether we actually make Christ Lord of our lives, is completely optional. This is the cheap grace Dietrich Bonhoeffer observed in the Lutheran church of his day. This same cheap grace is rampant in our day.

Antinomianism contributes to the creation of a sub-Christian culture devoid of personal responsibility. It undermines the healthy place of re-

7. David Pawson, *Once Saved, Always Saved? A Study in Perseverance and Inheritance* (London: Houghton and Stoughton Ltd., 1996), 1–2.

pentance and honest confession in the life of the believer and instead substitutes a legal fiction. The presence of cheap grace and cheap forgiveness, however, permeates the Christian community today.

Moralistic Therapeutic Deism

Christian Smith and Melina Denton first coined this term to describe the belief system of today's youth culture. Many American teenagers within the church hold to a theology that includes the following:

1. A God exists who created and ordered the world and watches over human life on earth.
2. God wants people to be good, nice, and fair to each other, as taught in the Bible and by most world religions.
3. The central goals of life are to be happy and to feel good about oneself.
4. God does not need to be particularly involved in one's life except when He is needed to resolve a problem.
5. Good people go to heaven when they die.[8]

This theological mind-set directly affects one's approach to conflict. For the teen culture, as well as many adults, life is about being happy, not having problems, and getting along with everybody else. Being nice to others includes not offending others by holding strong religious beliefs. In this paradigm, there is little room for accountability, confrontation, or repentance.

The New Universalism

Universalism, the idea all will be saved in the end, has always had a small following by some on the margins of the Christian church. It has

---

8. Christian Smith, "On 'Moralistic Therapeutic Deism' as U.S. Teenagers' Actual, Tacit, De Facto Religious Faith," paper, accessed April 4, 2013, http://www.ptsem.edu/uploadedFiles/School_of_Christian_Vocation_and_Mission/Institute_for_Youth_Ministry/Princeton_Lectures/Smith-Moralistic.pdf. See Smith and Lundquist Denton, *Soul Searching: The Religious and Spiritual Lives of America's Teenagers.*

been experiencing a resurgence in recent days. Richard Foster was asked to consider a new book on this topic. He made the following comment:

> Universalism is growing in popularity today, for it fits neatly into the modern non-judgmental live-and-let-live mood of our culture. And it has been a minor (very minor) current in Christian history. So I thought I'd see how persuasive the arguments might be in this new attempt to dust off an old heresy. How utterly disappointing! The same tired arguments and the same weak sentimentality about God's mercy winning out over God's justice.[9]

This new universalism, which is the same as old universalism, fits perfectly in our culture of tolerance. Contemporary Christian musicians sing about it:

> atheists and charlatans,
> and communists and lesbians,
> and even ol' Pat Robertson
> Oh God, He loves us all
> Catholic or Protestant,
> terrorist or president,
> everybody, everybody loved, loved, loved, oh
> la la la la la[10]

Popular authors write about it:

> [G]iven enough time, everybody will turn to God and find themselves in the joy and peace of God's presence. . . .There is a long tradition of Christians who believe that God will ultimately restore everything and everybody.[11]

---

9. Richard Foster, "Eternity," *Knowing and Doing: A Teaching Quarterly for Discipleship of Heart and Mind* (Springfield, VA: C. S. Lewis Institute, Fall 2003), www.cslewisinstitute .org/webfm_send/449.

10. Michael Gungor, "God is Not a White Man," 2008, accessed April 13, 2013, http://www.lyricsmania .com/god_is_not_a_ white _man_lyrics _gungor.html.

11. Rob Bell, *Love Wins: A Book about Heaven, Hell, and the Fate of Every Person Who Ever Lived* (New York: HarperCollins, 2011), 107.

By stressing the universal love of God without a biblical theology to undergird the various ways in which that universal love will not, in the end, save everyone, we have created a culture that is purely and unconditionally accepting.[12] Acceptance is a good thing when properly understood within a biblical worldview.[13] Pure and unconditional acceptance, outside of that context, is merely more propaganda from the father of lies.

The Perfect Storm

The convergence of these six factors has produced an evangelical environment that is fertile soil for today's common view of conflict. We now live in a world no longer governed by the authoritative truth of God's Word, where human beings without divine supernatural power can change themselves, where believers sincerely think it is the church's responsibility to usher in the fullness of the kingdom, where personal responsibility and personal holiness in conduct are viewed as unnecessary baggage on our journey of self-discovery, where being "nice" is of utmost importance, and where we now believe that we all win anyway. The archaic notions of ownership of sin, of sincere repentance, of contrite confession, of just restitution, and the hard work of mortification, putting to death the deeds of the flesh by the power of the Spirit, seem out of place.

Despite our modern attempts to alter it, the path of wisdom remains the same. God calls us to follow Him out of obedience to His Word and Spirit, to be salt and light in this present evil world, and to live responsibly and ethically as evidence of our love for Him, so in the end, we will receive the prize that belongs to those who have persevered to the end.

12. Carl Rogers is famous for the practice of "unconditional positive regard," which means people are to simply be loved and accepted as they are. There is never room within a truly Rogerian context to question the ethics of anyone's behavior. There really is no right and no wrong. Everyone is affirmed as they "do what is right in their own eyes" (Judg. 17:6).

13. The Scripture teaches us the inherent value and dignity of all people. All people are worthy of being loved and respected, regardless of their behavior. Jesus modeled this loving treatment of others in His public ministry. While Jesus truly loved all people, He, by the same sincere love that desired what was in their best interest, called them to forsake their sins and to turn to Him in true repentance and faith. He loved them too much to leave them alone.

Introduction

Life Under the Sun

Again I saw all the oppressions that are done under the sun. And behold, the tears of the oppressed, and they had no one to comfort them! On the side of their oppressors there was power, and there was no one to comfort them. And I thought the dead who are already dead more fortunate than the living who are still alive. But better than both is he who has not yet been and has not seen the evil deeds that are done under the sun.

(Eccles. 4:1–3)

Looking at life "under the sun" can lead to despair. Life on earth is so marked by the presence of oppression and strife, at times, we can wish with the writer of Ecclesiastes that we were never born. This world is not the way it should be. Our lives are deeply impacted by the painful presence of conflict. The nations are shaped by defining struggles in each of their respective histories. Family systems for generations to come will bear the residue of past discord. None of us is immune to the effects of this pervasive reality. We were born into a world filled with interpersonal conflict and in the throes of its core clash with its Creator. The fall shapes our reality and makes us long for the *not yet.* Just think how conflict has shaped your spheres of life. How many unresolved conflicts have been instrumental in defining the contours of your life?

- Have you or a parent ever left a job or a location due to unresolved conflict?
- Have you or a loved one ever left a church body due to unresolved conflict?
- Have you or someone you love ever left a marriage due to the inability to resolve conflict?
- How many friendships have you simply discontinued due to the presence of conflict?
- How has your extended family been shaped by the presence of conflict?

Where we live, whom we live with, whom we worship with, where we work, whom we spend time in relationship with, all of these have everything to do with whether we have been able to successfully resolve conflicts or have instead suffered as a result of our inability to find *shalom*.

Shalom, often translated as "peace," is more than the mere absence of strife or the cessation of hostility. In its fullest sense, shalom involves a sense of wholeness and completeness.

We experience shalom, in part, even as we live life under the sun. When the Son returns, shalom will be brought to consummation. Until then, as we wait for the Blessed Hope, we look for signs of the coming kingdom in our present lives. We follow the God of peace by seeking to be peacemakers. This is an integral part of the emerging reality of His coming rule and reign.

Another Book on Conflict?

If you're asking yourself, "why another book on conflict?"—I understand. Although there have been many recent books written on this subject, many of which have much to commend them, there is still room for an attempt to address not only the biblical path toward conflict resolution but also the *limitations of that process in light of the place we find ourselves in redemptive history*. We live in the *now*, this side of the *not yet*. This important aspect of our present reality has massive implications to our thinking about life as we know it. Conflict is a complex topic, and viewed through the lens of Scripture, is large and multifaceted. Many attempts at describing the biblical teaching on conflict have partly failed to succeed due to an inability to reflect the complexity of the subject matter at hand. This book will be most useful in conjunction with other books on this topic.[14]

The rabbis spoke of truth as a multifaceted gem that reflects different aspects, different refractions of light, as we slightly shift the paradigm. Truth is multiperspectival, rather than simple. So it is with the topic of conflict. Each expert in the field seems to have his or her own perspective, his or her "yoke" to be taken up by willing followers. We each have a paradigm. Humility demands we understand that we each bring a different facet of truth to better represent a proper understanding of a complex topic.

Born out of Experience

It is the crucible of personal experience that often underlies the observations and conclusions reflected in these pages. It is the quest for meaning, to understand the heart of God in the midst of suffering, that has driven my efforts to rightly comprehend the truth revealed in the Scripture. When crises hit, we are existentially forced to search for meaning. We sometimes search in vain for someone else that seems to "get it," someone who will help us make some sense out of our present feelings and experiences. This can be a lonely process. Many of the observations in this work are not consistent with popular teaching in the church of today.

14. Though there are many books explicitly on the topic of conflict from a Christian perspective, I would highly recommend three as foundational for a somewhat diverse study of the major thoughts. Dr. Kenneth Newberger's *Hope in the Face of Conflict* outlines his Judeo–Christian model of peacemaking. Jim Van Yperen's *Making Peace* is a helpful how-to book on the topic of reconciliation. Lastly, Ken Sande's landmark work *The Peacemaker* needs to be a part of any contemporary conversation about biblical peacemaking.

The Christian community in America at the beginning of the twenty-first century reflects its cultural context. Our theology has been impacted by the world in which we live. Some of the thoughts and conclusions in this volume, however, will contradict that common thinking. For this reason, I suspect some of the deductions I suggest may not be readily accepted in our current Christian culture.

Were it not for the life situations I, in God's providence, have been allowed to experience, this book could not exist. It has been in the midst of pain I have found the greatest need to understand God's goodness and His sovereignty. This, then, is not an academic approach to theodicy. Rather, this is a very personal apologetic, a defense of biblical truths I hold that *must be true* if life is to make any sense or have any meaning at all. Pain has a way of truncating our view of the situation. We seek immediate relief from our suffering and sometimes, in so doing, we cling to half-truths as answers. God has revealed Himself and His will to us in the Scripture. May God help us as His people to better understand those things able to be known, things He has given us in His inspired Word. This book seeks that end.

A Book for "Conservative" Evangelicals

In my journey through the Christian church I have learned much from exposure to various orthodox Christian traditions. You may notice I will quote from Christian thinkers of various traditions. For far too many years, we have been focused on an in-house fight, a theological conflict, if you will. At this point in the history of the church, it is time for all of us who hold to an orthodox evangelical belief in justification by grace alone through faith alone, inclusive of the additional qualification that the grace that saves is never alone, to stand together. As Ben Franklin said, "We must, indeed, all hang together, or, most assuredly, we shall all hang separately."

This Book Is Not . . .

- Based on the claim that conflict is somehow a good or natural part of human life (God can bring good out of evil, but evil is still evil and therefore not good).
- Supportive of the claim that Christians can and should live conflict-free lives.
- A how-to strategy for resolving all conflicts.

This Book Is . . .

- Based on the premise that conflict is directly connected to the fall of humanity.
- Based on the close connection between conflict, sin, and foolishness on one hand and shalom, righteousness, and wisdom on the other.
- Based on the premise that conflict is a temporary problem belonging to this time in human history, not to eternity.
- Based on the second coming of Christ as the way and the time in which God will finally resolve the problem of conflict.

Part 1

FIRST THINGS: GOD, SHALOM, & THE HISTORY OF CONFLICT

1

In the Beginning

For me, God and His nature are always the starting points. When I'm trying to understand something, I have learned to begin with thinking about what God is like. In the major conflicts in my own life, I have always been troubled by the disconnect between the God I've mostly heard about: the God who always loves everybody, forgives us unconditionally, gives us peace that passes understanding; and my own heart's desire for truth or justice or even vindication at some level. The "God of love only" has not always been very comforting to me. When my view of God as the Giver of perfect peace hasn't matched my inner thoughts and turmoil, I've wondered if I was just not getting it. Maybe I'm not really connected to Him, at least like others who seem so utterly unaffected by things others have done to them. I'm not experiencing this transcendent experience of release. Who is this God I so desperately want to be connected to?

The proper place to begin any discussion is at the beginning. In regard to the topic of conflict, the best place to begin is prior to the "beginning" mentioned in the first chapter of Genesis. *In eternity past, before God made the angelic hosts, mankind, or the universe, there was no conflict.* There was only God and in Him there was no shadow of conflict.

God

A proper understanding of God is foundational to life. God is the Creator and Sustainer of all things. All things derive from Him and have meaning only in relation to Him. The fear of Him is the beginning of wisdom (Prov. 1:7). A. W. Tozer once wrote,

> What comes into our minds when we think about God is the most important thing about us. . . . A right conception of God is basic not only to systematic theology but to practical Christian living as well. It is to worship what the foundation is to the temple; where it is inadequate or out of plumb the whole structure must sooner or later collapse. I believe *there is scarcely an error in doctrine or a failure in applying Christian ethics that cannot be traced finally to imperfect and ignoble thoughts about God.*[15]

We begin with theology proper—the doctrine of God. Before anything was made, God eternally existed. One God in three Persons has always been. We have come to know this God as He has revealed Himself to us in creation, providence, the Scripture, and finally in the person of the God–man Jesus Christ.[16] God, the Holy Spirit, has opened our eyes to see this revelation. In the beginning, before there was anything, God not only existed but also embodied certain characteristics inherent to His eternal nature as God. Among these revealed attributes of God are certain key pairings of qualities often incorrectly juxtaposed to one another. One attribute in each pair is often preferred at the expense of the other. We need to realize, however, that God embodies in His being both sides of these apparent contradictions, these paradoxes. There is no contradiction in God. There is no contradiction in these qualities in the Godhead. Think about the three following pairs of God-traits.

---

15. A. W. Tozer, *The Knowledge of the Holy* (San Francisco: Harper and Row, 1961), 9–10 (italics added).

16. This is the thrust of Heb. 1:1–3. The author explained the centrality and finality of God's ultimate revelation in and through the Son. The original language described this revelation as "in Son."

Diversity and Unity

God answers the question of the one and the many. There has been a debate among philosophers for centuries regarding which is ultimate, the one (unity) or the many (plurality or diversity).[17] In the Trinity, we find the only answer to this age-old question. Because of God's nature as one God in three Persons, all of creation is simultaneously unified and diverse. Read how Francis Schaeffer described this reality:

> The only answer for what exists is that God, the infinite-personal God, really is there. . . .This is not only an answer to the acute philosophic need of unity in diversity, but of personal unity and diversity . . . with the doctrine of the Trinity, unity and diversity is God himself—three persons, yet one God. That is what the Trinity is, and nothing less than this.[18]

Because God is three and one, He shows us that both aspects of diversity and unity are equally ultimate in the created order.[19]

How does this relate to conflict? If God embodies both unity (oneness), as well as diversity (threeness), then our differences (things that make us unique as individuals) cannot be seen as causal to the presence of conflict. In God, three distinct Persons have existed eternally in perfect harmony without a hint of conflict, but not at the expense of losing the individuality of any one Person of the Three.

---

17. When we say God fills the category of the many or of diversity, we are not implying some form of polytheism. There are not many gods, but One (Deut. 6:4). This one God, however, has eternally existed in three distinct, yet perfectly connected, Persons.

18. Francis A. Schaeffer, *He Is There and He Is Not Silent,* in *The Francis Schaeffer Trilogy: The Three Essential Books in One Volume* (Wheaton, IL: Crossway Books, 1990), 288.

19. An application of this principle helps to resolve disagreements in the church between individuals versus corporate aspects of salvation, sanctification, and body life. In God, we can see the simultaneous emphasis on each Individual Person and the unbreakable oneness that exists among the Godhead.

Uniformity is not required to prevent the presence of conflict.

Their diversity has not led to any conflict or lack of perfect unity. Therefore, as we will see, to attempt to blame the presence of conflict on the presence of diversity or differentness among us falls short of a reasonable explanation. God Himself disproves this idea.[20]

Justice and Love

God is also perfect in love and perfect in justice. God is altogether holy and righteous. Everything He does reflects whom He is. His acts cannot be separated from His character. Throughout church history, different theologies have exalted one of these divine attributes over the other. The result has been predictably problematic. Love and justice seem to be, from our finite fallen human perspective, opposite principles.[21] Nonetheless, the heart of the Christian gospel is that God's love has satisfied His requirement for justice in and through the cross of Christ. This is the great Christian mystery that love and justice can meet in the person and work of Jesus (Ps. 85:10).

These two groups of God's attributes must always be kept in balance if we are to have a proper apprehension of whom He is and therefore what He is like. The "love" principle and the "justice" principle must be held together as we consider the nature of God. This balance can be illustrated as follows:

---

20. John Wesley, "Upon Our Lord's Sermon on the Mount," *The Standard Sermons in Modern English,* ed. Kenneth Kinghorn (Nashville: Abingdon Press, 2002), 2:160. Wesley said, "God's Trinity and unity and unity in Trinity are disclosed to us in the very first line of his written word. This phrase translates literally, 'the Gods created'—a plural noun joined with a singular verb."

21. This is an example of antinomy, two apparently contradictory laws that together comprise a paradox.

Table 1. The Love and Justice Attributes of God

The "Love" Principle		The "Justice" Principle
love	AND	justice
mercy		righteousness
grace		holiness
goodness / kindness		sovereignty

John Wesley would have validated the addition of anger to the right side (the justice side) of the table above. He believed that the words "justice" and "anger" are "nearly synonymous" because "anger stands in the same relation to justice, as love does to mercy."[22] Wesley went on to say that anger at sin (those we commit and those committed against ourselves or others) is not itself a sin but "rather a duty."[23]

These two "sides" to the being of the Godhead are imbalanced at great theological peril. Bad Calvinism exalts the sovereignty of God at the expense of God's love and goodness.[24] The logical end of this theological projection is "divine determinism." Bad Wesleyanism exalts God's love and goodness at the expense of His justice.[25] The extreme logical end of this theological projection is "open theism" or even "process theology."[26]

22. John Wesley, "An Extract of a Letter to the Reverend Mr. Law," of *The Works of John Wesley*, ed. Thomas Jackson (Grand Rapids, MI: Zondervan Publishing House, 1958), 9:481.

23. John Wesley, "Thirty-seven Letters to a Member of the Society," in Jackson, *Works of John Wesley*, 12:291.

24. I'm using the term "bad Calvinism" to refer to the extreme of hyper-Calvinism that most biblical Calvinists reject.

25. By "bad" Calvinism or Wesleyanism, I mean an overly consistent form of either theological system that, in an attempt to remove paradox and antinomy, removes one side of the argument from consideration.

26. For a discussion of open theism, see Pinnock et al., *The Openness of God: A Biblical Challenge to the Traditional Understanding of God.* Open Theism is a view of God that makes love the defining attribute of God, at the expense of many others. It is based on a thorough commitment to libertarian free will to the point of asserting God does not foreknow what comes to pass. God is just as surprised as we are at what happens in history.

Sound theology of any persuasion must seek to uphold all of God's attributes revealed to us in Scripture, doing damage to none. When we seek to do this, from either side of the equation, we seem to end up with at least some degree of unresolvable mystery.[27] Should we be surprised that the Maker of heaven and earth is not fully grasped by His finite creatures? If we could grasp Him, the incomprehensible God, it seems He would cease to be God at all.

In much of the discussion of conflict resolution among the Christian community, the conversation loses the balance required between these two sides of the Godhead. In our attempts to resolve conflict, we need to be wary we do not somehow misrepresent *God as He is*. To attempt to make *God as we prefer Him to be*, rather than as He has revealed Himself, is the heart of idolatry. Any attempts to work toward reconciliation between differing parties must reflect this two-fold reality in God. God is perfect in love and perfect in justice. Therefore, both principles of justice and love must be included in proposed solutions to the problem of conflict. Fortunately, as we will see, the concept of shalom, the peace that God brings, is large enough to hold both principles.

War and Peace

The ultimate end of all things, as described in the prophetic writings of the Old and New Testaments, is a state of perfect shalom, which existed for eternity past and even in the garden prior to our fall. God often described Himself in Scripture as "the God of peace" (Rom. 16:20; Heb. 13:20). Jesus Himself pronounced "peace" to His disciples after His resurrection (John 20:26). Paul often described God as possessing and giving peace to His children, beginning or ending many of his letters with the double blessing of grace and peace.[28] In several explicit statements, the

27. Deut. 29:29 reminds us the "secret things belong to the Lord." In other words, there are things we are not to know or to speculate about. On the other hand, Moses continued, "the things that are revealed are for us and our children." We need to be content with those things God has chosen to reveal to us, hold fast to those, and walk in obedience before Him.

28. For further discussion, see 2 Cor. 1:2; Eph. 1:2; 4–3; 6:23–24; Phil. 1:2.

Scripture assumes that God's children will imitate Him in seeking peace.[29] Can we extricate the biblical concept of shalom, however, from Gentile, secular, and even American intrusions into our contemporary paradigm of "peace"?

God doesn't always appear to be the God of peace. The Old Testament and the New Testament often portray a far different portrait of Yahweh.[30] Though He is anxious to secure peace with His people through the means of the Levitical system He established, a foreshadowing of His ultimate salvific solution, He is also clearly a God to be feared by His people and all people on the earth. God destroyed the earth and everything in it by a flood. Other than Noah and his immediate family, all human beings living at that time perished in the torrents. The history of Israel and Judah is marked with God going before them in battle. God for them is a God of war who fights for the sake of His people. The nations of Canaan learned the hard way that resistance to the power of Jehovah was futile.[31]

So, which is it? Is God a God of peace or a God of war? Lest we think that He has progressed from a God of war to a God of peace,[32] we need only to read the account of the culmination of history when God, in one final and decisive victory, defeats forever sin, death, and the devil.[33] In the

---

29. For further discussion, see Rom. 12:18; Matt. 5:9; Phil. 4:6, 7.

30. These perceived differences have led to faulty conclusions in the church ranging from dispensationalism to the heresy of Marcionism. Marcionism can be shown to be foundational to the thinking and writing of Anders Nygren, the father of "unconditional love." An attempt to separate the God of the Old Testament and the God of the New has been declared heretical by the church in history, but this tendency nonetheless persists.

31. It is interesting to notice the command of Yahweh for his people to take Canaan and eradicate the current inhabitants from the land. Disturbing to our modern sensibilities, this command often specifically included women and children. How is this God connected to our modern idea of the God of peace?

32. This is the troubling idea of process theology that suggests God is somehow changing over time. He is becoming more loving and less judging as He progresses. This unfortunate trend in some postconservative theologies has likely contributed to some of the confusion about conflict and biblical conflict resolution.

33. For an excellent discussion of the warrior side of God, see Longman III and Reid, *God is a Warrior*.

end, God will justly judge not only the angels but also all of humanity. None other than Jesus Himself will sit as the Judge. All those who have refused His gracious offer in the gospel will receive the just penalty for their sins—eternal separation from God. Eternity must be preceded by a decisive defeat of the devil and all his followers, so that in the New Jerusalem there is no longer sin and conflict among us.

In short, God is both the God of peace who has made provision for peace with Himself in and through union with His Son, and the God of war whose holiness demands that He deal with all sin that is an affront to His rule.[34] He will triumph over evil and will ultimately "do right." Future justice carried out by God Himself is a key part of the hope of the coming eschaton. Final peace, shalom, will come through the war to end all wars, the decisive victory and the final judgment of evil.

Creation, Diversity Reflecting His Glory

So, God Himself is unity in diversity, perfect justice and perfect love, a God of war and a God of peace. But what of His creation? Creation itself, according to Scripture, is a reflection of the God who made it (Ps. 19:1; Rom. 1:20a). The God of perfect unity created a universe of such diversity that humankind has been kept busy for at least six millennia seeking to catalog all that He has made. God is most certainly not the author of uniformity but of unity within a rich diversity! One only needs to spend an afternoon in the natural landscape prepared by God to notice the tremendous beauty formed by this diversity of forms working together. The contrast and complement of differences played against one another give a richness and depth to all we experience. God loves diversity and openly displays His love and infinite creativity in and through all He has made. God is always working for unity in diversity. D. A. Carson said, "The Triune God loves diversity—so much so, as someone has remarked, that

34. Cf. Ps. 2.

when He sends a snowstorm He makes each flake different. We manufacture ice cubes."[35]

Our point here is to observe that before the fall, apart from sin, the created order represented a rich diversity even as it does today. God did not create a generic tree but a variety of trees that would each reproduce differently after their kind. Animals, as well, represented a range of species and subspecies, all differing even within their subspecies as to individual characteristics, just as it is today. Humankind was created with what we now know was a DNA that rendered this diversity certain among the human family. No two human beings, even identical twins, are in fact completely the same. Creation shouted then as it does now, "Diversity!" This diversity existed without sin, prior to sin. Therefore, diversity itself cannot be shown to be the reason for conflict.

We are often uncomfortable with diversity. Instead of embracing it, we push for uniformity. We want everyone to be like us, to agree entirely with us on everything, theologically or otherwise. We are, in this sense, intolerant of diversity. We resist the created order of the universe and yet we persist. God has made a rich diversity that makes all of life so wonderfully varied. He is so other than us. Creation reflects God's character as a God of unity within diversity.

Humanity, the Image of God

The height of the creative process was the forming of man from the dust and the subsequent completion of Adam with the forming of Eve. In this human couple, God placed His image. We can only imagine what it was like for Adam and Eve to live in unbroken relationship with God and each other. The reality of that relationship in full, what we lost in paradise, waits for us in eternity. For now, we vaguely sense in our collective unconscious the distant memory of Eden. They walked with God in the cool of the evening. They enjoyed all He had richly provided for their fulfillment and satisfaction. They clearly connected the things they enjoyed, even one

35. Carson, *Showing the Spirit*, 32.

another, with the God who had given them all things. They were free from the inclination toward idolatry present in us, their descendants. In short, as the writer of Ecclesiastes said, they were "upright" (Eccles. 7:29). The LORD Himself declared regarding them that His creation, in this regard, was "very good" (Gen. 1:31).

Humanity, as represented in this initial pair, a unity in diversity if you will, was free from conflict. This is a point often missed in the literature. Each spouse in the first couple was unique. They were of two different genders, which included not only anatomical differences but also likely additional nonphysical differences that continue to mark the difference between the sexes today. Masculinity and femininity existed in perfect harmony and complementarity in the keepers of the garden. The team functioned perfectly. They performed their tasks the Lord had given them as one. Neither one lorded authority over the other. There was no power struggle. In their uniqueness, their twoness, they also lived out oneness. So it was in the beginning. Man and wife, with all their created differences endowed by their Creator, living in perfect harmony and shalom.

Original Shalom

The created order was rich in diversity and beauty, reflecting the majesty of Him who called it into existence. Humankind was the crowning work of creation. Into this perfect environment, God placed a man and a woman, His image bearers who were to rule and reign over creation as His vice-regents and coworkers. All was well. In the beginning, there was shalom.

> The webbing together of God, humans, and all creation in justice, fulfillment, and delight is what the Hebrew prophets call *shalom*. We call it peace, but it means far more than peace of mind or a ceasefire between enemies. In the Bible, shalom means *universal flourishing, wholeness, and delight*—a rich state of affairs in which natural needs are satisfied and natural gifts fruitfully employed, a state of affairs that inspires joyful wonder as its Creator and Savior opens doors and wel-

> comes the creatures in whom he delights. Shalom, in other words, is the way things ought to be.[36]

Shalom was the air the first couple breathed every day in the garden. But then sin entered the picture and everything changed. Conflict entered the picture. Relationships became hotbeds for this new potential. The initial struggle between the first couple became a prototype of things to come. Since their fall, humanity has been engaged in a struggle with God and one another. In the midst of our current struggle under the sun, we long for peace. Within our collective memory of the way things were in the beginning, there is a sense of home. Shalom, then, is far more than the absence of hostility. It has everything to do with right relationships, with the absence of separation and distance from one another.

> At its most robust, the word [*shalom*] points to a situation in which God's authority and rule are absolute, where his creations—including human beings—exist in right relationships with him and with each other, and where there is no separation between God and man because of sin.[37]

The effects of the fall will be no longer when the final shalom brings us back to our original state of uprightness. Sin and all of its deleterious effects will be merely a distant memory after the perfect has come (1 Cor. 13:10). We all long for a return to Eden. However, it is at this point, in the midst of these deep longings, that counterfeit shalom offers us a less-than-biblical substitute.

Counterfeit Shalom

The prophet Jeremiah warned against the potential for false peace, counterfeit shalom. He railed against the prophets and priests of his day, who told the nation on the eve of its deportation from the land, "peace."

---

36. Cornelius Plantinga, *Not the Way It's Supposed to Be: A Breviary of Sin* (Grand Rapids, MI: Eerdman's, 1995), 10.

37. De Young and Gilbert, *Mission of the Church*, 197.

The leaders had failed to deal with the real problem of the nation and, instead, had substituted a shallow solution. "They have healed the wound of my people lightly, saying, 'Peace, peace,' when there is no peace" (Jer. 6:14).

In our desire for peace, we must always guard against the intrusion of lesser forms of peace, which are in fact not peace.

True peace, shalom, and wickedness cannot coexist (Isa. 48:22). It is noteworthy that in our day, we often hear that the goal of peace and security among the nations is achievable. How will this be attained while evil remains? This is apparently the thought that will prevail just prior to the Day of the Lord (1 Thess. 5:1–11). We must be careful we are not deceived. True believers long for the true peace that will come with the return of the Prince of Peace and must be vigilant to guard against lesser substitutes.

Much hinges on our understanding or misunderstanding of shalom. To the extent we have allowed Gentile thinking to intrude into our paradigm of peace, we will continue to miss the biblical goal of redemption and settle for second-rate substitutes. Consider the following false substitutes for shalom.

Inner, Subjective Peace of Mind

This is a very western, very American, concept of "peace." It is reflective of the narcissistic culture in which we live. It is highly individualistic and private. Peace as understood in this false paradigm is "inner peace" or "peace of mind." It has more to do with stoicism than with the portrait of shalom or *eirene* (its Greek equivalent) as described in the Bible. So often, we read this picture of peace into our interpretations of Philippians 4 and other oft referenced passages concerning peace. This concept closely resembles the highest good of stoicism, *apatheia*.[38]

38. Stoicism, not biblical Christianity, holds out the highest good as a state of being unaffected and dispassionate about the circumstances of our lives, *apatheia*. Maturity, according to stoicism, is to come to a place where regardless of any circumstance in our lives, we experience

Pretended Agreement

Instead of coming to genuine agreement through "the hard work of mutual submission and reconciliation," we simply go our separate ways either figuratively, literally, or both.[39] Within the Trinity, there is no agreeing to disagree. Shalom, in the fullest sense among men and women, involves a genuine unity of relationship and purpose. Differences are worked through to real agreement. How often have those who have "agreed to disagree" been parties to future conflicts that clearly reveal the lack of any real "agreement" in the first place?

Peace through Amnesia

This would better be termed "evasion." This is a quick and shallow solution to legitimate conflicts; it sells the birthright of shalom for the porridge of denial. Collective amnesia is not the goal of shalom. This is a counterfeit form of peace. True peace exists where conflicts are owned and worked through to a successful resolution that restores relationships. Reconciliation is shalom. Forgiving and forgetting are not.

Peacekeeping and Peacefaking

True shalom is founded on the presence of genuine peacemaking. The children of God are called such because of how they resemble their Father, the True Peacemaker. True peace is made, not kept. True peace involves the transforming work of the Holy Spirit in the lives of the parties involved. Peacekeeping is a counterfeit that substitutes rules and outward regulations that seek to create peace externally. There are two kinds of peacekeepers. Left-handed peacekeepers avoid conflict at all costs. These are the peacefakers. Right-handed peacekeepers try to force peace through aggression and heavy-handed confrontation tactics.[40]

---

uninterrupted inner peace and tranquility. It is common today for Christians to conceive of peace in a stoic way.

39. Jim Van Yperen, *Making Peace: A Guide to Overcoming Church Conflict* (Chicago: Moody, 2002), 170.

40. Van Yperen, *Making Peace*, 173.

Détente

Détente is a form of cease-fire and falls short of the wholeness brought about by true shalom. It is built fundamentally on mistrust between conflicting parties. It is not concerned with the relational goal that shalom promotes as central. It is rather content just to see the skirmishes stop. This is Rodney King's "can we all get along." True shalom is far more than a cessation of hostilities but a bringing together into one family those who were former enemies (Eph. 2:12–19). Shalom is not sleeping with one eye open.

Justice and Shalom

Most contemporary formulations of Christian forgiveness and reconciliation omit the human desire for justice. As we have seen, justice is an essential part of the character of God. God is not only perfectly loving but also perfectly just.

As image-bearers of God,
human beings have an inherent,
God-given desire for ultimate justice.

This God-given desire, however, is often portrayed as originating from our fallenness rather than from the image of God. The historic teachings of Judaism and Christianity, however, have maintained the hope for future justice as legitimate and a ground of hope for this life. Orthodox Jewish and Christian believers, throughout both histories, have maintained that final retribution is a key component in the final defeat of evil. When "peace" is substituted for shalom, one of the first casualties is justice.

Justice is part of our core. In our gut, human beings have an inherent desire to see right prevail over wrong. In fact, "depending on the severity of the evil, the need for justice in the human experience is so great that a lack of justice in the face of evil can collapse our entire emotional, psychological, and spiritual framework."[41] The concept of shalom is inclusive of this sense of justice and righteousness. "Shalom is intertwined with justice. In shalom, each person enjoys justice, enjoys his or her own rights. There is no shalom without justice."[42]

God, the God of all shalom, is a holy and just God. There is no contradiction here. God not only loves righteousness; He also hates evil. "God's justice is a reflection of His holy character. Therefore, 'for Him to let sin go unpunished is to approve of it; which is the same as a denial of holiness.'"[43] God is not dispassionate. He is not the stoic first cause. Instead, God deeply feels the plight of His creation. One of His feelings in regard to the creation is wrath. "Divine wrath does have an affective dimension. The God of the biblical revelation is a passionate God. . . . God is not affect challenged."[44] God cannot remain unmoved or unaffected by the injustice that has entered His creation. "This is a moral universe, which means that, despite all the evidence that seems to be to the contrary, there is no way that evil and injustice and oppression and lies can have the last word."[45]

Just as God reflects a core desire for justice, so do we, His people. We who are being recreated in His image feel a deep heart-level desire for the same. Our desire for justice is not only cognitive but also affective. In the same way that God is passionate for righteousness, we too long for the right to prevail. This God-given attribute is triggered and provoked in all instances of injustice, those involving others as well as those involving ourselves.

Just as indignation or guilt over the mistreatment of others stands as emotional testimony that we care about them and their rights, so does

41. Kenneth Newberger, *Hope in the Face of Conflict: Making Peace with Others the Way God Makes Peace with Us* (Three Sons Publishing, SDM, 2011), 84.

42. Nicholas Wolterstorff, *Until Justice and Peace Embrace: The Kuyper Lectures for 1981 Delivered at the Free University of Amsterdam* (Grand Rapids, MI: Eerdmans Publishing Co., 1983), 69.

43. A. H. Strong, *Systematic Theology* (Old Tappan, NJ: Fleming and Revell Co., 1907), 766.

44. Graham A. Cole, *God, the Peacemaker* (Downer's Grove, IL: Intervarsity, 2009), 72–73.

45. Desmond Tutu, *God Has a Dream: A Vision of Hope for Our Time* (New York: Doubleday, 2004), 2.

resentment stand as emotional testimony that we care about ourselves and our rights. This is a very important point to emphasize:

> Moral commitment is not merely a matter of intellectual allegiance; it requires emotional allegiance as well, for a moral person is not simply a person who holds the abstract belief that certain things are wrong. The moral person is also motivated to do something about the wrong—and the source of our motivation lies primarily in our passions or emotions. Intellectually believing something and actually feeling it in your guts emotionally are, of course, two quite distinct things.[46]

We feel the lack of shalom. Original shalom reflected the nature of God. In His infinite and unquestionable wisdom, God permitted the corruption of His creation by moral agents acting freely. He was not, however, caught off guard. Hidden within the mystery of God was the plan to redeem and re-create in and through the person and work of Jesus Christ. God would come. He would undertake the project of reconciling all things to Himself in and through Christ (2 Cor. 5:19).

God has allowed conflict to exist. Without His permission, it could not be. His plan, however, far supersedes the allowance of evil. He is able to overturn evil and bring life out of death.

Meet Bill and Dave

Dave and Bill were the best of friends. However, they haven't spoken to one another in over three months. Their conflict began shortly after Bill, a financial planner, offered to help Dave make a "better return" on his IRA. Since Dave signed up with Bill's company a little over three years ago, his net worth has been cut in half. To make matters worse, Dave recently lost his position at the plant. The money his family would have had access to is dwindling fast and the stress level is rising. The conflict has affected Bill and Dave's families. Jane and Carol haven't seen or spoken to each other in

46. Jeffrie G. Murphy, *Getting Even: Forgiveness and Its Limits* (New York: Oxford University Press, 2003), 19.

over four months. The kids in both families are confused and don't know how to respond to the break in their parents' relationship.

Bill and Dave are both members of a conservative evangelical church. When the conflict between them erupted, Bill's prior commitment to the doctrine of the holiness of God vanished in favor of a kinder, gentler, forgiving God. The fact that Dave claims to have been defrauded in his investment with Bill seemed to flavor his theology. "Everyone makes mistakes," he explained. "It wasn't intentional." When they met with the conciliator, Bill's "new view" of God was challenged, but he was unaffected.

Our theology has implications. Our true view of God is the one that comes out in the midst of conflict. Regardless of our previously professed view of God, the love-only God, the God of counterfeit peace, has a tendency to show up when the stakes are high. It is common for us, just like Bill, to create a "God" that fits our situation. It is much harder to hold to beliefs about God that bring personal accountability into our lives. Theology proper, the doctrine of God, however, matters.

2

The History of Conflict

Growing up, I don't remember a lot of conflict in my life. It may have been there. I'm sure it was, but I just think we were all working hard not to notice it. I was never comfortable with being angry, something my first counselor pointed out to me. He asked me, "How did your family handle anger?" I didn't know how to respond. "We were never angry," I said. "What conflict?" He also told me that I used the word "appropriate" quite a bit as I described my feelings about the situation that had led to my resignation from the church. That makes sense to me now. I feel as if the theme of my life has been trying desperately to live "appropriately." If I'm appropriate enough, perhaps then I'll be accepted. Appropriateness and anger didn't go together in my family.

I can't wait, honestly, for the experience that awaits us on the other side of this life. It's amazing to think that someday conflict will not be a part of our lives. We won't feel the tension, the pain, the unresolvedness that we feel now. God was there in the beginning, in the absence of conflict. So were Adam and Eve. Since things have begun to unravel in my adult life, it seems like conflict is the one constant. It's as if we're living in a fallen world, full of fallen people, and a world that is in desperate need of re-creation. I am so looking forward to the day when conflict will be no more. Come quickly, Lord Jesus.

Conflict was not in the beginning. At some point in history, that which was not came to be. It is to that distant place we return as we investigate the origin of conflict.

Conflict in the Heavenlies

Conflict did not begin on earth but rather in heaven, in the presence of God and the angelic hosts. The fall of some of the angels is something about which we know very little. We see only glimpses of this part of history, shadows of its details through historical figures that typify this rebellion against God's authority. What we do know is that conflict originated some time and some place prior to its entrance into human history in Genesis 3. Let's go back, as best we can, to this time before "time" as we know it to gain some insight into this thing we call "conflict."

Eternity Past

It is naturally difficult to conceive of things we have never observed. This is the case when we attempt to imagine what it must have been like in eternity past. Obviously, we weren't there. We have no empirical basis to know what this was like. Neither do we really have the ability to imagine an existence so unlike our present one, resulting from our fall in Adam, in which there was no sin. For eternity prior to the creation of anything, God has always existed in three Persons, in perfect fellowship, unity, and harmony within Himself. This was shalom. In other words, there was no conflict. There was never a disagreement about anything. All three Persons were in perfect agreement and united as one God. The Persons in the Godhead eternally enjoyed and delighted in one another. The Eastern Church has historically referred to this perfect relationship as a *perichoresis* or a "holy dance." An unbroken dance of joy and love, this is the Godhead. A God who is entirely self-sufficient, who needs nothing, this is Yahweh. God wasn't lonely. He didn't lack something that He needed for His own fulfillment. He, for reasons ultimately unknown to us, chose to create angels and all other things, knowing that with the creation of free moral agents, all that has unfolded was possible.

I Saw Satan Fall . . . The Beginning of Conflict

Somewhere prior to the scene in Genesis 3, the conflict came to be. We don't know when God created angels. Were they part of the creation process described in the Genesis account or something prior? Were they created in the gap that some scholars see between verses 1 and 2 of Genesis 1? What is relevant is that, at some point, there was God and a host of angelic beings who apparently had the capacity to fall. Angels were given wills that could be exercised to remain loyal to God or to turn against Him and His purposes.

We understand that at some point, the former leader of the angelic choir in heaven, Lucifer, became enamored with himself. He became envious of the glory that God was receiving and pride was born. Prior to this, pride did not exist. The Bible doesn't answer all our curiosities but simply states, "iniquity was found in him [Lucifer]."[47] This is the origin of the first conflict. Satan and those who followed him in his rebellion were cast down. Likely one-third of the total number of angels fell with Lucifer and two-thirds remained loyal to God (Rev. 9:1; 12:3–9). Jesus, preincarnate, was there. He said concerning this past event, "I saw Satan fall like lightning from heaven" (Luke 10:18). We don't know all the details, but we understand, nonetheless, that this historical event set in motion a new principle of opposition to God. This created the enmity that now underlies the existence of conflict in the world.

---

47. The fall of Lucifer is described in some detail in Isa. 14:12–21 and Ezek. 28:11–19. The passage in Ezekiel is actually a lamentation for the King of Tyre. It has been historically seen in the church to refer beyond the earthly King of Tyre to the power behind him, namely Lucifer. It describes for us the beauty of Lucifer, his nearness to God, his musical orientation, and that "iniquity was found in him" (v. 15).

Conflict among the Children of Adam

The conflict in the heavenlies, unfortunately, didn't remain in the heavenlies. The conflict spread to earth. At the suggestion of the enemy of God, humanity decided to join the opposition to God and His rule over all things. Adam and Eve chose autonomy over dependence and experienced the dire consequences of sin, death, and conflict with God and others. As the initial scene opens in Genesis 3 following the completion of creation, the serpent possessed by the devil is present in paradise.

In the Garden

Life in the garden was Edenic, utopian. There was no flaw in the created order that necessitated the coming fall. The man, Adam, and his wife, Eve, dwelt in perfect harmony with one another and with God for an undisclosed period of time. They experienced shalom, a complete wholeness and unbrokenness. Life was fully functional. We don't know if it was one day or many, but this perfect state of conflict-free living was brought to a tragic end. Without much explanation, the man and his wife were found in the midst of the garden near the tree the man had been forbidden by God to eat from, and there he was, the serpent.

From that point on, we see the fall of the woman and the man into sin by yielding to the suggestion of the serpent that God was withholding good from them. The temptation suggested by the serpent was they could find fulfillment and life apart from God. They were tempted to leave their place of dependence on God. When they yielded to the serpent's suggestion, literally all hell began to break loose in their lives. From that initial moment of disobedience, they both became acutely aware of the brokenness of their relationship with God and each other. They hid from God's presence with an acute and debilitating awareness of their guilt and shame.

When God came to Adam to discuss the problem of sin, the presence of conflict was now clearly present. When questioned, Adam blamed Eve and Eve blamed the serpent. Dissension, strife, blame shifting, denial, deceit—they're all there in Genesis 3. Conflict in all its ugliness had now become part of the human experience. Life was forever altered in that momentous event.

Life under the Curse

The entire history of the sons and daughters of Adam and Eve, of all humanity (excepting of course, the Lord Jesus), is one of constant conflict. The first family experienced conflict between the first two sons, which resulted in the first murder. Conflict continues to be woven into the fabric of life under the sun from the first family on. Conflict between the two seeds is part and parcel of the human experience.[48] Humanity, in one sense from then on, is no longer united as one, but rather divided into two seeds (Gen. 3:15). God Himself puts "enmity" between the seed of the woman and the seed of the serpent. Enmity is most definitely conflict language. In the third chapter of Genesis, we are no longer one with God or with one another. Instead, separation from God and each other became normative due to the presence of sin among the human race. We will further reflect on the two-fold division of humanity in the rest of this volume.

Things get so bad that God wiped out the human race and began again with Noah and his family. Conflict, however, was not eradicated in the flood. No sooner was the family off of the ark than the resumption of conflict was present among them. The history of mankind is a history of conflict: *individuals against individuals, families against families, and nation against nation.* The history books are essentially a record of this conflict. The Bible accurately records all of it in all its ugly details.

Life in Christ

With the coming of Christ, the promised Seed (Gal. 3:16), the kingdom of God began to break into the kingdoms of this world. The presence of conflict, correspondingly, was not eradicated but rather intensified in

48. Gen. 3:15 has been called the *protoeuangelion*, the first mention of the gospel. What Moses records as God's words is the proclamation of enmity being placed between the two seeds, the seed of the serpent and the seed of the woman. This conflict between the two seeds is a continued theme of the Scripture following this pattern; cf. Gal. 3:15–18; 4:21–31.

the life and ministry of Jesus. The kingdom of darkness resisted the coming of this kingdom of light. On a human level, the religious authorities, who ought to have represented God's kingdom, were at the forefront of the opposition to Jesus and all that He represented. Because they were not truly of the light, they resisted coming to the light and instead conspired to extinguish the Light of the world.

The opposition ultimately led to Calvary. In an attempt to extinguish the Light, the devil and his followers conspired to see a Roman cross do away with Jesus and His kingdom. They thought they had achieved their end. How wrong they were! In and through the cross, Jesus triumphed over sin and death and on Resurrection Sunday, over the grave. The kingdom of darkness and the prince of that kingdom were dealt decisive deathblows in and through the death and resurrection of Christ. Victory was won!

Following this central act of history, the sons and daughters of God, however, have continued to experience opposition from the "children of the flesh" (Gal. 4:29). Jesus warned his followers of the high cost of following Him (Luke 14:25–33). He described the great potential for conflict among relatives, extended and immediate family, and the world system in opposition to God as a whole. He assured them they would experience opposition as His followers.

Jesus, nonetheless, calls us to be "salt and light" in the world. We are to exemplify the otherworldly values and morals of the coming kingdom. We are not citizens of this world but rather citizens of the one to come. Our entire identity is intimately connected to Him as we experience the mystery of our union with Him. We experience conflict in this life due to our connection to Him. He calls us to follow Him in all areas of life, including suffering.

This present state of affairs, the *now*, though the kingdom of Christ has come in part, includes the presence of conflict. Conflict in this present life is inevitable. In redemptive history, we find ourselves sandwiched between the first advent of Christ, the Lamb of God who takes away the sin of the world, and the second advent of Christ, the Judge of all the earth. While we wait for His return, He has called us to "occupy" (Luke 19:15). Until He comes, we live as citizens of the coming kingdom in the midst of a "crooked and twisted generation" (Phil. 2:15). These two kingdoms are most definitely "in conflict."

The Final Conflict

Eschatological strategies that seek to eliminate the presence of conflict prior to the consummation of all things or leading up to or creating the consummation have been proposed throughout the history of the Christian church. Prior to the return of Jesus Christ, the final judgment, and His ushering in of the eternal state, will we be able to eliminate conflict? There was great optimism at the beginning of the twentieth century concerning this possibility.[49] As world wars and global conflicts began to multiply throughout the century, that optimism, however, began to fade to pessimism or even further to escapism.[50] Throughout the majority of the Christian church's history, it has maintained that the kingdom of God has come and is coming. However, it will not be ushered in fully apart from the return of the King, Jesus Himself.

Today, there are many attempts to create a utopia free from all the cataclysmic struggles portrayed in the Scripture as connected to the final days of life on earth as we know it. This is not a new phenomenon. In the first century, the Corinthian and Thessalonian believers were both confused about the return of Christ. In both cases, they held to an overrealized

49. Postmillennialism in many circles taught the kingdom would be ushered in by the church. It stood in stark contrast to premillenialism, which prevailed among most conservative evangelicals in America at the time.

50. The rise of the doctrine of the pretribulational rapture of the church, under the leadership of C. I. Scofield and other dispensational theologians, began early in the twentieth century. These escapist paradigms were seldom present in the church in the prior nineteen centuries of her existence. Overoptimism (postmillennialism) gave way to a new Pessimism (dispensationalism).

eschatology, as if the *now* was the *not yet.*[51] This sentiment is present today in many segments of both evangelical and main-line churches. The advent of the "missional" church has served to foster these ideas afresh.[52] Though we bring kingdom values to all of life presently, we ought to have a healthy caution against thinking for a moment that the answer to all that ails us will be found apart from the return of Christ.

When He returns the second time, it will not be like the first. He came the first time to offer Himself as an atoning sacrifice. The second time He comes as the Judge of all the earth, bringing salvation for all His own (Heb. 9:26–28). John's revelation of Him portrays His final war against all those who stand in opposition to Him. No longer is He the meek and mild Jesus, allowing Himself to be beaten and mocked. On that Day, He returns on a white horse, and we are right behind Him, making war against His enemies and ours. Look at the language of John:

> And I saw heaven opened, and behold, a white horse, and He who sat on it is called Faithful and True, and in righteousness *He judges and wages war.* His eyes are a flame of fire, and on His head are many diadems; and He has a name written on Him which no one knows except Himself. He is clothed with a robe dipped in blood, and His name is called The Word of God. And the armies which are in heaven, clothed in fine linen, white and clean, were following Him on white horses. From His mouth comes a sharp sword, so that with it He may strike down the nations, and He will rule them with a rod of iron; and He treads the wine press of the fierce wrath of God, the Almighty. And on His robe and on His thigh He has a name written, "KING OF KINGS, AND LORD OF LORDS." … And I saw the beast and the kings of the earth and their armies assembled to make war against Him

---

51. Eschatology refers to the teaching concerning last things, as well as the progressive unfolding of God's redemptive plan throughout human history. To have an overrealized eschatology is to wrongly and prematurely perceive experiencing things that are not yet come to pass.

52. The missional church is a collection of missional believers acting in concert to fulfill the *missio dei*—the mission of God in the world. "Missional living" is a term that describes a missionary lifestyle: adopting the posture, thinking, behaviors, and practices of a missionary even while remaining in one's community in order to engage others with the gospel message.

> who sat on the horse and against His army. (Rev. 19:11–16, 19 NASB; italics added)

Here vividly portrayed are Jesus and His bride coming to feast on the flesh of those who stood in opposition to Him. This radical portrait of Christ is completely foreign to our modern concept of Jesus. Nonetheless, the Revelation is true. He will come again to bring justice and equity to the earth. He, the Light of the world, will destroy the forces of darkness in the ultimate conflict!

Eternity Future

> The maker of heaven and earth has a project. By means of this project God will address the multifaceted problem posed by sin and its entailments. This project's goal is nothing less than the reclamation of creation, and the centerpiece of the project . . . is the person and work of Jesus Christ, the Son, Savior of the World.[53]

In the consummation of all things, there will be no more conflict. In the new heaven and the new earth, sin and conflict that arise out of our sinfulness will be a thing of the past. As John recorded:

> He will wipe away every tear from their eyes, and death shall be no more, neither shall there be there be mourning, nor crying, nor pain anymore, for the former things have passed away. . . . No longer will there be anything accursed, but the throne of God and of the Lamb will be in it, and his servants will worship him. They will see his face, and his name will be on their foreheads. And night will be no more. They will need no light of lamp or sun, for the Lord God will be their light, and they will reign forever and ever. (Rev. 21:4; 22:3–5; italics added)

Conflict will cease to exist, even as sin will cease to exist. This is the eternal state toward which all things are moving, shalom. We will be transformed and glorified, free creatures and yet unable to sin. We cannot com-

53. Cole, *God, the Peacemaker*, 85.

prehend this coming reality at present. But this hope we have through the apostle John:

> See what kind of love the Father has given to us, that we should be called children of God; and so we are. The reason why the world does not know us is that it did not know him. Beloved, we are God's children now, and what we will be has not yet appeared; but *we know that when He appears we shall be like Him, because we shall see Him as He is.* And everyone who thus hopes in Him purifies himself as He is pure. (1 John 3:1–3; italics added)

We cannot fathom what is to come. We only have glimpses of what will be, what it will be like for us in the presence of God, unhindered by the presence of sin and its effects. This is what theologians have often referred to as the *not yet*. In light of the glory that is to come, we could also refer to this coming reality as the *can't wait!*

Sometimes a picture is worth a thousand words. Figure 1 represents a historical timeline of conflict. We can clearly see that conflict is a temporary reality. In the consummation of all things, conflict will cease to exist.

Figure 1. The Historical Timeline of Conflict

Bill's Sunday School Memories

Bill grew up in a Baptist church. He has fond memories of his second-grade Sunday school teacher, Mrs. Culp. She used a flannel board and cut-out figures to teach the children week after week the stories of the Old Testament and of the life of Jesus. Bill attended the Christian school tied to his church from kindergarten through sixth grade. He heard often about the love of Jesus for him and made a profession of faith in second grade. He never worries about going to heaven because he believes that once someone receives Jesus, he is guaranteed heaven, no matter what he does in the future. All his sins, past, present and future, were forgiven the moment he believed. He knows that in Jesus all his "mistakes" are forgiven. Therefore, Bill doesn't understand why Dave seems to make such a big deal over their business issues.

If we believe conflict is only a temporary reality, this belief will have implications for how we approach conflict now. If eternity is ushered in through a final conflict led by none other than Jesus Himself, we may need to rethink our view of conflict and of Jesus. Maybe He's not quite like the meek and mild man Mrs. Culp taught about in Sunday school. Not only our doctrine of God but also our eschatology matters. Our view of the history of the world and of redemptive history flavors our approach to conflict. In the heat of the battle, the temporal seems to be more real than the eternal. This is not the biblical perspective.

Bill's insistence that he had a right to keep the money he had wrongly gained from Dave is inconsistent with the values of the eternal kingdom toward which they both are moving. Bill lives in a conflict-free world, believing because of Jesus and the cross, all his sins are covered in the blood and never to be discussed again.

3

God Responds to Conflict

I used to think that God was just like the Jesus I learned about in the Baptist church, while growing up. Meek and gentle Jesus always loved everyone, never got angry, always remained with us, no matter what we did. We were, after all, "eternally secure." Jesus was my fire insurance. He would prevent me from an eternity in hell like "nonbelievers." On the other hand, we sang songs about "being careful" that reminded us God was watching us all the time. That created a weird split within us. We grew up torn between trying to assure ourselves that God loved us and was fine with our behavior and the legitimate guilt we felt when we sinned. When my behaviors as an adolescent weren't things I was glad that He was watching, I began to develop a growing awareness that I didn't really know Him at all. This was the source of much confusion of soul.

When I was brought into a real relationship with God by the work of the Spirit, everything changed for me. For the first time, I actually had a sense that He was with me, not in the anxiety-provoking way I had known before, but as Someone who cared deeply for me and wanted to grow closer to me. I learned that He loved me and I experienced His love, at least some of the time. But I also learned that He was holy, much holier than I had ever previously been informed. I began to take seriously the connection between my professed relationship with Him and my daily living. Though

I was earnestly seeking Him now, I still struggled with my own sinfulness. I learned that sin, not just sin in general but the specific acts I committed, was something that created a problem between God and me. My sin, the sinful choices I made, affected God, affected me, affected our relationship. I wasn't sure exactly how. In any case, He wasn't just the always loving, always overlooking God anymore.

If God is all-powerful, can He, therefore, do *anything*? The simple answer to the question is, "no." He can't do anything, if that anything includes things contrary to His nature. For instance, He cannot lie. It is impossible for Him to do so.[54] God cannot sin. To sin is inconsistent with His perfection in righteousness and holiness. His character precludes Him from sinning. Therefore, when there is conflict with God, He is never the guilty party in the conflict. It is never His "fault." He is never the offender. He simply and always justly *responds* to conflict, the sinful opposition against His sovereign, just, and holy reign over all things.

If conflict with God is, by definition, sin, how does God respond to our sinful conflicts with Him? We might call this Godward aspect of conflict "vertical conflict" as opposed to "horizontal conflict," which is our clash with others. When we vertically conflict with God, what responses are available to Him? Can He respond from His justice? Must He always respond in love and mercy? Many have attempted to limit the range of "right" responses from God. The argument usually goes something like this, "a loving God would never . . ." or "a just God would never . . ." or worse yet "my God would never . . ."[55] These attempts to limit God to one

54. Cf. Num. 23:19; Titus 1:2; Heb. 6:18.

55. This last example is certain proof of the presence of an idol substituted for God. "My God" is usually a god created by sinful people that better fits their situation and understanding of how God ought to be. This is the god of our defining, not the God of the Bible.

of His attributes, the one we prefer over others, is at its core idolatrous.[56] Who are we to assess the rightness of God's responses to His creatures' sin?

God is not controlled by anything or anyone outside of Himself.[57] Therefore, He is never limited in His available responses by anything other than Himself. As we have seen, He is omnipotent, but He is not able to do certain things that are contrary to His nature. By definition, God can do whatever he chooses to do consistent with His nature in response to conflict. By definition, *whatever the Lord does is right.* If we find God responding to conflict at any time past, present, or future in a certain way, we have no other option than to conclude that His response to the conflict He faces is a "right" response.[58]

In this chapter, we want to survey God's responses to conflicts in history to determine the range of godly responses. Some experts in the field of Christian conciliation have argued that godly responses to conflict do not include reactions classified as escape responses or attack responses.[59] Observe the differing types of responses God utilizes as *appropriate responses* to the situations at hand. Our survey begins in an unknown time.

---

56. To make God in our likeness (or of our liking) is the very heart of idolatry. God is who He says He is. The only source we have for our concept of God is His self-revelation. We, as sinful humans however, have a propensity to re-create Him as we would prefer Him. It is common for us to simply omit certain of His attributes we find less appealing in the creation of "our god."

57. This is commonly referred to as His aseity. Notice that I did not say God is not affected by these things outside Himself. The stoic idea of impassibility, God is unaffected by things outside of Himself, continues to be popular today. God in Scripture seems quite definitely to be affected by things in Creation, but He is not controlled by anything outside of Himself. He is sovereign!

58. This is important as we seek to understand a biblical paradigm for conflict resolution. For instance, Peacemaker Ministries characterizes withdrawal (escape) and attack responses to conflict as sinful (at least for humans). These responses, at least for God, cannot be sinful as He utilizes them in His righteousness.

59. Specifically, Peacemaker Ministries' popular illustration, the slippery slope of conflict, depicts both escape and attack responses as ungodly responses. This chapter sheds light on the fact that God can be seen at various times in history responding to conflict in ways that do not fit the slippery slope paradigm.

The War in Heaven

As we noted previously, God initially created a host of angelic beings to serve as His messengers. Sometime after the creation of the heavenly host, a certain angel, Lucifer, was found to have iniquity in him. His heart was lifted up with pride. He became jealous of the glory that God alone received and sought in his heart to become like God, to be a recipient of the glory, just like God.

God's response to the heavenly rebellion was to cast Lucifer and the angels who fell out of His presence to the earth.[60] There was no grace for them. There was no redemption for them. God was just in simply condemning them to eternal damnation with no second chance. He will, contrary to popular opinion, cause them to burn forever in eternal torment in the lake of fire. This was the initial instance of conflict and of God's first response. No forgiveness. No second chance. No mercy. Pure justice in the condemnation of rebellious creatures begins the survey of God's responses in history to opposition against His reign.

The War on Earth

As we have seen, the war in heaven soon came to earth. How does God respond to the war on earth, the great conflict between humanity and Himself? In two fundamental ways, God interacts with humanity in our fallenness. As we can clearly see, not only do these two ways sharply contrast, but the outcome of those who interact with God in these two differing ways could not be more opposite. First, consider the good news of the gospel.

Conquest through Redemption

The gospel is the good news that God has responded in mercy to our sin. In and through the coming of the Messiah, His substitutionary life and death, His victory over death and the grave, His return to the right hand of the Father, having earned for us peace with God; we are brought

60. It is likely that one-third of the angels fell and were cast down with Lucifer (cf. Rev. 12:4).

back into a relationship with the God who made us. God's first option is to offer us a way back through confession, repentance, and faith. This is not a new development in the New Testament but clearly revealed in the Old. God comes to all people with an initial offer of forgiveness and reconciliation. He triumphs over us with His mercy and love. This is the glory of His grace!

Grace Resisted

Though the legitimate offer of salvation is extended to all, not all respond. Many resist His grace, suppress the truth revealed to them, and choose rather to live life apart from Him. For those who resist His grace and refuse to be transformed, there is no salvation. Contrary to popular belief, everyone does not ultimately go to heaven.[61] All are not saved, not due to an insufficiency on God's part, an insufficient provision in Christ, or a lack of calling them to return to Him. All are not saved because some refuse the grace of God, resisting His gracious offer to the end. Sadly, those who resist will perish in their unbelief, separated from the benefits of Christ, who alone brings us back to a right relationship with the Godhead. God will render a just verdict in the case against fallen humanity apart from Christ. This is the glory of His justice (1 Thess. 1:10).

God's response to sinful human beings is twofold. To those who repent and believe, who follow after Him seeking to be saved from the wrath to come, He gives full salvation and eternal membership in the Heavenly Family. To those who refuse His grace, He gives the just desserts of their condition in Adam, an eternity separated from Him. This is the great divide. At a macro level then, we observe that God's response to conflict between Himself and humanity is essentially twofold: giving mercy to some and judgment to others. His response is most definitely not a one-size-fits-all approach.

---

61. There has been a recent resurgence in the old heresy known as universalism. The same arguments are being resurrected to attempt to show that in the end, "love wins."

The Consummation of the Ages

Christ will come again to judge the living and the dead and to usher in the final state of things for all eternity. How will God ultimately respond to conflict at the end of time? This division between the sons and daughters of God and the children of Adam, who refuse the grace of God in Christ, will be indelibly applied in the eternal state of each. Each will be "confirmed" in their final state. The devil and his angels who began the ultimate conflict will once and for all be defeated. The One who brings this new reality is none other than the Lord Jesus Himself.

The Defeat of Sin, Death, and the Devil

The fate of the devil and his angels is sure. For demons, there is no salvation, no forgiveness, no reconciliation, and no second chance. Their fate has been sealed since before the creation of the world as we know it. Somehow, in God's mysterious providence, He has allowed these demons destined for ultimate destruction to interact, meanwhile, in the affairs of men. Their work is included under the sovereignty of God, however, and they are not permitted to act without His assent.[62] God has patiently endured their evil works and will soon be finished with allowing them to perpetrate diabolical schemes. Eschatologically, their days are short and they know it (Rev. 12:12).

The Final Separation of Sheep and Goats

No less than the Lord Jesus described the final separation that is to come. As the True Shepherd who knows His own, Jesus will instruct his angels to sort the great multitude of humanity into two groups. The horror of those on that day who find themselves "unknown" to the Savior is graphically depicted in the words of Matthew 7:

> Not everyone who says to Me, "Lord, Lord," will enter the kingdom of heaven, but he who does the will of My Father who is in heaven

---

62. The case of Job clearly shows God's permissive will over the activities of demonic forces. Satan cannot bring calamity into Job's life without the permission of God.

> will enter. Many will say to Me on that day, "Lord, Lord, did we not prophesy in Your name, and in Your name cast out demons, and in Your name perform many miracles?" And then I will declare to them, "*I never knew you*; DEPART FROM ME, YOU WHO PRACTICE LAWLESSNESS." (Matt. 7:21–23 NASB; italics added)

Jesus painted a picture of this future event:

> But when the Son of Man comes in His glory, and all the angels with Him, then He will sit on His glorious throne. All the nations will be gathered before Him; and *He will separate them from one another*, as the shepherd separates the sheep from the goats; and He will put the sheep on His right, and the goats on the left. . . . These will go away into eternal punishment, but the righteous into eternal life." (Matt. 25:31–33, 46 NASB; italics added)

Here is the great divide. The sons and daughters of God, the "sheep," enter into eternal life in the very presence of God, and those who refused His mercy, the "goats," enter into eternal punishment.[63] For one group, the justice of God is fully satisfied in and through the redemptive work of Christ and the active application of that redemption by the Holy Spirit. For these, God's response is not merely salvation, but adoption into the Family of the Trinity. For the others, the justice of God is fully satisfied in the eternal condemnation of sinners—two very different responses to conflict.

God is just. As one writer wisely commented, "A universe without final retribution, even a hell, would be a morally indifferent one."[64] Wittgenstein said to one of his students bemoaning the church's rejection of Origen's denial of the existence of hell, "Of course it was rejected. It would make nonsense of everything else. If what we do now is to make no difference in the end, then all the seriousness of life is done away with."[65]

63. This is not just a time of correction as some have recently contended but rather an eternal separation.

64. Cole, *God, the Peacemaker*, 78.

65. Ibid.

The Final Comfort: Conflict Resolved

In the end, conflict will be resolved. Conflict is itself temporal and temporary. It did not exist in eternity past and will not exist in eternity future. In the consummation of all things in Christ, conflict will be finally eradicated. This is the blessed hope connected to the return of Jesus. A world without barriers between humanity and God, or between humanity with one another, ultimately awaits us. God's final response to conflict, therefore, is the eradication of it.

A Survey of God's Responses to Conflict

A brief survey of some of the particulars of the history of conflict clearly shows God's varied rejoinders to different situations. God's reaction is not a one-size-fits-all response as He interacts with the various scenarios He has been involved with historically. Notice the variety of responses in the following partial and selective review of biblical history:[66]

Heavenly Rebellion: Judgment

When the angelic host followed the rebellion of Lucifer, God's response to the heavenly conflict was one of judgment. Though He did not immediately destroy the angelic beings, their fate was unalterably determined. There was no grace or mercy available for fallen angels.

Fall of Humanity: Judgment Tempered with Mercy

God responded with the mercy and grace of the gospel of the Seed of the Woman to come in the midst of divine judgment against the new reality of sin in the human race.

The Flood: Judgment and Grace

When men became wicked continually (Gen. 6:5), God determined to destroy all humanity and all of the animals in a great flood. God graciously

66. This survey, for obvious reasons, is not exhaustive but representative of a varied set of responses from God to the presence of conflict against Him.

saved Noah and his family out of the flood, along with the pairs of animals necessary to repopulate the earth. God again demonstrated mercy in the midst of judgment.

The Tower of Babel: Frustration of Plans

When humankind sinfully sought to exalt itself, to proverbially reach to heaven, God came in judgment and brought confusion and frustration to their effort. The confusion created through His intervention stopped the project in its tracks.

Jacob: Wrestling with a Supplanter

God's conflict with Jacob culminated in a wrestling match where the Angel of the Lord struggled all night with the "supplanter." As a result of the struggle, Jacob's name was changed to "Israel," and his character began to be transformed. God's response to conflict here was to allow Himself to be engaged in a wrestling match with a man.

Pharaoh: Hardening (Judgment)

God, through Moses, offered Pharaoh repeated opportunities to let the Israelites go. Pharaoh resisted God, hardened his heart increasingly over time, and God in response hardened him.[67]

Aaron and the Israelites: Judgment

When Moses went up the mountain to meet with God, the children of Israel grew restless and convinced Aaron to participate in the idolatrous worship of a golden calf. Three thousand men of Israel were killed that day by the Levites, according to God's command.

Moses and the Striking of the Rock: Forfeiture of Blessings

The second time Moses attempted to deal with the complaints of thirst by the people, God specifically instructed him to speak to the rock. Moses, in his anger, struck the rock, misrepresenting God to the people. For this

---

67. Five times it is said that Pharaoh hardened himself, and five times God hardened him.

action, Moses and Aaron forfeited their privilege of entering the Land of Promise. God responded to conflict by enforcing consequences for the action of Moses.

Philistines (Goliath): Defeat and Death

David defeated the Philistine champion in God's strength and by His power. God responded to the conflict with the Philistines and many other opposing armies gathered against Israel by bringing military defeat and destruction.

David: Consequences Tempered with Mercy

When David's sin with Bathsheba and Uriah was exposed, God dealt with David, mixing both mercy and judgment. The child they conceived died soon after its birth. David continued to have family strife as a result of his disobedience. But God truly forgave David and restored to him "the joy of his salvation" (Ps. 51:12). David also experienced God's mercy.

King Saul: Withdrawal

Saul's episode with the Amalekites was the final straw. The kingship was stripped from Saul. God removed His presence from Saul as did Samuel, God's prophet. Saul remains a vivid example of how God at times withdraws from individuals who will not be transformed.

The Nation: Judgment, Reasoning, Mercy

God's interaction with the nations of Israel and Judah is a complex history. In summary, however, we can see that God interacts with His people in diverse ways. Sometimes He brings judgment. The ultimate examples of this response were the Assyrian and Babylonian conquests and captivities. At other times, through the prophets, God pleaded with the people, calling them to repentance and warning them of impending judgment. When the nation repented, God came in mercy to them.

The Pharisees: Warning and Judgment

When Jesus arrived on the scene, the religious system was dominated by the Pharisees and the Sadducees, the corresponding legalists and liberals of the day. Jesus, on behalf of the Godhead, pronounced judgment (woes) on the Pharisees in their hypocrisy (Matt. 23). He called them to repent in light of the kingdom that had come upon them. Some did repent and found God's mercy. Others did not repent and faced God's judgment.

Peter: Grace and Restoration

Peter denied the Lord three times. This was a serious offense to renounce his connection with Jesus. Jesus responded to Peter's denial (his offense) with grace, calling Peter to resume his role among the burgeoning church. Peter was not judged nor was he disqualified from leading in the church.

Saul of Tarsus: Confrontation and Mercy

Jesus confronted Saul on the road to Damascus. He brought this persecutor of the church to His knees, showed mercy to him, and made him the apostle to the Gentiles and the largest contributor to the writing of the New Testament.

Ananias and Sapphira: Judgment and Death

Ananias and Sapphira lied to the Holy Spirit about the price of the property they had sold. They were struck dead on the spot. There was no grace to cover their transgression, at least in terms of the removal of the temporal consequence. Here we see an example of God's attack response to conflict by taking their lives.

The Corinthians: Judgment and Death

Similar to Ananias and Sapphira, the Corinthians who had mistreated the poor among them at the agape feasts were dead, "sleeping." God's response to their sin against others was to take their lives (1 Cor. 11:30).

The Great White Throne: Final Judgment and Reward

This is the final response of God toward conflict. For all those who have loved His appearing, He will reward them with eternal life in the kingdom. For all those who have opposed Him and resisted His gracious offers, He will give them the just desert of their works (Rev. 20:11–15).

Summary of God's Responses

God has utilized diverse responses to vertical conflicts with Him. He reserves the right as the sovereign God to answer conflict with a variety of just and holy responses. He does not, of necessity, need to respond to any given situation in only one way. He is perfectly just when He pronounces or brings judgment on the unjust. He is perfectly just when He "shows mercy to whom He shows mercy" (Rom. 9:15). The point, then, is that God is not constrained to one response. At times, He withdraws. At other times, He pursues. Still at other times, He attacks. This survey of God's responses to conflict becomes highly relevant data as we begin to consider our own responses to conflict. How then, as children of God, should we live? If God's response to conflict is so varied, how should our response to conflict reflect His presence in our lives?

God's inclination is redemptive. Though He at times responds differently, He reveals Himself centrally as a God who is rich in mercy and abundant in forgiveness. This is His dominant posture toward humanity:

> The LORD, the LORD, a God merciful and gracious, slow to anger, and abounding in steadfast love and faithfulness, keeping steadfast love for thousands, forgiving iniquity and transgression and sin, but who will by no means clear the guilty, visiting the iniquity of the fathers on the children and the children's children, to the third and the fourth generation. (Exod. 34:6, 7)[68]

---

68. This is the recurring triad of the LORD's character traits. He is gracious (*channun*), compassionate (*rachum*), and full of steadfast (*hesed*), loyal love. *Channun* comes from the Hebrew word *chen*, "favor or grace, literally to bend towards." *Rachum* derives from *rehen*, womb, and describes "a deep compassionate love rooted in a natural bond, as in a mother's love for her helpless child." *Hesed* is "God's covenant faithfulness and loyal love toward us, His for-us-ness."

The emphasis in the equation falls on redemption as He keeps steadfast love for thousands. He is, as Peter wrote, "unwilling that any should perish" (2 Pet. 3:9). God, unwilling to simply lose any, pursues a relentless campaign of grace toward mankind. As one writer observed, it is significant that God Himself is always the Initiator. We don't go after Him. He always comes to us. He is the Ultimate Pursuer.

> At every point, God comes down to us, and at every point, this world is the focus of God's gracious activity. God initially created this world for humanity and gave the first human beings a share in the communion of the Trinity in this world. After the fall, God gave his promise that in this world he would act to bring about redemption. That redemptive action began as the Son personally came down to this world, to live, die and be raised so as to give us a share in his own relationship to his Father. When the Son returned to the Father, he sent the Spirit to this world to dwell personally within believers, thus uniting us to the Trinity. . . . [I]n the next great redemptive event (yet to happen), the Son will come down a second time to this world. . . . Finally, Scripture indicates that at the close of history God the Father will bring his dwelling place, heaven itself, down to this world. . . . First, the Father sent the Son down; then the Father and Son sent the Spirit down. Later God will send the Son again. And finally, stunningly, the Father will come down, bringing heaven and all the heavenly host with him . . . God's final act will be to change his address.[69]

Even as God is a redemptive God, so we His people have been given the ministry of reconciliation. Though we, like He, may have varied responses to conflict, our heart's desire is for all men to be not only reconciled to Him but also to one another. This is the heart of peacemaking.

Bill and Noah's Ark

One of Bill's favorite stories while growing up was the story of Noah and the Ark. He had a picture of the story that hung in his room as a

69. Donald Fairbairn, *Life in the Trinity: An Introduction to Theology with the Help of the Church Fathers* (Downer's Grove, IL: InterVarsity Press, 2009), 225–227.

young boy. He loved thinking about Noah and the animals on the boat. He never considered that the story had a darker side. He didn't like thinking the entire population of the earth, with the exception of eight people, had perished in the flood.

Bill had a selective memory when it came to reviewing the various ways God has interacted with conflict in history. When the conciliator pointed out several biblical examples of God bringing judgment rather than mercy, Bill was shocked. At first, he argued against the relevance of these Old Testament stories. "I'm a New Testament believer," he explained. In the midst of the struggle with Dave, his theology of God and his memory of God's dealings with various biblical characters had been altered. So it is with all of us. We are tempted to revise history to better suit our situation. In so doing, we exchange the God of Israel for another god.

Part 2

CONFLICT DEFINED & DELINEATED

4

So, What Is Conflict?

I know that we all use the word "conflict" all the time to describe things that may not necessarily involve sin. I get that. As you read this chapter, please don't think for a minute that I don't get the common use of the word. I know we have and will continue to use the English word to describe things that aren't in themselves sinful. But I honestly think, after a lot of soul searching, that our use of the term in many situations can't be reconciled with what the Bible speaks of.

What has been one of the most difficult things for me to walk through has been the way in which our common thinking about conflicts and their solutions have been pushed onto me. In the midst of the most painful experiences of my life thus far, I've had plenty of ignorant, yet well-meaning, Christians offer unsolicited advice on how to resolve "personality conflicts" or "differences of opinion." For me, the attempt to define the terms we use to describe "conflict" consistent with the usage in Scripture has been really important. If we're not talking about the same thing, it is no wonder to me that we are suggesting different solutions. And yet, they persist. "Just take him out for breakfast." "Don't talk about the things that have happened in the past." "Just move on." "Forgive and forget." I interject, "You don't understand. There is nothing I want more than a restored relationship. But resuming a relationship by pretending that what has happened never happened doesn't give me back a real relationship. It's all so phony." I've overlooked tons of things that can be chalked up to differences of personality or opinion. I'm confident that those who care for me have done the same. We all do that and need to continue to do so. But it seems like there are things that require a different path. That's all I'm talking about by trying to narrowly define "conflict" in the pages that follow.

Thus far, we've examined the history of conflict and of God's response to those sins committed against Him. Conflicts with God, "vertical conflicts," are only half of the story. We now turn our attention to "horizontal conflicts," interpersonal conflicts between us as fallen human beings. As we broaden the discussion, we need to attempt to define the term. How can we best understand conflict in our interpersonal relationships? What does the Bible, our ultimate authority in all things, have to say about this subject?

There are three clear risks in attempting to define conflict. If we define it too broadly, we will likely feel compelled to see every disagreement about what to eat for dinner as a conflict that requires third-party intervention. On the other hand, if we define it too narrowly, much of what occurs in our daily lives will not be viewed as conflict at all. We can quite easily drift into a sentimental mind-set that refuses to see the elephant of conflict sitting in the middle of the room. If we define conflict in overly biblical terms we will likely be charged with being old-fashioned and naive. To see sin under conflict, for many, is to revert to an unthinkable paradigm of right and wrong, something our more developed sense of tolerance recoils from.

The Definition of Conflict

Before we can undertake a discussion of conflict resolution, we need first to look at the meaning of the English word conflict. In our twenty-first-century usage some dictionary definitions of conflict are:

con-flict (kon flikt') **n.** A **battle**; **clash**; a disagreement of ideas, or interests, opposition to someone or something.[70]
verb (used without object). 1. to come into **collision** or disagreement; be contradictory, at variance, or in opposition; **clash**; 2. to **fight** or **contend**; do **battle**.
Noun. 3. a **fight**, **battle**, or struggle, especially a prolonged **struggle**; **strife**; 4. controversy; **quarrel**: *conflicts between parties;* 5. discord of action, feeling, or effect; **antagonism** or **opposition**, as of interests or principles: *a conflict of ideas;* 6. a striking together; **collision**; 7. incompatibility or interference, as of one idea, desire, event, or activity with another: *a conflict in the schedule.* (emphases added)[71]

It is apparent that conflict involves some sort of fighting about something. Notice the terminology used above to describe conflict: *battle, clash, collision, fight, struggle, strife, quarrel, antagonism, opposition, collision.* Conflict equals fighting. It may be civilized or uncivilized in the way the fight is conducted, but the fight is still a fight.[72] This notion of conflict as a fight most likely explains why at the mere mention of the word, many of us become hypervigilant. We, therefore, frequently utilize alternate terms to describe conflict that help us ramp down the emotional impact. We speak of "disagreements" or "differences of opinion." The common English use of conflict, however, seems to involve more than this.

Why is it then that in much of the literature, Christian or otherwise, the seriousness of conflict is minimized? Have we redefined conflict to make it less threatening? The danger here, initially, is that *we trivialize the concept of conflict.* Most people react with a certain amount of anxiety to the presence or mention of conflict. Because of this uncomfortability with the concept, we have various means at our disposal of reducing our

70. *Webster's Deluxe Edition Dictionary and Thesaurus*, 11th ed. (Reisterstown, MD: Nichols Publishing Group, 2001), s.v. "conflict."

71. *Dictionary.com*, s.v. "conflict," accessed April 13, 2013, http://dictionary.reference.com/browse/conflict.

72. The difference between litigation and other legal attacks and illegal forms of attack (assault, slander, etc.) are in form, not substance.

discomfort. One of our favorite means is minimizing. Conflict is reduced to a lower, less threatening level of disagreement or difference of opinion.

The second danger is of *divorcing the idea of conflict from any sense of any wrongdoing.* We are living in a day that grants divorce due to the presence of "irreconcilable differences."[73] These same dissolutions are also called "no-fault" divorces. One wonders how pervasive this line of reasoning has permeated our cultural mind-set. Have we, beyond the sphere of divorce law, created a cultural reality of no-fault conflicts in general? If conflict with God is "sin," can we rightly use the word "sin" to describe our conflicts with one another? Read what Karl Menninger had to say in 1973:

> As to sin, we have transferred that old-fashioned breast-beating and guilt-seeking from churches to the psychiatric clinic. And trouble enough it was to do, too. There were, and there still are, reactionaries who threaten hell on earth and then worse hell after death. . . . Sin hasn't disappeared, you say—it has merely been called something else or swept under the rug. It is still with us. In us. And all about us. We can't do without sin—apparently—or without the notion of it, so you seem to say. With all that guilt and penance and accountability stuff. "But some of us *are through* with it. Old-fashioned sin *is* out." . . . Sensible people don't feel guilty for sinfulness or "sins" anymore, and thank God they don't. What sort of morbid, morose, artificial, synthetic gloom was that moral smog in which our ancestors lived? Do you want to continue it?[74]

If sin is an archaic way of conceiving conflict, how should we as modern thinkers think about it? More sophisticated theories of conflict speculate at some of the roots inherent in conflict. Several roots, which we shall examine, have been suggested.

73. Apparently, the term "no fault" was first used in English literature in 1509. It is an interesting phrase with widespread usage in our contemporary culture. We are consistent in our insistence that no one be at fault, so we have created a standard ground on which marriages are dissolved. When a marriage dissolves, it may or may not be primarily one spouse's fault. It may, in fact, be the fault of both parties. One thing that is almost certain, however, is that it is not a "no-fault" situation.

74. Karl Menninger, *Whatever Became of Sin?* (New York: Hawthorn Books, 1973), 174–175.

A common and consistent assumption in secular literature is that conflict is good. The struggle is a good and necessary part of making progress in society.[75] Is this assumption consistent with all we have said thus far concerning conflict? If conflict really is good, why would God's ultimate plan involve its eradication? Why does biblical history reflect a world that existed prior to conflict? Why does the blessed hope connected to the glorious return of Christ involve the ushering in of true peace on earth, the end of conflict?

Implicit in every definition of conflict is its proposed solution.

For example, if conflict is seen as the result of limited resources, the solution will be some form of providing more resources. If it is viewed as fundamentally about power or wealth imbalances, the solution naturally would involve some way of redistributing power or wealth. If it is seen as a natural result of diversity and differences, some have suggested the answer of uniformity. If it is seen, however, as the result of sinful and foolish choices made under the influence of demonic forces, it would suggest an entirely different solution.

Christian Definitions of Conflict

The twenty-first-century church has begun afresh to address this topic of interpersonal conflict. Though the historical church has been deeply marked by the presence of conflict, the "modern" church, for almost a century in many sectors, has carried on the masquerade of being a conflict-free zone.[76] We are far more tolerant than our forebearers. The New Testament ideals of unity and love have been used to drive the recognition of strife among God's people underground. Conflict occurs in all

75. This is consistent with our naturalistic worldview, as influenced by Darwin, of life as "the survival of the fittest."

76. The history of the Christian church is a history of constant conflict. The church has been divided over doctrinal issues, struggles for power, and defining the boundary between those inside and those outside.

Christian families, churches, organizations, and at every level of all these institutions. In this present world, fallen as it is, conflict is most definitely "inevitable."[77] Just as Jesus promised, "in this world you *will have* tribulation" (John 16:33; italics added).

Strife and division are not new things. Conflict is evident among God's people in both testaments and is a constant part of the grand narrative of Scripture. The early church, which so many are idealistically calling the church to return to, was fraught with conflict.[78] Quarrels and disputes abounded between the Gentiles and the Jews, between the poor and the rich, and between the more charismatic and less charismatic individuals and groups within the early church. Conflicts within and conflicts without, the early church was so marred by the presence of strife that it often teetered on the verge of extinction. If it weren't for the preserving grace of God, the church would not have lasted until this present day. Despite apostolic commands forbidding them, God's people continue to quarrel with one another.

Many books have been written concerning conflict resolution from a Christian perspective. One Christian writer bemoaned that Christian books on conflict share "a characteristic with secular ones." He went on to point out that, "Neither addressed or investigated two related questions: How does God make peace with us, and what would that model look like if we adopted it for peacemaking between people?"[79] In answer to this question, we have sought to examine conflict with God first, and only then, to begin to develop a definition of conflict or a strategy for its resolution.

---

77. Ken Sande, *The Peacemaker: A Biblical Guide to Resolving Personal Conflict,* 3rd ed. (Grand Rapids, MI: Baker, 2004), 290, and Van Yperen, *Making Peace*, 102.

78. Shortly after the description of common life in Acts 2, we see the church hopelessly divided over the issue of racism (Acts 15). One race, the Jews, was being favored over another, the Hellenists, in the distribution of the widows' fund. The early church was not the utopia some claim.

79. Newberger, *Face of Conflict*, 9.

In this recent renewal of honest dialogue about conflict in the church, several individual believers and Christian organizations have been at the fore. Ken Sande, the founder of Peacemaker Ministries, offered the following definition of conflict. Conflict is, "*a difference in opinion or purpose that frustrates someone's goals or desires.*"[80] Is conflict, however, in its essence, merely "a difference in opinion or purpose" as Ken suggests? Can someone have their goals or desires frustrated and remain free from conflict?

Jim Van Yperen defined conflict in two primary ways. He first described conflict as *a broken relationship.* He pointed to this relational aspect of conflict as follows:

> *Relationship* implies a common life shared by a common language—the ability to communicate thoughts, actions and feelings in truth and love. [*After the fall*] relationship*s* once unified by love and nurture were now, due to sin, separated by hatred and hostility.[81]

So, in his thinking, sin has moved us from love and nurture to hatred and hostility in our relationships. The second aspect he identified is the principle that conflict is *a spiritual collision.* Behind the scenes, in most if not all conflicts, is the reality of spiritual forces who are eager to destroy relationships and organizations in order to discourage and, if possible, destroy believers and their cause.

A third expert in the field is David Augsburger from Fuller Seminary. He said, "Care-fronting has a unique view of conflict. It sees conflict as natural, normal, neutral and sometimes even delightful. . . . Conflict in itself is neither good nor bad, right nor wrong. Conflict simply is."[82]

There is no consensus. What is it that defines conflict? Can some of these factors be present and yet conflict be avoided? The Scripture seems to say so. What is it, then, that makes conflict happen? Where does it come from?

---

80. Sande, *The Peacemaker*, 29.

81. Van Yperen, *Making Peace*, 97–98.

82. David Augsburger, *Caring Enough to Confront: How to Understand and Express Your Deepest Feelings toward Others,* 3rd ed. (New York: Regal, 1989), 11.

The Roots of Conflict: Where Does Conflict Come From?

If conflict comes to be, where does it begin? What are the factors, the components that seem to underlay the presence of conflict? These are the roots, those things that make the sprouting of conflict possible. Consider some leading contenders as roots that lead to conflict:

Humanness

Many authors have suggested that conflict is inherently connected to our humanness. Alexander Pope said, "to err is human."[83] Is it inherent in being human that we would err or that we would have conflict? One Human, at least, never erred. Two other humans, prior to their fall in the Garden, had never erred. So perhaps, Pope's line needs to be amended to say, "to err (after our fall in Adam) is part of (fallen) humanity." Humanity in itself, apart from sin, as seen thus far only in the person of Christ and briefly in our first parents, is not destined to err.

Second, if conflict is inherent to being human, what hope do we have for our eternal destiny? Will not conflict be absent among glorified humanity in the New Jerusalem? Won't we be human in eternity? Does that make us then able to sin or even worse, as humans, prone to err? We can readily see there is a conceptual problem with ascribing erring to humanness. We would do well to put the emphasis on the fallenness rather than simply on the humanity. Humanity, in and of itself, is an insufficient explanation for the presence of conflict.

It is humanity corrupted by the presence of sin that is at the root of conflict.

Scarcity (Limited Resources)

Many theories of conflict center on the problem of limited resources or at least on the perception of limited resources. Isn't this a description of the conflict that happens between a brother and sister who both want the same toy? If we simply had a toy for each, then we would eliminate the

83. Alexander Pope, *An Essay on Criticism* (London, 1711).

source of the conflict, or would we? If conflict is the result merely of limited resources or even of unevenly distributed resources, then much of the effort to bring inequality to an end would solve the problem of conflict.[84]

Perhaps the classic example of this idea is seen in the dispute between the herdsmen of Abram and Lot (Gen. 13:5–17). The land could not sustain them both and there was strife. Was the strife between the shepherds being caused by the land being too small? Or did the constraint of the land and the difficulties created by overcrowding simply serve as a provocation toward a strife-filled response from the heart of the shepherds? We can certainly imagine a situation in which a scarcity of resources does not result in conflict. *Conflict is not a necessary outcome of a shortage of resources.* Children can lack toys and share the few they have peacefully.

Unmet Needs

Some have proposed a needs theory of conflict. If my needs are not being met in a given situation, one of the likely outcomes is some form of conflict. Under this paradigm, my unmet needs cause the coming conflict that is based in the failure to meet those needs. Observing third world or homeless populations can refute this theory. Though conflict occurs in the midst of needy populations, it is entirely possible for those in greatest need to avoid turning on one another as a result. Can legitimate needs go unmet and conflict still be avoided? Many places around the world suggest, "yes."

Unmet needs alone do not create the necessity of conflict.

One difficulty with the needs theory of conflict is found in differentiating real needs from supposed needs or even mere desires. Desires frequent-

84. This is the myth of socialism. Redistribution of wealth has never brought about the purported peace it has promised. Socialism and Communism have both been colossal failures. Neither has been able to raise the standard of living among those less fortunate to the degree that nations with the rule of law and free markets have been able to achieve. See Richards, *Money, Greed and God: Why Capitalism Is the Solution and Not the Problem*. For a graphic representation of this truth, see www.gapminder.org. This is not to say, however, capitalism is the ultimate answer. The only real answer to all of the problems we face is found in the coming kingdom of God.

ly masquerade as needs and when unmet, easily grow into demands. Most of our conflicts are not over food, clothing, and shelter. We fight over things *reclassified as needs*. We argue about sex, money, power, prestige, and so on. We act as if the lack of these things that seem so essential for our survival will in fact kill us. Getting our needs met, however, does not guarantee the elimination of conflict. As we have seen, the initial conflicts in heaven and earth arose in the midst of a place of perfect provision, a place where there was no lack.

Diversity (Differences of Opinion or Goals)

Others look at conflict and trace the origin back to the diversity that is part of the fabric of humanity. People are different. They value different things. So, is this diversity responsible for the existence of conflict? We can see this in Ken Sande's definition: "*a difference in opinion or purpose that frustrates someone's goals or desires.*"[85] Is it not possible to dwell together in our diversity without the presence of conflict? As we've seen, diversity connects back to the Trinity and is evident in all that They created and proclaimed "very good." A diverse creation, before the fall, had nothing in it that tended inherently toward conflict. To have differences is not to have conflict.

It is quite possible to live in unity with our diversity apart from conflicts.

So, differences are not sin. Differences are not conflict. Differences are often, however, the soil in which conflict can grow. Frequently, the differences between us lead to sinful thoughts about one another. Envy and jealousy, just as in the case of Lucifer, are often the underlying heart problems driving ongoing conflicts. It is often the differences between us that exacerbate our envy. This, however, is not our fate. We don't have to experience conflict in our diversity.

85. Sande, *The Peacemaker*, 29.

Desires (Wants)

This component of desire, of us wanting something, seems to be a necessary precursor to the presence of conflict. If diversity exists, even among fallen humans, even in the midst of limited resources or scarcity, even in the midst of needs going unmet, conflict will not necessarily sprout. Desire, however, is another story.

Is desire bad? Not at all. Though the Christian church in its history has often struggled with ascetic tendencies, there is plenty of good Christian literature available today that demonstrates the Bible's affirmation of the goodness of desire rightly placed and rightly sized.[86] God uses the "desires of our hearts" to bring about much good in our lives. To eliminate desire is not a Christian pursuit.

There are many good desires, as well as many bad desires. In the realm of those things we desire that are good (e.g., a solid marriage, a good job, a reasonable income, a peaceful church, believing children, etc.), we need to be reminded that these desires in keeping with God's standards for us are good desires. Further, the desire for pleasure (sexual fulfillment in marriage, a good meal, beautiful environments, etc.) is also part of God "giving us richly all things to enjoy" (1 Tim. 6:17 NASB). None of these desires, in themselves, are bad. The problem seems to arise when we want these good things too much, *inordinate desires*, or when the things we crave are unhealthy and unholy in themselves, *inappropriate desires*. Either unhealthy or healthy desires can readily be elevated to the level of a demand.

86. A good example of this is Thomas, *Pure Pleasure: Why Do Christians Feel So Bad about Feeling Good?*

The Sprouting of Conflict: Elevated Desires and Sinful Demands

The core problem of the fallen, yet being renewed, human heart is a tendency toward idolatry. *Our desires don't stay at the level of desires, but escalate to demands.* Notice the progression toward idolatry in James:[87]

> What is the source of *quarrels* and *conflicts* among you? Is not the source your pleasures that wage *war* in your members? You *lust* [*desire*] *and do not have*; so you commit *murder*. You are envious and cannot obtain; so you *fight* and *quarrel*. (James 4:1–2 NASB; italics added)

To illustrate this principle in James, consider a scene at an amusement park involving a young girl of five and her proud parents. It's a hot day—really hot. The family has been walking through the park all day, and it is now three in the afternoon. Just as the family rounds the corner near the carousel, the young girl spots a street vendor with a cart full of ice cream. Immediately, she desires a cool treat. Her salivary glands already flowing, she asks her father, "Daddy, may I have an ice cream?" So far, so good. Nothing wrong with desiring an ice cream on a hot, crowded day at an amusement park.

The scene continues. "Well, sweetheart, it's three o'clock and we'll be eating dinner in a few hours. Let's wait and get something to eat at dinnertime." The girl grows irritated. "But Daddy, I want one now. Can't I please have one now?" Her father replies, "Later honey, we'll get you one later." Her irritation rises, "Daddy, I want it now." No more "please." No room for politeness. She needs that ice cream and she needs it now. You get the picture. If unchecked, this sweet little girl's demand can escalate into a conflict that will impact the whole park. She may choose to punish her father, just like James said. "Daddy, you're mean. I don't love you. You're a bad Daddy!" We use the example of a child because, at heart, we are all capable of immature childlike responses when it comes to the realm

87. I'm indebted to Ken Sande and Peacemaker Ministries as well as Tim Keller for understanding this principle of idolatry. See Sande, *The Peacemaker*, 100–114, and Keller, *Counterfeit Gods: The Empty Promises of Money, Sex, and Power, and the Only Hope That Matters*, ix-xxiv.

of conflict and sinful demands. Adults engaged in sinful conflict often resemble the tantrums of five-year-old girls in amusement parks that wanted their ice cream, and wanted it now.

The root of our conflicts is found in sinful, elevated desires that have become demands.

This is true in the case of vertical as well as horizontal conflicts. Unmet needs, scarcity, humanness, and diversity can and do place additional pressure on the situation, but these pressures do not inevitably lead us to sin. We don't have to sin. We sin when we decide that those things we *want* are things we *must have*. Further, when anyone stands in our way of obtaining those things "rightfully ours," we "need" to remove them as an obstacle. So we slander and gossip to destroy those who frustrate our desires (James 4:11, 12). We kill them so that the obstacle will be removed, and we can get what we want. As Ken Sande wisely pointed out, "all idols demand a sacrifice."[88] If I don't get what I want, someone's going to pay!

When Lucifer, in the presence of God, lacked nothing and desired something that was not his to have, iniquity was found in him. There, in the very presence of God, in the throne room of heaven, in need of nothing, sin came to be found in his heart. It was this sinful demand to be like God that led to his expulsion from the presence of the Lord. Are we saying that conflict is sinful? In a word, "yes!" Demands for things God has not allowed us to have are central to the concept of sin. This was the problem in the garden. Eve began to desire things God in His perfect love for her had forbidden her to have. There is no better descriptor for this principle than *sin*.

The Biblical Terminology of Conflict

The word conflict only occurs twice in the King James translation of the New Testament and does not occur in the Old Testament (Phil. 1:30; Col. 2:1). When we expand the concept of conflict to include common

88. Sande, *The Peacemaker*, 108.

biblical ideas, such as strife, contention, division, and quarreling, we find the presence of conflict throughout the Old and New Testaments. The bulk of the Old Testament is a description of the conflict between God and His people, as well as of the conflict between the people of God and other nations. Think for a moment how pervasive the presence of conflict is in the story of God's people under the Old Covenant. Conflict is virtually on every page.

A common theme in the New Testament is the conflict between the flesh and the spirit. Notice the components that Paul saw as constituting the works of the flesh:

> Now the *deeds of the flesh* are evident, which are: immorality, impurity, sensuality, idolatry, sorcery, *enmities, strife, jealousy, outbursts of anger, disputes, dissensions, factions, envying,* drunkenness, carousing, and things like these, of which I forewarn you, just as I have forewarned you, that those who practice such things will not inherit the kingdom of God. (Gal. 5:19–21 NASB; italics added)

Life in the flesh is not just a life filled with sins of sensuality or other destructive pleasures (carousing, drunkenness, etc.). The works of the flesh (i.e., sin) also include: enmities, strife, jealousy, outbursts of anger, disputes, dissensions, factions, and envying. In other words, the life of the flesh is a life marked by the presence of conflict and its underlying principles of envy and jealousy.

From Paul's perspective, conflict involves sin.

It was not only the apostle Paul who connected the concept of conflict with the deeds of the flesh. The half-brother of Jesus and leader of the church at Jerusalem, James, did the same thing (James 3:13–18). James showed the demonic roots of jealousy and ambition that lead to conflict. He contrasted this worldly wisdom, foolishness, with the true wisdom that comes down from above. We'll return to this contrast between wisdom and folly, but it is crucial, at this point, to see that conflict is not only sinful and fleshly, but in James' mind driven by demonic forces as well.

So, is all conflict sinful? *In the absence of sin, there is no conflict.* There may be disagreement. There may be differences in opinion. There may be scarcity of resources, unmet needs, power imbalances, and so on. But, *where sin is absent, conflict cannot and will not exist.* This is a reality not often reflected in the literature on conflict, Christian or otherwise. The notion that all conflict involves sin would be thought by many today to be primitive and rather unsophisticated. Nonetheless, it seems to be the perspective of the authors of Scripture led by the Holy Spirit. Ultimately, the reader needs to draw his or her own conclusion.

All these factors lie below the surface barrier of the soil that conceals them from our view. They are like fertilizer, which when combined with water and sunlight, feeds the growth of our desires into sinful demands. At some point, sin sprouts (see Figure 2).

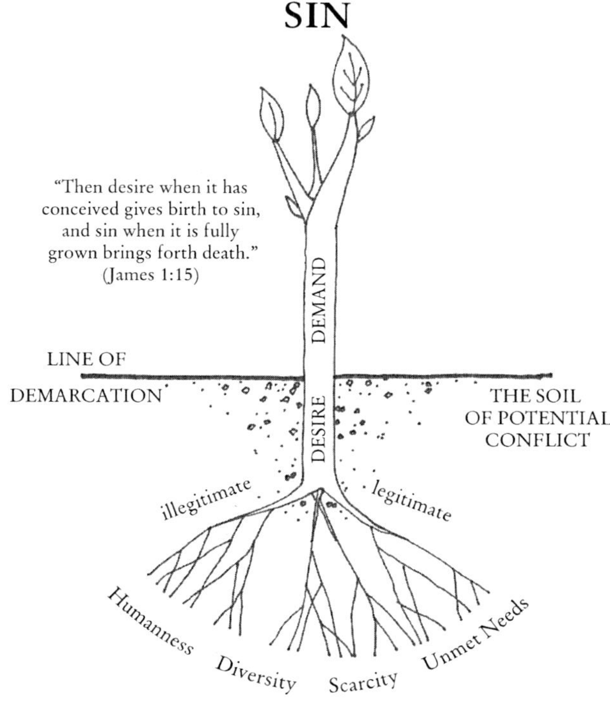

Figure 2. The Sprouting of Conflict

The Fruit of Conflict

When a conflict sprouts and blooms, the fruit is usually quite clear. For a long time prior to the conflict we now see blooming before us, the seeds of desire and demand have been slowly growing beneath the soil. *Conflicts, in the hidden soil of the heart, have been fed, watered, and otherwise nurtured for some time prior to the emergence of the visible fruit.*

The seeds that lay dormant were likely stirred up by the presence of demonic influence in and through the foothold of the "flesh." In the hidden part of the heart, demands have been fed and allowed to grow. At some point, just as the seedling pushes through the surface of the soil, so the young conflict emerges into the light. Sins that were previously "heart sins" hidden under the surface now become openly expressed. An offense is committed against another and against God.

Toward a Christian Definition of Conflict

Conflict consists in things of substance. To push the understanding of conflict down to such a trivial level as a disagreement about where to go for dinner, earliness or lateness to engagements, or which color of car to buy is to miss the point.[89] These issues do not rise to the level of conflict as this book is seeking to define it.[90] Pushing the understanding of conflict down to the level of disagreement leads many contemporary Christian authors to teach that conflict itself is not bad.

89. In current psychological understanding, these types of differences in our marital relationships are actually understood as unresolvable conflicts rooted in personality and background differences. We don't ever resolve these conflicts, but instead in love for one another, learn to manage them so as not to allow them to be ground for real conflict. Dr. John Gottman, based on thirty-plus years of research with couples, said sixty-nine percent of marriage conflicts are of this nature.

90. English is sometimes an ambiguous language. We use the same family of words to describe an international war as an "international conflict," a church split as a "congregational conflict," a serious fight between a husband and a wife as a "marital conflict," and differences of opinion over where to go for dinner. Much like the word love, conflict in the English language is a term with too broad of a denotation to be helpful in clearly defining categories.

> The Bible does not teach that all conflict is bad; instead, it teaches that some differences are natural and beneficial. . . . Many of these differences are not inherently right or wrong; they are simply the result of God-given diversity and personal preferences. When handled properly, disagreements in these areas can stimulate productive dialogue, encourage creativity, promote helpful change and generally make life more interesting.[91]

Disagreement is not always sinful. But, is conflict synonymous with disagreement? The two have been shown to be distinct and different concepts.

Others agree that conflict and disagreement should not be regarded as synonymous. Many times, "'disagreement' may be a cop-out when the conflict is far more serious."[92] The same authors went on to say that neither is "all conflict neutral or beneficial" and add, "the Bible teaches that many disagreements are the direct result of sinful motives and behavior."[93] Many disagreements rise to the level of conflicts. They, nonetheless, do not cross the threshold apart from the presence of sin. These situations marked by the presence of *actual offenses* are rightly called conflicts, as distinguished from mere disagreements or differences. With requisite and appropriate humility, consider the following working definition of conflict:

> *A conflict is the presence of a broken relationship that has resulted from the commission of sinful actions growing out of inordinate or sinful desires on the part of one party, the offender, against the other, the offended.*

A conflict is not a conflict until sinful actions are committed against another person and God Himself. Though Jesus taught us that sins of the heart are just as serious as outward acts before the presence of a holy God, sins of the heart against one another that remain only in the heart, gener-

91. Sande, *The Peacemaker*, 24–25.

92. Kenneth O. Gangel and Samuel A. Canine, *Communication and Conflict Management in Churches and Christian Organizations* (Eugene, OR: Wipf and Stock Publishers, 2002), 129.

93. Gangel and Canine, *Communication and Conflict*, 25.

ally do not escalate to the level of conflict.[94] It takes sinful actions (actual offenses) for a true conflict to emerge.

Testing Our Hypothesis

The book of Proverbs makes a few explicit statements about the source and nature of conflict. Let's use those as a check to see if we are, indeed, on the right track with our thinking about conflict (italics added):

- "*Hatred* stirs up strife, but love covers all offenses" (Prov. 10:12).
- "*Pride* leads to conflict; those who take advice are wise" (Prov. 13:10 NLT).
- "A *hot-tempered person* starts fights" (Prov. 15:18a NLT).
- "*Fools' words* get them into constant quarrels" (Prov. 18:6a NLT).
- "*Wine* produces mockers; *alcohol* leads to brawls" (Prov. 20:1 NLT).
- "Fire goes out without wood, and quarrels disappear when *gossip* stops. A *quarrelsome person* starts fights" (Prov. 26:20–21a NLT).
- "*Greed* causes fighting" (Prov. 28:25a NLT).
- "An *angry person* starts fights; a *hot-tempered person* commits all kinds of sin" (Prov. 29:22 NLT).
- "*Stirring up anger* causes quarrels" (Prov. 30:33).

In this brief review of Proverbs, there is a pattern. Conflict, or strife, or quarrels are caused by heart problems of hatred, pride, quick tempers, sinful communication patterns, substance abuse, and greed. All of these heart issues are defined biblically as sinful. Perhaps it is right to suggest that conflict, which sufficiently rises to the level to accurately be called conflict, is intrinsically sinful. As we will see, it is not only sinful but also foolish.

94. See Jesus' teaching in the Sermon on the Mount for this principle (Matt. 5:17–48). Sins of the heart (lust, hatred, etc.) are said to be just as serious before God as the outward sins that correspond to them (adultery, murder, etc.).

Two Different Definitions of Conflict

Bill feels bad that Dave's investments didn't pay off, but he is convinced that he did nothing wrong in the situation. Despite Dave's repeated attempts to tell Bill in two detailed letters the various ways in which he had failed to be honest with Dave, Bill maintains his innocence. "I don't know why Dave is so upset," Bill tells others in the church. "I'm only human," he has repeatedly explained to Dave.

Dave feels deeply wronged by not only Bill's failure to disclose the nature of the investment, but by his continued misinformation about Dave and Carol to others in the church. Jane has shared her concerns about the situation as a prayer request several times with the ladies in her small group. She has explained how concerned she is that Dave and Carol are too legalistic. "They call everything sin."

If conflict is sin, this changes everything. No longer do we talk as if we just make mistakes or that we are only human. A biblical understanding of the nature of conflict and its relation to sin changes everything. Dave and Carol feel clearly that Bill, initially in his falsehood related to their investments, and later with Jane, in their false communication to others about the situation, have sinned against them. To them, this is not just a personality conflict or just about their differences, but about the actual ways in which they have been harmed by the actions of Bill and Jane. They don't feel comfortable attending the church anymore due to the sidelong glances and whispering among others.

5

Conflict, Sin, and Responsibility

"Boys will be boys." "It takes two to tango." These slogans drive me nuts. When I found myself embroiled not just in a conflict, but also in a struggle to maintain my own sanity, to find reasons to keep going, there was certainly no shortage of people offering me advice. "Just kiss and make up." "You boys just need to fix this." I've always been the type of person that is more than willing to take responsibility, overly so, for things going wrong. The primary struggle for people with my disposition is feeling worthless. I had always been willing to fall on my sword to take the fall before. My resignation from my position as the pastor was familiar territory. "If I leave, you can continue to keep the church going," I told the one who had done me in. Though part of me knew I wasn't the problem, the other part of me suspected that it was me, that it was always me.

Taking the blame for things that were not my fault led me to despair. I should have remained in my position. If the church didn't make it, so be it. It would still have been better for me to fight. One of the key problems I encountered was an unskilled mediator trying to help resolve the situation with an unsophisticated view of conflict. Before he came to work with us, he had the three key people involved in the conflict do soul-searching homework. Looking back, it is no surprise to me that when we met to discuss the sins that the Lord was convicting us about as we completed our homework assignment, I was the only one of the three who was confessing.

Conflict emerges when sinful or inordinate desires that have become demands lead us to commit sin against God and one another. In every discordant situation, there is the need for any who would seek to bring healing and shalom to the parties involved to be able to appropriately and equitably identify roles and responsibilities in the situation. It is this difficult task of sorting that we now consider.

Roles and Responsibilities in Conflict

One of the most difficult tasks in working conflicts through to just, and sometimes, reconciled outcomes is the task of sorting out roles and responsibilities. Conflicts can grow and become quite complicated in the number of individuals in different roles connected in some way to the overall situation. It is important to remember *all sin is interpersonal.* Though many in our day would claim sin only hurts the sinner, as we will see, it inevitably affects others connected in various ways to the offender.

Roles

Conflicts follow somewhat predictable patterns in the way people and groups interact. Because of this regularity, there are typical roles that will emerge in a conflicted situation.[95] It can be helpful for the parties involved, including other third parties, to sort out the roles of each individual involved in a given conflict. What follows are the most common roles we would expect to find.

The Aggressor (Offender, Perpetrator)

Often in a conflict, there is one person who is at the heart of it all. The aggressor is the one who is motivated to both begin and perpetuate

95. These roles are typical in a generic sense. As we will see throughout this work, every conflict is highly unique. While using these general role categories, we need to be aware of the potential for stereotype bias to hinder a more accurate assessment of the situation.

the conflict.[96] The aggressor has an agenda, a definite end in mind albeit subconscious, as he seeks to "defeat" his opponent or "target." He may initially have sought to achieve a personal desire. He may perceive this goal to be blocked by the target. The target is often someone who failed to meet a perceived need or, at the very least, was perceived to be in the way or hindering the obtaining of a growing desire. Frustrated desires have created a perceived need for someone to pay. The most likely candidate to pay the price is the target, the victim.

The aggressor is the one on the attack. His or her methods or motives may vary. Nonetheless, his or her role is able to be determined as we look at the direction of the conflict itself. The conflict is moving from the aggressor toward the target.[97] Sometimes, as we'll discuss below, conflict is the result of mutual aggression. In these two-way conflicts, the aggressors are mutually targeting one another.

The Target (Victim, Aggrieved, or Offended Party)

In a conflict, often there is one person, sometimes more than one, who is the target of the aggression. The word "victim" could be used, but the potential baggage that comes with this identity is worth seeking to avoid. Perhaps you're reading this book because you have been targeted by an aggressor. Perhaps, the conflict you find yourself in was not of your own making, nor is it something you have any desire to be a part of. Nonetheless, you find yourself smack dab in the middle of a conflict and unfortunately the arrows seem to all be pointed at you. You're not alone, nor are you the first. Targets may or may not have done something prior to provoke the aggression. There are examples of targets with prior

96. This role may or may not be obvious upon initial analysis. Many aggressors are masters at manipulating truth. An undiscerning, though otherwise well-intentioned, peacemaker can often be misled by the aggressor to see the target as the "problem," the origin of the conflict. Being skilled at projection is part and parcel of the character flaw in some aggressors.

97. Biblical examples of this abound. To name just a few, think of these examples: King Saul and his aggression toward David; Haman and his aggression toward the Jews; Cain and his aggression toward Abel; and Reuben, Simeon, and Levi toward Joseph.

provocation and the proverbial "innocent victim." Often, in the conflict there are those identified as targets. They are drawn into the conflict by the aggressors.[98]

The Accomplice (Conspirator)

In a conflict, there are often accomplices who have differing levels of alliance with the aggressor(s). These levels of involvement vary greatly, all the way from simply providing a sounding board for the grievances of the aggressor to picking up those grievances and moving to the front of the prosecution of the target. A common problem among accomplices is receiving slander and gossip. Many Christians do not understand that by participating on the receiving end of these practices, they are sinning themselves. Just as there are different levels of involvement, so are there different degrees of responsibility and culpability as the accomplice becomes more and more a part of the aggressors targeting of the accused. Some accomplices are in full knowledge of their role. Others unwittingly fill this role. The nonabusive parent and other adults aware of the situation are often silent accomplices to the abusive parent.[99]

The Bystander

There are often many bystanders to a conflict. Some are "innocent," as we often say. Some are not so innocent. Nonetheless, there are most often more people looking on to the conflict than simply the parties immediately involved in it (the aggressors, the targets, the accomplices). What we do affects others around us. Often children are the bystanders in a home where conflict is present. Church members are usually bystanders in the

98. There are many biblical examples of these targets of conflict: Jesus being targeted by the leadership among the Jews of his day; Mordecai and the way that Haman specifically targeted him as appropriate for the gallows; and David, the anointed future king, targeted by Saul and the spirit that influenced him as the appropriate outlet for his murderous rage.

99. The classic biblical example of this is found in the circumstances surrounding the betrayal and crucifixion of Christ. Judas is an accomplice with the Sanhedrin in their plot to execute Jesus of Nazareth, who threatened their existing power base. He is a coconspirator, an accomplice, in the plot.

midst of conflict among the leadership. Citizens of nations at war look on as battles are fought between them.[100]

There are, however, accomplices who attempt to appear to be bystanders. It is common for those more culpably connected to the presence of the conflict to pretend to be neutral bystanders. This is the myth of neutrality.

The Authorities

Sometimes the authorities over a given context are also parties to the conflict itself. In most cases, the persons in conflict will have some form of authority over them. Authorities in situations of conflict have a definite role to play and a responsibility that corresponds to their position.[101] In a family conflict among siblings, parents often have the proper authority to intervene. In a church conflict, local leaders often have authority to bring to bear. In conflicts among leaders in churches, bigger picture leaders at the district or denominational level often have authority to assist the parties involved in conflict. In any case, those with delegated authority from God have a role to play, even if they choose to do nothing. All authority comes from God. Whether those in authority acknowledge this principle or not, it is nonetheless true they are in their position with power and influence over someone else, having been given their position by God Himself. They are, therefore, ultimately accountable to Him and will give an account to Him for the way they have used the authority given to them. They are stewards of God's authority.

Those with God-given authority over conflict situations have power to influence the outcome toward justice. Sadly, many in this position opt

100. Think about the crowd of Jews who were supportive, for the most part, of the ministry of Jesus. Many were there when the false charges from the accomplices of the Pharisees were leveled at Him. These bystanders did not share the disdain for the Rabbi they had learned so much from. And yet, as is often the case, they did nothing to stop the murderous plot.

101. In the case of the conflict that led to the crucifixion of Jesus, the Roman and Jewish authorities (Pilate and Herod) had God-given authority. Sadly, none of those leaders exercised their God-given authority for justice as they together conspired to put an innocent man to death. For our sake, however, God used their neglect as leaders to ultimately resolve our conflict with Himself.

for a nonconfrontational position, one that will provide a false shalom, rather than true reconciliation. It is common for authorities to do damage control, rather than the hard work that may be required to reach right outcomes. As Edmund Burke said, "The only thing necessary for the triumph of evil is for good men to do nothing." This aptly applies to those in authority.

God

As the Creator and rightful Owner of everything and everyone, God is intimately involved in interpersonal conflicts between His image bearers.

God is a party to every conflict.

When a believing husband and wife quarrel, God is affected as the Father of each party. The prayers of the husband, in particular, are said to be hindered when he fails to "dwell with his wife according to understanding" (1 Pet. 3:7). The reason his prayers are hindered is connected to the care and concern that God has for the husband's wife. As a good and protective Father, He cannot be unaffected by any mistreatment of His daughters whom He loves. In a similar way, God is involved in every conflict among humanity.[102] All of life is lived *coram deo*, before the face of God.

Satanic Forces

Because conflict is inherently connected to the principle of sin, we would do well to note the connection between the enemy of our souls and the presence of conflict among us. All conflicts include the presence

102. It is beyond the scope of this book to fully explain this point. However, the implication here is that God is not impassible as stoics have portrayed Him. He is not only transcendent over creation but is also immanently connected to all and everyone He has made. God feels our conflicts. God is never dispassionate or unaffected. He is not impassible, if we mean He is emotionally unaffected by the affairs of humanity below. This is a great mystery. We ought to be careful in saying this, however, so as not to unintentionally advocate heretical views of God, such as pantheism or panentheism.

of demonic influence working behind the scenes to kill, steal, and destroy the body and witness of Christ (John 10:10).

Types of Conflict

In addition to typical roles in conflicts, there are also three common types of conflict situations with many variations on these three.

Mutual (Two-Way) Conflicts

Some conflicts are indeed mutual. Both parties have sinned against one another in a reciprocating fashion. Though by definition, there will always be an initial offense and a first offender, often the mutuality of the conflict is the overriding nature of the situation. Who started the cycle of interactive conflict is relevant data, but in these conflicts the initial offense is less central to the nature of the conflict. Sometimes, then, conflict is two-way, mutual.[103]

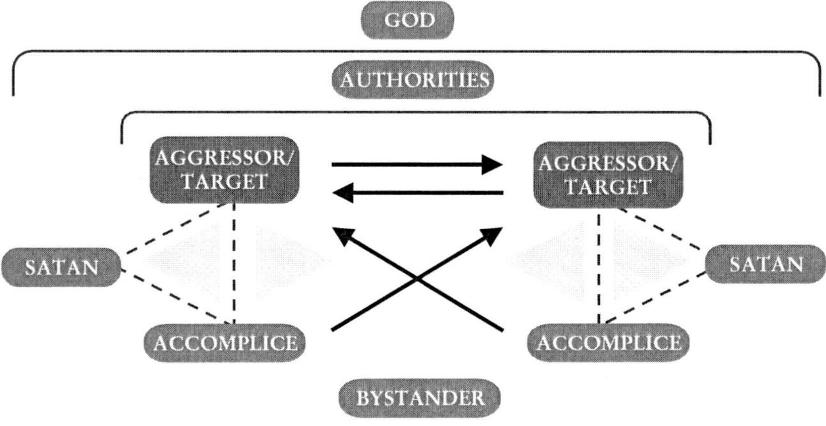

Figure 3.1. Two-Way Conflict

103. There are examples of this kind of two-way conflict in Scripture. Paul and Barnabus had an "honest" difference of opinion about the usefulness of John Mark and whether he ought to go on the missionary journey with them. They sharply disagreed *with one another*. Paul later wrote to the church at Philippi to entreat two women, Euodia and Syntche, to "agree in the Lord" (Phil. 4:2). These two women, who may have been deaconesses, had served together with Paul in the work of the gospel. They had apparently become estranged from one another for a reason unknown to us. Paul encouraged them *both* to be reconciled.

One-Way Conflicts

Often conflicts are not two-way but are substantially one-way in nature. Sometimes an aggressor seeks to harm a given target. The target is sometimes innocent of any direct contribution to the conflict but is drawn into the conflict by the aggressor.[104]

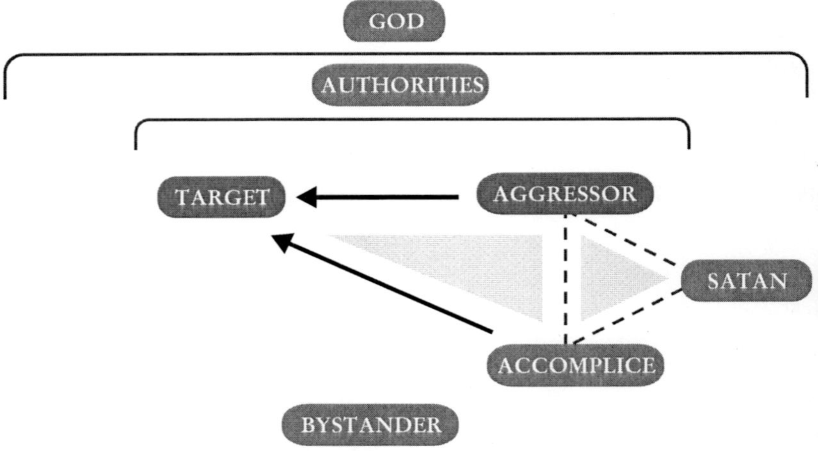

Figure 3.2. One-Way Conflict

Mobbing

Mobbing involves group aggression. This is multiple aggressors working together, à la William Golding's *Lord of the Flies*. Typically, in such a mob there can be a form of "group think." Each individual gives up a large portion of his rational capacity for the sake of the group and what "we" think or know to be true. There may or may not be a main aggressor

104. Scripture gives many examples of this as well. Jesus was the target of the Pharisees and the Herodians, who sought to kill Him. Jesus was not responsible for originating the conflict, though at times His truth threatened to expose them for what they really were. He did not seek their destruction, but they clearly sought His. Haman also initiated aggression toward Mordecai, illustrating a one-way conflict.

initially instigating the group dynamic. Nevertheless, at some point, the group loses the ability to think for itself. It believes its own perpetuated reality.[105]

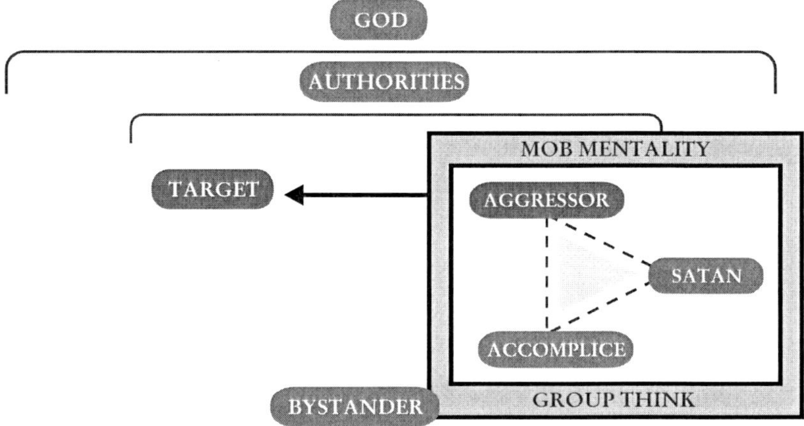

Figure 3.3. Mob Conflict

Responsibilities in Conflict

When attempting to resolve conflict in a God-honoring way, the concept of equity or justice needs to be as prevalent as the principle of mercy. Far too often, the Christian community has failed to understand the differing roles in conflict and to assign just responsibilities to those differing parties.[106]

105. A biblical example of this is the crucifixion mob. The crowd was initially worked up by the religious leaders (the agressors) who sought to destroy Jesus. The whole crowd gathered (the mob) despite the lack of any real evidence or credible witnesses and in unison demanded, "crucify him!" Another historical example can be found in the group think that characterized the ranks in the Nazi regime, which carried out some of the greatest atrocities against human beings in history.

106. The classic example of this failure is the church's unjust dealing with cases of domestic abuse. It has been far too common in some Christian circles for church leadership to perpetuate abuse among women and children in the name of forced forgiveness toward their abusers. Instead, abusers should be held responsible for their actions, and if appropriate, forgiveness should be granted in the context of safety, repentance, and changed behavior.

The church and Christians have consistently pursued this task of sorting with two unconscious principles in play. Both "one-size-fits-all" and "all-have-sinned" thinking pervade many current cataloguing processes. These two simplistic paradigms undermine the just and equitable distribution of responsibilities, leading to a lesser likelihood of obtaining a fair outcome.

One Size Fits All

Conflicts are all unique. When we try to oversimplify conflict and reduce conflict resolution or the conciliation process to a simple formulaic approach, we do disservice and injustice to the parties involved in any specific conflict. This one-size-fits-all approach is highly problematic and unlikely to produce God-glorifying results. It is essential to sort through the conflict with wisdom and discernment provided both by good practices of listening and interviewing in combination with the wisdom and discernment that the Spirit gives. Cookie-cutter approaches to conflicts and their resolution fail to discern the unique nature of each situation. There is no substitute for the hard work required to carefully, deliberately, and objectively process data to come to a more accurate assessment of the case before us, in all its specificity.

All Have Sinned

Evangelical Christianity teaches on the basis of Romans 3:23 and other clear passages that "all have sinned and fall short of the glory of God." The problem of sin finds only one solution in terms of salvation. This is found only in the gospel of Jesus Christ, the God–man who was sacrificed as a perfect atoning sacrifice for the forgiveness of sins. All evangelicals agree on this point. This is a true statement at all times, both in the midst of conflict, as well as in the absence of a specific conflict situation. Why is this relevant to this discussion?

It has become common practice for some in attempting to deal with conflict situations to spotlight this truth as the core truth that needs application. It goes something like this. Party A and Party B are involved in a conflict. We know from Scripture that Party A and Party B are both sinners. Therefore, we conclude that Party A and Party B are both culpable and responsible for the conflict and should equally repent, or forbear, or forgive the other. This simple formula presumes that there is no such thing as an innocent target in a conflict on the basis of the nonexistence of an innocent person.

"We're all sinners," the pastor says to the wife who is in his office for the umpteenth time with bruises and other evident signs of physical abuse. "Certainly, you know that you must have something to do with the dynamic in your home. If you were submitting to your husband as the Scripture tells you to, he would not become so angry. Do you feel that you need to own your sin of disrespect toward your husband and seek God's and his forgiveness of your failure to live in obedience to God's requirements?"

This may be an extreme or even ridiculous example of this principle, but this and others less obviously like it are daily occurring in the evangelical community.

Assigning Proper Responsibilities

In an ultimate sense, only God knows perfectly and exhaustively the specific part each one plays in a given conflict situation. However, it is possible, even within our human limitations, to sort through conflicts, even complicated ones, and assign appropriate responsibilities to different parties. To do this, we must attempt to approach the task of sorting and assigning responsibilities with as much freedom from stereotypes and preconceptions as possible. This is not the place for snap judgments or hasty conclusions. We must, as objectively as possible, gather data from the parties and relevant eyewitnesses, suspend judgment, and avoid any premature conclusions. Once we have gathered sufficient data, we can begin to identify actual offenses and assign responsibilities accordingly.

We may find the situation before us is essentially mutual, that equitable sorting would dictate a fifty-fifty picture of responsibility. We may only do this, of course, if the objective data supports this finding. On the other hand, we may determine the data suggest a one-way, 100-zero or nearly one-way, ninety-ten distribution of accountability. Assumptions and hasty conclusions are our biggest enemies and potential pitfalls in this process. In any case, rightly understanding the situation and rightly assigning responsibility, though hard work, is a God-given stewardship.

Sin and Conflict

As we have seen, true conflict does not exist without the presence of actual sin, real offenses. If conflict is dependent on the committal of sin, how do we rightly assign responsibility for differing types and levels of sin involved in conflicted situations? To provide the basis for justly distributing responsibility, we need to introduce the difference between primary and secondary offenses.

Primary Offenses

There is a difference, not in essence but in degree, between primary and secondary sins. To illustrate the difference, let's use the clearest example of this principle. In the case of ongoing domestic abuse, the pattern is incredibly predictable. The abuser, typically but not always the husband, sinfully takes out his frustrations on his wife in various forms of abuse. Physical, emotional, verbal, psychological, or sexual offenses against her are committed. In this example, the husband is clearly the aggressor. He is initiating and perpetuating the violence. His offenses, what he commits as part of the overall campaign of domination, are the primary offenses in the conflict.

Secondary, Reactive Offenses

Lest we be confused, all sin is sin. Sin of any sort is serious and requires genuine repentance, forsaking, and forgiveness. Having said that, it is common in conflict situations for one party to commit lesser offenses in the course of the battle and under the provocation of the aggressor. If we utilize a paradigm of sin that does not attempt to understand this distinction, we are in jeopardy of inequitably assigning responsibility for the situation.

Secondary offenses are the reactive responses to the primary sins committed against us that may be rightly considered sin, but always need to be considered within the overall context of the relational conflict and overall patterns of sin.

To return to the example of domestic abuse, it is typical in an abusive situation for the victim, or target, to reach a breaking point and lash out in some way against the victimizer. For instance, in the midst of yet another incident of physical abuse, having been beaten and knocked to the ground by her husband, a wife cries out, "Damn you." Her provocation triggers an additional beating from her husband. Fast-forward the situation to the pastor's office the next week. The pastor, upon hearing of the woman's use of profanity and disrespect toward her husband, exhorts her to repent. The husband is, likewise, encouraged to stop his physical abuse. The controlling paradigm however is that both parties have sinned. She swore in her anger. He beat his wife. How are these similar sins?

This example is illustrative of the failure to distinguish between primary and secondary offenses. The man beating his wife is the primary problem in this situation. While we could split hairs to rightly call profanity or disrespect against her husband sinful, her response is a reasonable response, albeit potentially less than entirely sanctified to the extremely sinful situation at hand. This is all we mean by secondary offenses.

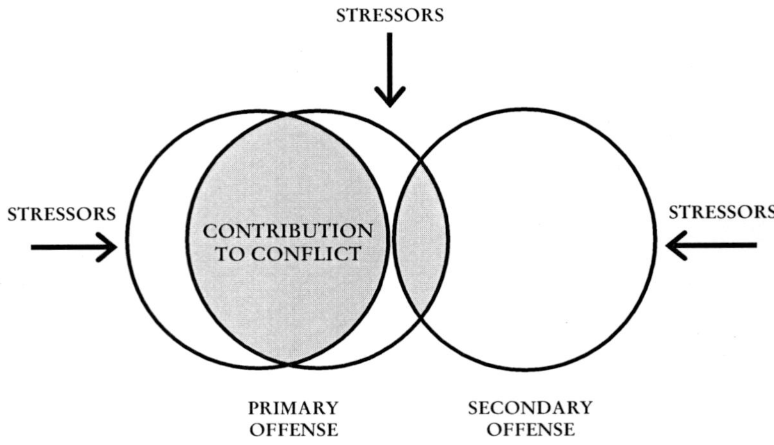

Figure 4. Differing Contributions to Conflict

Myths about Sin That Don't Help the Process

Though the presence of conflict is being connected to the presence of sin, we need to be careful as we proceed. Equitable sorting out and assigning individual responsibilities are hard work. The following myths related to common doctrines of sin will not prove helpful in seeking to resolve broken relationships.

Sin is Sin: The Denial of Degrees of Sin

The essence of the lie is this: Sin is sin. There are no degrees of sin. This is a fairly common evangelical myth. This teaching is often based on a misinterpretation of the Sermon on the Mount. In that sermon, Jesus contrasted the common view of the day regarding God's law with the true essence of the law. He contrasted contemporary Jewish views of marriage and divorce with God's heart. He contrasted the common view of love, which excluded enemies, with God's requirement to love our neighbor. He contrasted adultery of the heart, looking at a woman lustfully, with the contemporary view of adultery as only a physical act.

Taking this last example, we can see this myth in real life. If looking at another woman lustfully is the same as adultery, one has already committed spiritual adultery in looking lustfully at her, wrongfully desiring her. Jesus did intend to teach us that this lusting in the heart is, in fact, sin. However, the paradigm often goes on as follows. "I've already sinned anyway. I might as well continue in sin at this point and pursue the actual adulterous relationship with the woman." This all follows under the myth that "sin is sin." The practical problem with this idea is in using this falsehood, the devil moves us deeper into sin. "I've already sinned, I might as well keep going." The truth, however, is that the sooner I come to my senses and turn from the sinful path, the less damage will be done with God and others.

There are degrees of sin. There are corresponding degrees of consequences for those degrees of sin. When Jesus taught the principle that looking at a woman was the same at the heart level as adultery, he was referring to the *essence* of sin. When he said to hate someone in our heart was the same as murder, he was referring to the *essence* of sin. He did not mean to teach by these sayings there is no difference between lustful desire and consummating the act of adultery or there is no difference between the presence of hateful thoughts in the heart and the commission of actual murder. Sin isn't just sin; the particulars and the level of sin are relevant. As one writer expressed it:

> All sin is equally wrong, but not all sin is equally bad. Acts are either right or wrong. They are either consonant with God's will or not. But among good acts some are better than others, and among wrong acts some worse than others.[107]

The church has throughout most of its history maintained that there are, in fact, degrees of sin. Sin is sin, but there is a critical difference between different types and expressions of sin committed by individuals in the context of a given scenario.

---

107. Plantinga, *Not the Way,* 21.

There Are No Innocent Victims

This is the myth that denies the possibility of innocence or of even partial innocence. The argument goes something like this: All people involved in conflicts are sinners by nature. Therefore, no one is truly innocent and each party must have contributed to the conflict.

Is that true? Does that logically follow? If two sinners are in conflict, can we conclude that both are at fault or that neither is innocent? To disprove this myth, consider the following examples of "innocent victims."

Jesus is the ultimate innocent victim. Never committing any sin, He was crucified unjustly. Abel did nothing to deserve his murder at the hands of his brother Cain. The envy and murderous intent that led to Joseph's betrayal at the hands of his brothers was not his fault. What did Tamar do to deserve the brutal rape of her brother Amnon? How was she responsible for the growing desire in Amnon to have what God had clearly forbidden, a sexual relationship with his sister? What did Mordecai do to deserve the rage of Haman against him? Was Bathsheba responsible for enticing King David by taking what many think was a ceremonial bath on the rooftop that day, not knowing she was being observed? Certainly, Uriah was innocent of any wrongdoing.

There are no innocent people. All of us have fallen short of God's standard and His glory. There are, however, people in given situations who are *innocent targets* of the aggression of others.

Sinners Can't Help Sinning: The Antinomian Myth

A key doctrine that emerged in the Protestant Reformation of the sixteenth and seventeenth centuries is total depravity—all people by virtue of their connection to Adam are born dead in sin and incapable, in themselves, of doing good in an ultimate sense. So, people are not basically good or in themselves capable of moral reform. Total depravity reminds us that we are desperately in need of the grace of God to will and to do according to His good pleasure (Phil. 2:13). We can't do it on our own. On our own, we are dead in trespasses and sins (Eph. 2:5). The grace of

God goes before us, enabling us to repent and believe on the Lord Jesus Christ.[108] We need God's grace to enable us to respond to the gospel.

But what happens at conversion? According to the teaching of the New Testament, we are made "new creatures in Christ" (2 Cor. 5:17). We have a new identity altogether different from our former life of sin (1 Cor. 6:11; Eph. 4:20–24). The Christian life is one of marked change from the former way of living. True Christianity always involves transformation from the inside out, more and more into the likeness of Christ (2 Cor. 3:18; Rom. 8:29). Antinomianism, cheap grace, obscures this truth.

Antinomianism removes accountability from the table. The ground of any godly process is truth. The establishment of truth is essential to the process of equitably sorting through responsibilities. In a grace-only paradigm, it is entirely too easy to simply lie or somehow distort the facts of the case to avoid potential consequences. We are sinners. Though we still struggle with sin, the good news is that Christ has come to not only set us free from the penalty of sin but also its power![109] In a world of no responsibility, where cheap grace reigns supreme, there is simply no possibility for biblical peacemaking. This is a serious and damnable error that still prevails in the church. We can and should cease sinning. When we spurn the grace of God and reject his provision that leads to our holiness, we are fully accountable for our actions that follow in conflict situations.

The Myth of Neutrality

There is one additional myth. Thirty-eight individuals looked on as twenty-eight-year-old Kitty Genovese was brutally stabbed and killed. No one did anything to intervene. On March 13, 1964, at three o'clock in

108. Wesleyans and Calvinists agree that grace goes before. The difference between the two positions is in the extent of the grace that goes before (prevenient). For Wesleyans, grace is given to all to enable them to respond to the gospel. For the Calvinist, grace is only given to some, the elect. Both sides of the debate agree, though, no one can respond to the gospel in their own strength.

109. This reminds us of Augustus Toplady's great line in "Rock of Ages," that the blood of Christ shed for us would "cleanse me from its [sin's] guilt and *power* (italics added)."

the morning, the young woman was killed in plain sight and sound of her thirty-eight "neighbors."[110] This event has become a landmark in the field of social psychology. Researchers have labeled this phenomenon the Genovese syndrome or the bystander effect. Various scientists have sought to understand the why of the unwillingness to help Kitty on the part of all these passive onlookers. Did each of them conclude that someone else would help? Did they each assume the others would do something and therefore, their intervention was not needed? "Someone else will surely stop it." Social psychologists speculate about these possibilities under a theory of diffusion of responsibility. Diffusion of responsibility means that duty has become so diffuse, so thin, that no one in society any longer owns individual accountability. Everyone, apparently, is perhaps too busy looking out for number one to care about others anymore.

This is eerily parallel to the parable of the Good Samaritan told by Jesus (Luke 10:25–37). In the allegory, several religious leaders stepped over or around the wounded man lying in the road on their way to greater service of God. "It's not my responsibility," they perhaps said within themselves as they ignored his plight. We, like these characters in the story, have also developed an overindividualized ethos. We have apparently bought into the lie that our sin only affects us. We tell ourselves we are not connected socially, that holding people accountable for their actions or intervening to help victims of others is "none of our business." We are a highly disconnected and dispassionate people in this regard.

This Western mind-set is foreign to the landscape of the Bible. The Bible makes bold statements about our interconnectedness. For instance, Paul within the analogy of the body stated "when one member suffers, we all suffer" (1 Cor. 12:26). We Americans have a different and opposite motto, "It's not my problem." We are obsessed with our own personal comfort and happiness. Unfortunately, the societal work of conflict resolution within the larger picture of the Christian community often cramps

110. Remember, the parable of the Good Samaritan is in response to the question, "Who is my neighbor?"

our style. We don't want to get involved in helping to do the hard work of "restoring someone to usefulness in the kingdom" (Gal. 6:1). If it doesn't directly impact us, then we are comfortable ignoring the injustice all around us.

At its worst, this apathy is reflective of our *moral indifference*. The opposite of love is not hate, but indifference. When we are bent on staying in the middle, on remaining neutral, we are in danger of drifting into this ethical position of indifference. In the midst of conflict involving others, we often insist on our neutrality. "If it doesn't involve me, then I'm staying out of it altogether." "What happens under their roof is their business." This presumes that we can be neutral. Neutrality is an ethically impossible place to remain.

Jesus warned us about neutrality. He said quite clearly, "Whoever is not with me is against me, and whoever does not gather with me scatters" (Matt. 12:30). Jesus clearly articulated this principle of antithesis. Two utterly opposed and contrary things, such as good and evil, God and His enemies, light and darkness, wisdom and foolishness, cannot be rendered compatible. The Bible in the Old and the New Testament defines our responsibility to advocate for the oppressed. God is not neutral and His people are to reflect His value system. We've come a long way, however in modern Evangelicalism in creating a kinder, gentler, and morally indifferent deity. Our "God" stays out of conflicts and doesn't take sides. He would never do anything so unloving as judge the wicked for their wickedness. This theology is reflective of our noteworthy lack of firsthand experience with evil and oppression. Miroslav Volf pointed to the shallowness of our theology:

> To the person inclined to dismiss it [divine judgment], I suggest imagining that you are delivering a lecture in a war zone (which is where a paper that underlines this chapter was originally delivered). Among your listeners are people whose cities and villages have been plundered, then burned and leveled to the ground, whose daughters and sisters have been raped, whose fathers and brothers had their throats slit. The

> topic of the lecture: A Christian attitude toward violence. The thesis: we should not retaliate since God is perfect noncoercive love. Soon you would discover that it takes the quiet of a suburban home for the birth of the thesis that human nonviolence corresponds to God's refusal to judge. In a scorched land, soaked in the blood of the innocent, it will invariably die. And as one watches it die, one will do well to reflect about many other pleasant captivities of the liberal mind. [111]

Often in conflict situations, the bystander is brought into the fray, at least in part. Refusal to side with the wronged party under the stance of neutrality is culpable. Neutrality in the face of serious injustice is morally reprehensible.

***To attempt neutrality is, by default,
to side with the perpetrator.***

To do nothing is a failure to condemn the practice of the oppressor and a simultaneous failure to validate the pain and suffering of the oppressed.[112] Yet, how often is it that bystanders refuse to take a side only to do what Proverbs warns of, "to listen to one side without hearing the other" (Prov. 18:17)?

It is often the case, in conflicted situations, that the perpetrator by nature is more willing to download their distorted account of the circumstances to others. Many innocent bystanders lose their innocence when they receive these slanderous and inappropriate charges against others. Frequently, they never check with the other party to confirm the information they have so gullibly received. In this way the not-so-innocent bystanders are actually accomplices. To become an accomplice is to lose

111. Miroslav Volf, *Exclusion and Embrace: A Theological Exploration of Identity, Otherness, and Reconciliation* (Nashville, TN: Abingdon, 1996), 304.

112. If I am "fine" and carrying on a relationship as usual with someone's abusive spouse, what message am I sending to their victim? By acting as if nothing is wrong, I am at some level condoning it and allowing the abuse to continue. We need moral courage to step forward and be counted on the side of justice and opposed to injustice.

professed neutrality and to prove the point that, at a profound level, our neutrality has always been mythical.

> I swore never to be silent whenever and wherever human beings endure suffering and humiliation. We must always take sides. Neutrality helps the oppressor, never the victim. Silence encourages the tormentor, never the tormented.[113]

Sorting It All Out

There is a strong correlation between conflict and sin. This is not a simplistic approach to the problem but an honest attempt to fully integrate the biblical paradigm into our discussion. In many ways, modern views of conflict are too simple. Resolution of conflict, particularly among professing Christians, is often seen as just forgiving and forgetting. So, in suggesting that the model for reconciliation be simplified, it does not imply that it be made simplistic or naive.

The Bible tells us over and over sin is a problem, a serious one. Sin has consequences directly connected to its practice. Treating sins with the appropriate level of sobriety and concern is important for both the perpetrator and the victim. On both sides of the equation, honesty really is the best policy. Truth demands we sort things out in correspondence with what has actually happened. Accurately understanding roles and differing contributions and responsibilities in conflict situations is part of rightly representing the values of the kingdom to come.

I'm the Victim

Bill explains to the conciliator, "I'm the victim. Do you realize how much sleep I've lost over this situation? I haven't been able to focus on my work and am losing clients as a result. Don't you see how Dave's false accusations are ruining my reputation?" After the first meeting with Bill

113. Elie Wiesel, acceptance speech of Nobel Peace Prize (Oslo, Norway, December 10, 1986).

alone, the conciliation team thought that he was the victim, and Dave and Carol were being legalistic and unforgiving toward Bill and Jane.

Fortunately, the conciliators made sure to hear the other side of the story from not only Dave and Carol but from others in their circle of friends at the church (Prov. 18:17). The more they listened to the additional data, their view of the situation changed dramatically. They not only drew different conclusions about Bill and Dave's contributions to the conflict, they also began to understand the contributions of their spouses and others in the church who had taken up Bill's cause and had spread false rumors about Dave and Carol to others in the congregation.

The pastor of their church who felt inadequate to help the two families resolve their conflict was grateful for the help from the conciliation team they called in to help. Fortunately, he had been introduced to their services at a recent conflict resolution seminar. He ended up being a key part of the solution to the situation and a real support to Dave and Carol as they processed through the sense of injustice and anger they felt toward Bill and Jane.

6

Conflict in the Real World

My personality style is prone to make every effort to keep the peace. I had been through the Peacemaker seminar several times. I taught the material to our small congregation at the outset of our church plant, in the hope of avoiding the pain we had just previously gone through in a church split. I knew things that were "too serious to overlook" needed to be lovingly confronted. I had done this several times with each of the people involved. Nothing was working. The conflict was getting worse. My emotional state was declining day by day.

I would pray without ceasing. "Lord, you know the situation we are in. Help me to see my contribution to this situation. Help others to see theirs as well. Lord, if You don't intervene, this is going to get ugly." When the mediator arrived, I had some hope that we could right the ship. We began with worship. I was trying to focus on the Lord but felt deep inner anxiety about what was coming next. The mediator allowed one of the men to pour out his venom at me for what seemed like an eternity. Pure contempt. Pure disdain. I was worthless, and he was making sure I understood it. The mediator did nothing. His accomplice sat there in silence, looking innocent.

The back wall was blue. In future counseling sessions of EMDR,[114] the color blue was connected to the intensity of the pain. I hate that color blue.

After that first intense meeting with the parties involved, however, I found myself in the hospital with what I had feared was a heart attack. It wasn't my physical heart. The pain and numbness was in my right arm, not my left. My side of the bed was soaked in sweat that morning. My shirt was completely drenched. It stunk. My wife was scared. This wasn't going to work. The mediator wasn't going to solve our problems. "But Lord, you are sovereign over the affairs of men. You can turn the hearts of kings. Surely, you can change all hearts involved and grant us the grace of repentance and renewal." This is a mystery I don't understand. Why does God, who has the ability to grant the grace of repentance, not intervene? I identified with Asaph as I puzzled over God's apparent silence in the midst of my collapse.

I thought the worst was over, that the enemy had decided to leave me alone. The unresolved conflict that led to my resignation was now five years ago. It was a new day. I was excited to be reentering the ministry. The day my pastor called me was one I'll never forget. I was cleaning out the storage room. The phone rang. It was the pastor. He wanted to talk to me about coming onto the staff of the church we had attended for five long years since my resignation. For five years, I mostly avoided serving in the church—just sat in the pew trying to survive, trying to get over my previous experiences. I had gotten to know him by helping him sort out a recent confusing conflict situation and had gained a measure of his trust sufficient for him to offer me the position. He and I met at a coffee shop to "seal the deal." I agreed to take the position he had offered. No one knew this was happening. Someone did.

Within days of his offer to bring me onto the staff, He received a phone call from a local pastor seeking to warn him about my "character problem."

114. EMDR stands for eye movement desensitization reprogramming, a counseling technique that utilizes bilateral stimulation to help the brain reprocess traumatic experiences. In the midst of an EMDR session, the client often reexperiences aspects of the trauma.

There was no way for this pastor to have known he had just offered me the position. If I believed in coincidence, this would be a substantial one. I don't. There is a network of highly coordinated intelligence seeking to destroy and discredit us. That network is able to highly influence the actions of others around us. I made it through the attack that day, knowing that my enemy in the unseen world was real. I wonder when he'll strike again.

Conflict, as we have defined it, emerges as a result of personal desires growing into the commitment of offenses against others. Correctly sorting through roles and responsibilities in conflict situations is critical to the task of justly working toward right outcomes. What about God's role in interpersonal conflicts? We've already said He is never at fault and He is never unaffected by our plight. How, then, does His unique place as the Creator and Sustainer of all things relate to the presence of conflict here on earth? What about the enemy? How does he relate to conflict?

God's Sovereignty and Conflict

If conflict exists, it does so by the permission of God. He allows trials to come into the lives of His dear children. Conflict almost certainly causes pain and suffering. When we approach the subject of God's sovereignty and suffering, we necessarily move into the realm of theodicy, the struggle to understand God's goodness juxtaposed to His permission of evil.[115] From the beginning of time, men and women have grappled with the apparent disconnect between God's sovereignty over all things and the existence of evil.

The simple problem of evil is usually stated as a three-part question. If God is all-powerful and God is all-loving, why would a loving God allow evil to exist if it is within His power to disallow its existence? The answers range from denials of God's sovereignty to denials of God's goodness and every human attempt at reconciling these apparently contrary principles

115. Theodicy is the defense of God's goodness and omnipotence in light of the existence of evil. It is often referred to as simply the "problem of evil."

on the continuum connecting these two extremes.[116] The short answer to the problem is God is sovereign, God is loving, and for reasons known only to Him, our God allows pain and suffering in our lives, fully holding the perpetrators responsible for their actions and yet often working to bring good out of evil.[117] This does not make evil good. Evil is always evil. Isaiah cautions against wrong thinking in this area. He says, "Woe to those who call evil good, and good evil; Who substitute darkness for light and light for darkness; Who substitute bitter for sweet and sweet for bitter" (Isa. 5:20 NASB)! Evil doesn't become good because God is able to bring good out of the situation. It is still evil. The perpetrator of the sinful act is still accountable before a holy God.

However, God is able to work together in all things, even sinful things, to produce good results in the lives of those He has called according to His purpose (Rom. 8:28). His express purpose is, "to conform them to the image of His Son" (v. 29). God, then, is able to take evil and sin and all things in our lives and produce from the ashes a beautiful conformity to Christ in our character.

A classic example of this is Joseph and his brothers. His brothers, driven by envy, nearly killed him. In a moment of conscience, however, they decided rather to sell him to a passing caravan. They then perpetuated a lie to cover their actions, allowing their father to feel the grief connected to the supposed death of his beloved son.[118] About twenty-four years later, through a providential famine, the brothers were brought to an encoun-

---

116. Denying God's sovereignty is proposed in current process theology and open theism. Denying God's goodness is a common error of some contemporary Calvinists (e.g., R. C. Sproul Jr. as quoted in Keathley, *Salvation and Sovereignty: A Molinist Approach*, who said that in terms of the origin of sin, "the trail leads ultimately back to God.").

117. For further study, see Stackhouse Jr., *Can God Be Trusted? Faith and the Challenge of Evil.*

118. The power of family secrets is evident in this story. The brothers kept their dirty little secret for all those years and were unmoved by the prolonged grief of their father. This showed the callousness of the brothers' hearts caused by their foolishness.

ter with the brother they had betrayed.[119] Remarkably, Joseph forgave his brother's treachery, making an important statement as he did so. Joseph, in Genesis 50:20, said concerning what had happened, "As for you, you meant evil against me, but God meant it for good in order to bring about this present result, to preserve many people alive" (NASB).

Joseph displayed the ability to discern two different intentions in the same event. His brothers meant harm to him. The Lord, in those same events, had a plan to not only ultimately do him good, but to save the entire nation, including his brothers and father. This is a helpful perspective in prolonged or unresolved conflict. God allows conflict in our lives and somehow mysteriously overrules the sins of those who offend us to bring about His holy purpose.[120] These two are simultaneously working, the secret and sovereign will of God and the sinful purpose of men. D. A. Carson commented,

> As Joseph explains, God was working sovereignly in the event of his being sold into Egypt, but the brothers' guilt is not thereby assuaged (they intended harm to Joseph); the brothers were responsible for their action, but God was not thereby reduced to a merely contingent role; and while the brothers were evil, God himself had only good intentions.[121]

Jesus is the ultimate example we are called to imitate. As He interacted with opposition in His earthly life, He trusted in the sovereignty and goodness of God. Our suffering is intimately connected to Him. It is an intimate part of our fellowship with Him (Phil. 3:20). Our well-being in adversity and conflict is directly connected to our perspective. Do we have

119. The following are key dates in the life of Joseph. He was seventeen when he was sold into Egypt. He was thirty when he was made overseer under Pharaoh. He was thirty-nine when his brothers first came to Egypt (second year of the famine, or nine years after being made overseer). He was probably forty-one or so (twenty-four years after being sold to Egypt) when the brothers came a second time and Jacob came to Egypt. He was 110 when he died. Therefore, he lived for another seventy years after he and his brothers and father were reunited.

120. This never justifies evil nor makes God the author of it.

121. D. A. Carson, *How Long O Lord? Reflections on Suffering and Evil* (Grand Rapids, MI: Baker, 1990), 206.

the same mind that was in Jesus who saw past the present affliction to the great joy that was to come as a result (Heb. 12:2)? God is sovereign over conflict in our lives. Just like Jesus, the Man, we can trust Him.

The Conflict behind the Conflict

Conflict is never devoid of demonic influence. Beyond our normal ability to discern with our five senses lies a vast network of angelic beings. Some of these angels have remained loyal to God and to His service. They constantly work to restrain evil and to protect the lives of God's people. On the other hand, there is a sinister network of fallen angels (demons), who seek to thwart the purpose and plan of God under the leadership of Lucifer. Though dealt a decisive blow in the cross of Calvary, these demonic powers have not yet finally or fully been removed from the earth. They are ever working behind the scenes to seek to bring about the destruction of God's greatest creation, humankind. They hate the image of God in us.

Many books on conflict make no mention of these unseen spiritual forces of wickedness all around us. It's as if we don't believe they exist. Have they convinced us they're not there? "The greatest trick the devil ever pulled was convincing the world he doesn't exist."[122] The devil's foremost strategy is to convince us he is not there; there is nothing beyond the data we can gather with our five senses. This is part of the current antisupernatural bent that characterizes our modern culture. We are a nation of materialists and skeptics. A recent Gallup poll revealed that while "nine in ten Americans still believe in God . . . only forty-three percent (43%) of Americans believe the devil to be a 'living entity,' as opposed to a symbol of evil."[123] If we do not believe *in* him, we are powerless to *resist* him!

---

122. Charles Pierre Baudelaire, "The Generous Gambler" (London, 1864). This quote was picked up by C. S. Lewis in his famous work, *The Screwtape Letters*.

123. John A. Murray, "C. S. Lewis and the Devil: Admirers of 'The Screwtape Letters' Range from Monty Python's John Cleese to Focus on the Family," *The Wall Street Journal Online* (August 5, 2011), http//:online.wsj.com/articles/SB10001424053111903454504576486441729097076.html.

Paul unapologetically concluded our wrestling, our true conflict, is not with our fellow man, but rather with beings not of this world (Eph. 6:10–12). Paul is not alone in this thought. Jesus Himself recognized and confronted the conflict behind his conflict with Peter. As He sought to explain the way of the cross, Peter under Satanic influence resisted Him. Notice Jesus' response to Peter and to Satan:

> From that time Jesus began to show his disciples that he must go to Jerusalem and suffer many things from the elders and chief priests and scribes, and be killed, and on the third day be raised. And Peter took him aside and began to rebuke him, saying, "Far be it from you, Lord! This shall never happen to you." But he turned and said to Peter, "*Get behind me, Satan*! You are a hindrance to me. For you are not setting your mind on the things of God, but on the things of man." (Matt. 16:21–23; italics added)

Jesus indisputably saw the presence of Satan in this encounter with Peter. He went so far as to confront Satan and his influence in Peter. Was Jesus delusional or superstitious? Or did He see things for how they really were?

This is not the only direct reference to the devil's work, even in the twelve. Just prior to the night Jesus was betrayed, Luke recorded, "Then Satan entered into Judas called Iscariot, who was of the number of the twelve" (Luke 22:3). So the inspired understanding of the role of Judas, the son of perdition, is that he did what he did under the influence of Satan. Our conflicts are never solely with flesh and blood.

Both Peter's correction of Jesus and Judas' betrayal of Jesus to the leaders of Israel were done verbally. The devil and his followers use various means to tempt us to sin and to keep us down when we fall. In all these things, at both the supernatural and natural levels, communication plays a key role in the process. One of the names for Satan is the devil, *diabolos*, in the Greek (Rev. 12:9). This term is derived from the verb *diaballo*, "to accuse or malign," and is thus translated as "the accuser" or "the slanderer." The devil is the originator of communication intent on destroying others. He often uses human beings as dupes to do his bidding. The tongue is his weapon of choice. How often is diabolical communication a significant part of a conflict? Its presence belies the presence of the enemy.

The prevailing wisdom of our day is naturalistic. Even among believers, many of us have been intimidated by the scientific community to abandon, or at least downplay, our supernatural worldview. Christianity is by definition supernatural. The entirety of our faith rests on the reality of the supernatural, a personal Holy Spirit, not a mere force or power. In our conflict situations, it is easy for us to follow the natural path so prevalent in our culture. We can use the best human techniques the growing science of mediation has to offer. The whole while, however, we can be completely oblivious to the presence of evil behind the curtain. We have a real enemy. His name is Satan. He has many fallen angels in his ranks. When we find ourselves in conflict, we would do well to recognize his presence.

How Should We Then Live?

If God is working out His overarching purpose in our lives, not only despite but also through the sinful conflicts we face, how should we then interact with those situations? What is our proper response to conflict as sons and daughters of the living God?

Overlooking and Forbearance

The faithful follower of God, frequently and as a default response, forbears the offenses of others. "It is a man's glory to overlook an offense" (Prov. 19:11). "Love covers over a multitude of sins" (1 Pet. 4:8). "Whoever covers an offense seeks love, but he who repeats a matter separates close friends" (Prov. 17:9). "Love is not easily offended; it is not touchy" (1 Cor. 13:5). All human relationships exist between imperfect and incomplete people. Though we are being made perfect, none of us has arrived (Phil. 3:12–14). If we are all still affected by our fall, our relationships will at times reflect this reality. All interpersonal relationships are relationships between sinners.[124]

Because we are imperfect, we will inevitably offend one another through unintentional or intentional ways. The very best of human relationships cannot endure a standard of perfection. If it were not for the countless times we simply grant one another charitable judgments, we couldn't even have relationships at all. This happens every day in our marriages. One spouse, for any number of reasons or even for no reason at all, offends the other in minor ways. In healthy marriages, couples are not quick to take offense or to hold on to minor offenses, but rather cover them over in love within the context of the overall life situation. Couples give mercy and grace to one another as the air they breathe within their relationship. This is a healthy, happy marriage.

This principle of overlooking or forbearance then is our first line of defense. Not only in marriage but also in all significant relationships, it is our default response to perceived or minor slights or attacks. We rightly factor into the situation all that we know about the other person and his character. "It's not like him to respond that way. I wonder what stresses he is under at work?" And we simply overlook the offense. When someone inadvertently steps on our toe at Wal-Mart, we simply overlook it. We presume that the action was unintentional, and we cover over the action, get over the pain in our big toe, and finish our shopping. The example of someone unintentionally stepping on our toe, however, is at the lowest end of the continuum of conflicts. For such minor offenses, "the offended party simply bears the insult. The offense is set aside, lovingly covered for Christ's sake. For petty and unintentional offenses, this is the proper and

124. This is not to validate the thinking that says, "We are all sinners. We will inevitably sin. We cannot not sin, because we are sinners." Though we are sinners not yet glorified, progress toward holiness in this life is not only possible but an essential aspect of true Christianity. The Bible, contrary to some theologies, not only calls us "saints" but calls us to be them.

loving way to forgive—unilaterally, without confrontation and without stirring any strife."[125]

Overlooking is a unilateral decision on the part of the person offended to bear the cost of the offense without any additional process of reconciliation between the parties.

We unilaterally forgive, without any apology, minor offenses committed in the context of otherwise loving relationships. There is nothing further that needs to be done. Because of the speed at which we do this on a daily basis, we may not think through the assumptions included in overlooking an offense. When we overlook offenses, we implicitly agree that:

- The minor offense actually occurred.
- The minor offense actually caused the offended person a degree of pain.
- The person who committed the minor offense is actually responsible for committing it, even if unintentionally.

Denial is an unhealthy pretending by either the offender or the offended that the offense didn't occur.

We can see that overlooking offenses is quite different than denial. Denial violates the three presumptions of overlooking and, instead of contributing to healthy relationships, sets us up for future conflict. It is at its essence "peacefaking." As C. S. Lewis wisely pointed out,

> There is all the difference in the world between forgiving and excusing . . . the trouble is that what we call "asking God's forgiveness" very often really consists in asking God to accept our excuses . . . if we forget this, we shall go away imagining that we have repented and been forgiven

125. John MacArthur, *The Freedom and Power of Forgiveness* (Wheaton, IL: Crossway Books, 1998), 122.

when all that has really happened is that we have satisfied ourselves with our own excuses.[126]

Forgiving inherently involves honesty about our sin, as opposed to excusing or denying it away.

For minor offenses, things less than the primary focus of this book, our default strategy is to overlook, cover over, and unilaterally forgive and forbear. This will take care of most of the daily minor slights we experience in our imperfect relational world. For things we cannot or should not overlook, the Bible gives us a different path.

Confrontation

Paul told the church at Ephesus to, "Take no part in the unfruitful works of darkness, but instead expose them" (Eph. 5:11). Older translations say, "have no fellowship." The believer is to walk as a child of the light. As such, it is the obligation of the Christian to not only avoid taking part in works of darkness, but rather to expose them. Americans, generally, are conflict avoidant. Our culture's incessant preaching of tolerance has likely impacted us. It is just not appropriate anymore to expose people or to confront them in their patterns of sin and darkness. We think we are more loving than that.

True love cares too much to leave people alone.

When we expose sin, we expose people. We confront people, not just sins in the abstract. People commit offenses. When we confront, we don't just confront the sin, we confront the sinner.

Confrontation is a core concept in most theories of biblical peacemaking. Many Christian cultures understand Matthew 18 to be the primary text on conflict and accordingly understand confrontation, à la verses 15–20, as the essence of the process. Much has been written with some merit but not without some important reservations. Others have suggest-

126. C. S. Lewis, *The Weight of Glory and Other Addresses* (NY: HarperCollins, 2001), 178–180.

ed a Matthew-18-only paradigm is unbiblical.[127] Some have wisely connected Matthew 18 to other key passages that pertain to the process of confrontation. Matthew 7:1–5 wisely instructs us to examine ourselves prior to confronting others. It is so easy for us to judge others without self-awareness of our own contributions to conflicts.[128] This is why Paul wisely told the church in Galatia to approach this task with humility and gentleness (Gal. 6:1). Confrontation is certainly biblically prescribed in the Old Testament and the New: "A bold reproof promotes peace" (Prov. 10:10 NLT). Reproof alone, however, is not the answer to the problem of conflict. God's ultimate goal of reconciliation will often, but not always, include human confrontation. Without fail, it involves confrontation of a higher order.

The ultimate Confronter is the Holy Spirit Himself.

The Holy Spirit lives in us if we are believers and is constantly working in our hearts to bring awareness of our sins in need of reparation. The confrontation process emphasized in many Christian circles can be a very human-level, horizontal confrontation. Prayer for enemies, on the other hand, engages the vertical dimension of confrontation. God is able to do in the human heart what we cannot. Jay Adams was correct when he listed the first step in church discipline as self-examination.[129] As Paul told the Corinthians, "If we would judge ourselves, we would not be judged" (1 Cor. 11:31). If only we would respond to the Spirit who lives in us, listening to His gentle voice calling back into relationship with Himself, the

127. See Newberger, *Face of Conflict*, 299–310.

128. One valid criticism of much contemporary peacemaking is an overemphasis on "taking the log out of our eye" as a prerequisite before confronting others. Many targets are well aware of the propensity for fallen people to play the hypocrite, to fail to see their own sin as they focus so intently on sins committed against them. However, this passage has been misapplied and misunderstood to place inordinate responsibility on victims rather than perpetrators. Often, victims see and own their logs quite clearly (more clearly than their aggressors). What is needed is not their awareness of minor offenses, but their aggressors' awareness of the main sins, the primary offenses, involved in the conflict.

129. Jay E. Adams, *Handbook of Church Discipline* (Grand Rapids, MI: Zondervan, 1986).

Son, and the Father. If only we would stop quenching His work among us, grieving His heart. Peacemaking literature is replete with discussions of confrontation on a human level. However, there is no substitute for the self-awareness and conviction the Spirit alone can bring to the heart of a believer. He is the ultimate Peacemaker who is able to perform an inside job.

But what of our responsibility to confront? The Holy Spirit alone can bring inward graces of repentance and honesty to a heart. Is it, therefore, not our responsibility to confront others in accordance with the Scriptural mandate? Some of us hide under a veil of "love" that never confronts. Is it loving, however, to allow someone to continue on a path toward their own and others' destruction? True love, biblical love, must confront. Love is never indifferent. The opposite of love is not hate but apathy. True love feels a compulsion to confront those things that are harmful in others just as we do in ourselves.

> Moral indignation, even moral outrage, may on occasion be proof of love—love for the victim, love for the church of God, love for the truth, love for God and for His glory. Not to be outraged may in such cases be evidence, not of gentleness and love, but of a failure to love.[130]

True peacemaking ought never to be at the expense of justice. True love and true justice both include honest confrontation of injustice. As Stanley Hauerwas says of true love,

> It is an active way to resist injustice by confronting the wrongdoer with the offer of reconciliation. Such reconciliation is not cheap, however, since no reconciliation is possible unless the wrong is confronted and acknowledged. . . . The task of peacemaking cannot ignore real wrongs, past or present.[131]

---

130. D. A. Carson, *Love in Hard Places* (Wheaton, IL: Crossway Books, 2002), 85.

131. Stanley Hauerwas, *The Hauerwas Reader*, ed. J. Berkman and M. Cartwright (Durham, NC: Duke University Press, 2005), 323, 325–326.

So, when things are too serious to overlook or forbear, we confront in accordance with the biblical process. Confrontation in these cases is our biblical duty.

> For any of us to turn a blind eye when a person hurts us or others, to remain silent when someone is doing wrong, to fail to confront and call upon such persons or groups to change their ways is not showing love. It is evidence of a lack of love and of indifference. In fact, *it could be argued that silence represents tacit approval, even complicity in their behavior.*[132]

Many helpful suggestions have already been offered to guide us in the process of confronting others.[133]

When we have brought loving correction, our job is not finished. Our task, following sufficient loving confrontation, shifts to prayer. This prayerful posture toward those we have confronted, who have yet to repent and seek reconciliation, remains with us. We need not and cannot continue indefinitely in a mode of confrontation. In fact, with some, it will become apparent that all our attempts at confrontation are for naught. It is futile to continue to do the same thing and expect different results. We carry with us the shared burden that the Lord feels for a lost and defiant world. The Bible provides a realistic approach to the management of conflicts. It does not fall prey to the utopian spirit of the age.

Every conflict in this life will not have a healthy or complete outcome.

We are living in the *not yet.* The shalom we justly long for someday, when brought forward prematurely into today, creates a snare. It trips us up and causes us to stumble.[134]

---

132. Newberger, *Face of Conflict*, 244.

133. Sande, *The Peacemaker*, 143–184.

134. Consider the stumbling of Asaph in Psalm 73 as exemplary of this principle. Asaph tripped over the current prosperity of the wicked around him, concluding he had wasted his time and effort in pursuing holiness. It is upon reflection of the future justice of God (the *not yet*) that Asaph regains his footing.

Sons and Daughters of the Living God

In and through Christ, we have been brought into the first family of the Trinity, and as *full* sons and daughters with *all* the rights and privileges that belong to us as such. Family members most often resemble one another. We say, "I can see your mother in you" or "she has her dad's eyes." So it is with God and His sons and daughters. We are being more and more conformed to the image of His dear Son and therefore will bear an increasing resemblance to Him as His Spirit transforms us over time (Rom. 8:29). So again, how should we live in light of this primary Familial relationship?

God is the Standard

For all eternity, God has existed. Each and every one of us is intimately and unavoidably connected to Him. Even if we want to pretend He doesn't exist, the Bible exposes our fraud. All humans know God and are therefore without excuse for not glorifying and worshipping Him as their Creator (Rom. 1:18–23).

God is the ultimate starting point for everything. Beyond that, God is also the standard of all things, of all reality, of all truth. When the Scripture makes statements like, "God is light," or "God is holy," or "God is just," or the most popular one, "God is love," it means to say that God is the very source of our understanding of this attribute. It is not as if something like love or truth or light or holiness exists in the abstract and that somehow God has this quality about Himself. *He defines the categories.* If we want to know what love is, we look to God. The categories we represent with language are less than adequate attempts to describe the indescribable. God is wholly other. If He had not condescended to reveal Himself to us in Creation and Scripture, we would be helpless to even attempt to use meaningful terms to describe Him.

This whole discussion may seem unnecessary. Don't all Christians, by default, begin with God as the reference point? Sadly, the answer to that question is an unfortunate "no." It's not a new problem. Long before the advent of the human potential movement of the sixties, human beings removed God as their reference point. Today, it is very common for us to begin not with God, but with ourselves.

Even As God . . . Like Father, Like Sons and Daughters

God is the standard against which all other things are measured. He is the measure of all things. In both Testaments, the Scripture consistently teaches that God's people, His children, are to mimic Him in their behavior. A summary statement of this principle is found in Leviticus 19:1. There, God tells the nation, "Be holy, *as* I am holy." Holiness in conduct for the nation of Israel is to resemble God's holiness. This same holds true for God's mercy and love. Jesus says, "Love one another *as* I have loved you" (John 13:34; italics added). He says, "Blessed are the merciful, for they shall obtain mercy" (Matt. 5:7), connecting God's mercy toward us and our mercy toward others.

Our conduct is to mirror the conduct we observe in God. We are to be like Him.

We also notice that the writers of Scripture consistently emphasized the order in which we ought to understand these principles. *Our conduct always follows and is a response to God's.* We never initiate. God always goes before us. All we do is but a response to Him. John said concerning the direction of love, "We love Him because He has first loved us" (I John 4:19). This direction is important. God is always first, then His creatures. Love comes from God. We would not know love, would never have experienced love, and would therefore not understand the first thing about how to love if He had not loved us. All we know about love is in direct relationship to His love that we have seen and experienced. So love and every other divine attribute are first found in Him and then are to be sought after by those who follow Him.

God is, and we imitate Him. Notice this principle so clearly taught by Paul in Ephesians, "Therefore *be imitators of God,* as beloved children.

And walk in love, *as* Christ loved us and gave himself up for us, a fragrant offering and sacrifice to God" (Eph. 5:1–2; italics added). Just as children naturally learn behaviors from their parents, so we as children of God will imitate our Father in His actions. God goes first. We follow. We do what He does. We follow His lead. This is the essence of the Christian life.

The Sermon on the Mount is Jesus' answer to the question, "How shall we then live?" Near the conclusion of the ethics portion of the sermon, we see Jesus drawing from this principle of God as the standard. Here, He specifically addressed the topic of God's love and ours.

> You have heard that it was said, "You shall love your neighbor and hate your enemy." But I say to you, Love your enemies and pray for those who persecute you, so that you may be sons of your Father who is in heaven. For he makes his sun rise on the evil and on the good, and sends rain on the just and on the unjust. For if you love those who love you, what reward do you have? Do not even the tax collectors do the same? And if you greet only your brothers, what more are you doing than others? Do not even the Gentiles do the same? You therefore must be perfect, as your heavenly Father is perfect. (Matt. 5:43–48)

Jesus teaches us that we love our enemies as God loves His enemies. God sends blessings down to those who oppose Him, not only to those who love and serve Him. In a similar way we are to be perfect, reflecting our relationship to Him as sons and daughters of the living God.

Not only is God first, He is also greatest. In each and every category of ethics, God is not only the standard of conduct, but He will be the only One who perfectly fulfills the essence of holiness. He is the Holy One. He is God and there is no other. This is an important point of understanding as it relates to Christian ethics. Because God is perfect in all things, *He always outdoes us.* His love is always better and more complete than ours. His mercy is more merciful. His justice is more just. *We can never outperform God in any of these categories.* Our best imitation of Him falls short of His glory, and it would be absurd to think we could ever exceed Him in our ethical living.

This, however, is precisely the trap we can fall into if we follow the logic of the day. We must be careful not to allow humanist ethics to intrude into our discussion. Man is not the standard. We don't make the definitions. The sentimental theology of tolerance dominates our culture, even among many evangelical believers. It is no longer shocking to hear someone questioning God's right to dictate the standard of conduct among us. Our culture freely judges the Almighty as "not loving enough." We ask, "How could a loving God send anyone to hell?" This resurgent universalism inverts the order of all things. Man becomes the standard and God needs to fit our paradigm of fairness.

Biblical ethics is different. God shows us what proper living looks like, and we follow His example by the power of His indwelling Spirit. This principle is assumed in most of the passages that describe our role in the process of peacemaking. Look at some of the most commonly quoted passages on forgiveness as examples of this principle. Paul wrote, "Be kind to one another, tender-hearted, forgiving one another, just *as* God in Christ also has forgiven you" (Eph. 4:32 NASB; italics added). He wrote similarly, "So, as those who have been chosen of God, holy and beloved, put on a heart of compassion, kindness, humility, gentleness and patience; bearing with one another, and forgiving each other, whoever has a complaint against anyone; *just as* the Lord forgave you, so also should you" (Col. 3:12, 13 NASB; italics added). So we are to imitate God by being tenderhearted and forgiving toward one another in the same way as God has been tenderhearted and forgiving toward us.

There is a direct correlation between God's character and conduct and our own.[135] God's actions are primary. Our actions are to conform to His standard of conduct. This point is crucial and often misunderstood. The vertical dimension in all aspects of ethics takes precedence and priority

135. The Christian community is not in agreement with this statement. Many have sought to make a sharp distinction between our relationship with God and our relationships with other people. The prevailing thought is human relationships cannot be compared or be conducted on the same level as our relationship with God. This position doesn't fit well with the teaching of Scripture and, in particular, the teaching of Paul and the Lord Jesus.

over the horizontal. If we rightly understand God's love or His justice or His mercy, we rightly understand the standard to which human conduct should aspire. This is the essence of biblical sonship. Our conduct evidences the reality of our Family ties. Just as Jesus taught, "Blessed are the peacemakers, for *they shall be called the sons of God*" (Matt. 5:9; italics added).

God Is Our Pattern in His Response to Opposition

We are to imitate God as His children. The commandments in Scripture to us are connected to God and His character. In other words, God is not asking us to do something He Himself doesn't or wouldn't do. God is not a hypocrite. God never lives by the motto, "Do as I say, not as I do." For this reason, we have spent considerable time seeking to understand God's varied responses to conflict. God's first response to conflict was judgment. There was no second chance, no mercy extended, no grace given. By definition this was a holy and right response. We have for so long been told God is love (only) that we may have difficulty putting our arms, let alone our minds, around the descriptions of God's responses to those who oppose Him.

If God is varied in His response to conflict, would we not expect His children to imitate Him in this pattern? Why would we expect a Holy God who wars against sin and the enemy to instruct His children to be pacifistic?[136] If God is a warrior, are we to be otherwise? There are certainly responses that belong properly to God alone.[137] It is not ours to take the life of anyone who opposes us.[138] This is His prerogative alone. But we need to reexamine the notion that God, who responds as He clearly does, asks His children to respond otherwise. He does not and cannot ask us to

136. The pacifism inherent in many Anabaptist theologies has had an impact in the broader church. Much of the literature on biblical peacemaking has been flavored with this philosophical bias.

137. Clearly, the sinful responses of murder and suicide are out of bounds to us. God alone has the authority to take a life. This may, however, call into question the basic premise that underlies Peacemaker Ministries' "slippery slope of conflict."

138. E.g., Ananias and Sapphira.

be more gracious, more loving than He is. If God withdraws from conflict at times, would He not instruct us to do likewise? If He moves toward those who oppose Him, would He not expect us at times to advance? Should we resemble our God or not? Like Father, like sons and daughters?

Dave's Question

Dave and Carol have been pulling their hair out over this situation. They are both experiencing significant stress and at times have turned on one another in the midst of the situation (something Jane prayed about in her small group after she heard they were having "marital problems"). Dave asks the conciliator, "What more can I do? I've tried repeatedly to explain to Bill in letters and e-mails the nature of my concerns. Many people in our circle of friends have told me to just get over it. They've warned me about the consequence of not forgiving Bill and Jane. But, to be honest with you, I don't feel as if I can just overlook this. It seems too serious to just gloss over."

Dave and Carol are actually gracious, forgiving Christian people who have overlooked lots of slights from people in the past and have even forgiven serious sins committed against them by their siblings after a healthy honest process of confession and reconciliation. Bill and Jane have unfairly painted them as being legalists. Dave and Carol feel the need to confront Bill and Jane for their own sake as well as for the future health and growth of their former best friends. They are concerned that Bill and Jane "getting away with this" as they have in former similar situations is creating a pattern in their lives, moving them away from a real honest relationship with God.

Part 3

TWO PATHS IN CONFLICT

7

Wisdom and the Fool

I was a staunch believer in biblical counseling, the nouthetic kind. I had no place for psychology but rather saw it as an unwelcome intrusion into the conversation about truth. "All we need is God's Word. It tells us how to live, how to work through adversity, how to ask our soul, 'why so downcast?'" I had no category for what I was experiencing. I felt deep sadness, cried a lot. Didn't do much else for about four or five months. I would stare out the window for hours on end just numb to life. I would jump at any loud sound. Backfires would make my heart start to race. I wasn't sleeping very well. I had vivid dreams, more accurately nightmares, of things that had happened. I was reexperiencing things that had been extremely painful. The list of symptoms continues.

You can imagine how shocked I was to discover that this set of symptoms I was living out every day had a name. But remember, I didn't believe in psychology. So, it couldn't be the case that what I was daily experiencing was the condition known as complex post-traumatic stress disorder (CPTSD). I didn't believe in CPTSD; that was psychobabble. "Anyway, people with something like that have been through really traumatic experiences, like 9–11. I hadn't. Except for that time I was hit on the fifth level of a five-level overpass." The woman behind me said, "I thought you were going over." I somehow drove the Hyundai home and stood at the front door of our

Chino townhouse shaking. I had been through some pretty painful church experiences in the past as well. But nothing that would affect me like this. Those things were in the past; I had put them behind me a long time ago. Or had I?

Then I stumbled across various websites that connected CPTSD with bullying over an extended period of time. "Bullying is for kids on the playground. That term couldn't apply to me." Or could it? I continued to dig and learned about things I had never heard of nor would I have previously believed. I saw the connection between "bullying" and "narcissism" in psychological literature that was beginning to offer some helpful explanation. Then, it opened up to me—the connection between bullying, narcissism and what the Bible calls foolishness. I saw it on every page of the Psalms. The Psalmists were being directly affected, like me, by people who had harmed them. They were suffering physically, emotionally, spiritually in the same way that I was. The enemies in the Psalms are "fools." But it's not nice to call someone a "fool." It's so "inappropriate."

Thus far, we have seen that we, as children of God, are to follow His example in conflict. To follow Him is to walk on His path. There is another option. If we choose, we can walk the broad path toward destruction. He offers each of us a choice. The ramifications of that choice are soberly eternal. *There are only two kinds of people in the world.* Those who turn from their sin in repentance toward God and reliance on the Holy Spirit, follow Him as His redeemed children. Those who refuse are, by default, left in the lineage of Adam's race. This logic is far too black and white for our modern pluralistic, relativistic, and tolerant society. Doesn't love win?

Two Kinds of People?

It sounds so backward in our modern culture. How can we reduce humanity into two categories? Certainly, we must have a more nuanced approach than to use this dichotomist paradigm? This is the offense built into the teaching of Jesus. He left us with the clear sense that there were only two options, two fundamental choices. He contrasted the narrow path and the wide road (Matt. 7:13–14). He emphasized the importance between sheep on His right and goats on His left (Matt. 25:31–46). He taught us that the wise man builds his house on the rock, while the foolish man builds on sand that cannot sustain the coming storms (Matt. 7:24–27). Jesus saw things clearly in two categories. Jesus was Jewish. His view was consistent with His knowledge of the law, the prophets, and, in particular, the writings.

The view of humanity divided into two did not originate with the coming of Christ nor did it end with His ascension. The entirety of the Old Testament and, in particular, wisdom literature is replete with this description of a two-fold humanity. The cry of the Old Testament is to find the "fear of the LORD which is the beginning of wisdom" (Prov. 1:7). Wisdom is the antidote to foolishness. Several years after the ascension of Jesus, his half-brother James, the leader of the church in Jerusalem, picked up his brother's theme when he described the two types of people, "God opposes the proud, but gives grace to the humble" (James 4:6b). Surely, it's not that simple? The proud and the humble? Where is the middle ground?

Conflict resolution is only ultimately possible on the path of wisdom.

This is a crucial reality, a key part of this conversation regarding conflict. Among fools, there is no conflict resolution. By definition, fools will not work through conflict or practice the spiritual disciplines required to bring conflicts to a biblical outcome. At first, we shy away from statements like these. It's not nice to call people "fools." Didn't Jesus even warn us about calling someone a fool, suggesting that to do so would put us in danger of hell fire (Matt. 5:22)? However, we can't bring Proverbs into our discussion without seeing the contrast between the wise person and the fool. If Jesus meant by his statement that we cannot use the term "fool," we may as well take the entirety of the wisdom literature out of our Bibles and dismiss it as irrelevant or even passé in terms of dealing with conflict resolution in this New Testament era.

Who Is the Fool?

Biblically speaking, there are only two basic kinds of people.[139] Many times we think along the lines of the two people groups as the *saved* and the *lost* or the *Christian* and the *unchristian*. These contrasting terms suggest that humanity is divided into two primary parts. Paul spoke of the children of the promise as opposed to the children of the flesh (Rom. 9:8; Gal. 4:22–31). In the garden, immediately after the fall, the first gospel promise spoke of the enmity between the two seeds (Gen. 3:15). These two subgroups of humanity exist under various names. The composition of the two groups is known only to God. One group is saved and the other unfortunately is not.

The Bible is quite clear that universalism is false. Not all will be saved. Some will be lost. This "savedness" or "lostness" is directly connected to Christ and our relationship to all He is and all He has done and to a vital connection, or union, with Him. As John Calvin rightly said, "As long as we stay disconnected from Jesus, all that He is and has done benefits us nothing."[140] So, the key issue in this regard is the reality or nonreality of our connection to Jesus.[141] The two groups could best be referred to as the *in-Christ* group and the *disconnected-from-Christ* group. Our connection to Christ is intrinsically connected to the way we live in the world.

---

139. See Allender and Longman, *Bold Love*. Allender and Longman nuance this view to include four kinds of people (one wise and three levels of foolish): the wise, the normal sinner (simple person), the fool, and the evil person.

140. John Calvin, *Institutes of the Christian Religion*, ed. John T. McNeill, trans. Ford Lewis Battles (Philadelphia: Westminster Press, 1960), 1:537.

141. Here's the real debate, not between losing salvation and eternal security, but between those who see this union as only legal versus those who see this union as both legal and relational, or primarily relational. If this union is more than legal, even as marriage is more than a wedding, the ongoing connection to Christ is foundational to the state of the union. For this reason, many in both Arminian and Calvinist paradigms have rightly emphasized the need for the believer to persevere to the end and be saved.

Another way of describing this division of humanity is through the lens of the wisdom literature. In this portion of the inspired Scripture, the primary categories used to describe the two types of people are the descriptors of *foolishness* and *wisdom*.[142] In the wisdom literature of the Old and New Testament, the category of fool is not used in a pejorative sense. It is merely the term used to describe the traits that exist in *someone who refuses to be made wise* or *someone who refuses to be transformed*. A summary of the concept of the fool in Proverbs reveals that the fool[143]

- Despises wisdom and correction (1:7)
- Hates knowledge (1:22)
- Is complacent (1:32)
- Slanders others (10:8)
- Lacks common sense (10:21)
- Likes doing wrong, has fun doing wrong (10:23)
- Belittles neighbor (11:12)
- Thinks own way is right (12:15)
- Broadcasts foolishness, brags about it (12:23; 13:16)
- Acts before thinks (i.e., is impulsive) (13:16)
- Deceives self (14:8)
- Makes fun of guilt (14:9)
- Plunges ahead with reckless confidence (14:16)
- Has a hot temper, vents anger (14:29; 29:11)
- Despises parental discipline (15:5)
- Has no good advice to give (15:7)
- Feeds on trash as opposed to knowledge (15:14)
- Has no heart for learning (17:16)

---

142. I highly recommend Jan Silvious's book, *Fool-Proofing Your Life: An Honorable Way to Deal with the Impossible People in Your Life*, as a more thorough discussion of this teaching concerning the fool in wisdom literature.

143. Proverbs uses four primary terms translated as "fool" or "simple": *pthiy* refers to the simple or naive person, a fool in the making; *kesil* refers to closed-mindedness or dullness; *nabal* refers to impiety and a lack of spiritual perception; *ewil* refers to the hardened fool whose character has been formed over time.

- Causes parents pain (17:21, 25; 19:13)
- Has no interest in understanding, only wants to air own opinion (18:2)
- Spouts off before listening to facts, speaks without thinking (18:13; 29:20)
- Is dishonest (19:1)
- Insists on quarreling (20:3)
- Spends whatever he or she gets (21:20)
- Despises the wisest advice (23:9)
- Has sinful schemes (24:9)
- Trusts own insight (28:26)

Characteristics of Fools

A picture of the person the Scripture calls a fool begins to emerge.

Godless / Lawless

"The fool says in his heart, 'There is no God'" (Ps. 14:1a). Fools live life as if there is no God, no One to whom they are ultimately accountable. This does not mean that fools are irreligious. Though fools inwardly deny the sovereignty of God over them by saying to themselves, "He doesn't see" or "He won't judge," fools throughout the history of humanity have often been religious overachievers. The Pharisees and Sadducees who opposed Christ were the religious leaders of the day and yet they didn't understand elemental things of God.[144] Fools may say in their hearts, "There is no God," but to others, they often claim a close relationship with Him.[145] Fools live in a state of pretended autonomy. No one is truly autonomous, but fools live as if they are.

Fools despise God's law. God's regulation of their lives makes them bristle. Because they think they are free from God, they live life as if there is no law. Living "above the law" is an understatement. More accurately

144. Notice Jesus' mild rebuke of Nicodemus in this vein (John 3:9).

145. This is the root sin of the Pharisees, the leaven of hypocrisy (Luke 12:1).

expressed, they live life "apart from any law." As Thom Oden lamented, "Corrupted modernity chafes under restraint and accountability. . . . it displays a kind of adolescent refusal of parenting."[146]

Self-consumed (Narcissistic, Prideful) [147]

Proverbs repeatedly connects the fool with the character flaw of pride. Fools are so self-focused that they have a hard time seeing anyone else. They are overly confident in themselves. Their pride is blinding. They sincerely believe that their way, their perspective, and their perception are right. Therefore, they are often immovable in their positions. Narcissists, by this same principle, refuse to own anything they do to others. It is never their fault. They are always misunderstood. Though they may well have been the key initiator in a conflict, they see themselves as the victims of others. It is always about them.[148]

Self-deceived, Deceptive, Slanderous

Fools have a hard time with the truth. They are deceived deceivers. They have very little self-awareness. Fools also tend to be deceptive in their interactions with others. They commonly engage in deceptive and slanderous strategies to tear down the reputation of others they perceive to be a threat. Because they are a law unto themselves, they are masters at situational ethics. The rules that normally govern behavior and appropriateness do not apply to them.

---

146. Plantinga, *Not the Way*, 126.

147. The biblical category of fool correlates closely to psychological literature describing the "narcissist." In the DSM-IV TR, the standard for psychiatric and psychological diagnosis, the criteria that comprise narcissistic personality disorder are as follows: grandiose sense of self-importance, fantasies of unlimited power and success, believes self is "special," requires excessive admiration, sense of entitlement, interpersonally exploitative, lacks empathy, envious of others and believes others are envious of him or her, arrogance, and haughty behaviors or attitudes. For a clinical diagnosis of Narcissistic Personality Disorder (NPD), an individual must, from early adulthood, show a pattern of at least five of these nine traits.

148. See Hotchkiss, *Why Is It Always about You? The Seven Deadly Sins of Narcissism*.

Simultaneously to a direct attack on their target, fools often employ indirect attacks. This assault against others is often in the form of character assassination, discrediting their perceived opponent in the eyes of others. The Psalms are replete with this pattern of fools slandering and maligning the righteous. Fools speak freely without regard for the objective truth. They are convinced their views are reality. They seek to bring others into this actuality.

Unchanging (Unteachable)

"Pride renders fools unteachable. They know it all. You can't tell them anything. They are 'wise in their own eyes'—a sure sign of folly."[149] Foolishness is a prison that traps its victim. It renders change impossible in that it so fills the heart of its victim with a sense of "rightness" that immediately discredits the thought of possible "wrongness." Fools look back on their past actions and think, "If I had it to do over, I wouldn't do anything any differently."

Impulsive, Angry, Destructive

Fools often have a very short fuse and can be provoked quite easily. When provoked, they can either vent their anger or channel the anger they feel into a destructive plot to harm those they perceive to oppose him. Tell fools, "no," and observe what happens. Fools are impatient with planning and discussion and simply want to get things done "now."

Fools are destructive. They seek to destroy others they perceive to be a threat to their ego and influence. They will directly attack enemies, attempting to destroy any ego strength in them. Targets of fools will often have little left in terms of any self-image, following prolonged interaction with their foolish oppressor. Fools leave a wake of destruction behind them. There are casualties along their path.

---

149. Plantinga, *Not the Way,* 124.

Lazy, Complacent

Fools don't like hard work and discipline. They are often looking for a short cut. This, in combination with their ethical dullness, can lead them to do things that are unethical or even illegal. The hard work that others would put in to achieve difficult goals is something fools think they are above putting in. They live with a sense of entitlement. They deserve better and shouldn't have to work hard for things like others. They should, however, still receive honor greater than those who work hard.

Inhuman (Unfeeling, Unempathetic, Sociopathic)

Some fools, at some level, actually enjoy the suffering they cause in others. They have a hard time understanding their own feelings and a corresponding difficulty empathizing with the pain of others. Because they are less affected by the suffering of others, they are able to continue in their course without the hesitation most people experience when they observe their painful effect on others.

The Hebrew term *ewil* suggests someone who has hardened over time into a rigid pattern of life. Foolishness over time moves toward this category. The modern psychological diagnosis of Narcissistic Personality Disorder may be similar to this ancient idea. A personality disorder occurs when someone gets "stuck" in one way of interacting with others. Not to say all fools are necessarily narcissists, but the trajectory of foolishness, especially over time, as in the sense of the Hebrew *ewil*, is quite serious. Foolishness also closely correlates with the paradigms of bullying and abuse.

Who Is the Wise One?

Contrast all that we have said about the fool with the wise as portrayed in Scripture. Wisdom begins, we are told, with the "fear of the Lord" (Prov. 1:7). Unlike the fool who says in his heart there is no God, the wise person builds his life on the reality of God and centers on living life with the awareness of his relationship to Him as his Creator and ultimate King.

A summary of the concept of the wise person in Proverbs reveals that the "wise person"

- Loves those who bring correction (9:8)
- Receives instruction, grows through teaching (9:9)
- Harvests in the summer, saves for a future day (10:5)
- Restrains his lips, is slow to speak (10:19)
- Will be the master of the foolish (11:29)
- Wins souls (friends) (11:30)
- Speaks to bring healing to others (12:18)
- Accepts parental discipline (13:1)
- Gives instruction to others like a life-giving fountain (13:14)
- Has the king's favor (14:35)
- Doesn't have mockers coming for advice (15:12)
- Listens to constructive criticism (15:31)
- Appeases the anger of the king (16:14)
- Is known for understanding and pleasant, persuasive words (16:21)
- Has wise, persuasive speech coming from a wise mind (16:23)
- Will rule over the dishonorable, earn a good reputation with the Master (17:2)
- Seeks knowledge, is ready to learn, is teachable (18:15)
- Grows wiser through instruction not punishment (21:11)
- Makes parents glad (23:34)
- Becomes mightier than others, grows stronger and stronger (24:5)
- Turns away anger (29:8)
- Stores up for the future like an ant (30:25)
- Makes his house in the rocks like a badger (30:26)
- Marches in formation without a king like locusts (30:27)
- Gets into the palace of the king like a lizard (30:28)

Characteristics of Wise People

The survey of characteristics above from Proverbs can be grouped into seven key attributes that constitute biblical wisdom.

Correctable

The wise respond well to correction or rebuke. Because humility is present, the wise have a right estimation of themselves. They see the evidences of God's transformation in their lives and of His gifts, but they also clearly see their own imperfections. The wise are self-aware.[150] Bring correction to the wise, and they will thank you for it. That doesn't mean they will thank you in the moment that you bring a rebuke. But thoughtful and wise people ponder loving rebukes and process the content of things shared with them about themselves and their conduct within a vital relationship with the Holy Spirit of truth and honesty about themselves. The wise not only respond well to others' correction, but to the Spirit as He brings constant awareness of areas needing additional transformation in their lives.

Teachable

The wise are not know-it-alls. They have cognitive modesty rather than overconfidence.[151] They are quick to receive other perspectives. They are open to new perspectives and are able to grow and learn. They are also open to the possibility that their current paradigm may be flawed in some way.

Planning / Preparation

Instead of a sense of entitlement, the wise are willing to work hard and to exercise self-discipline to achieve desired goals. They are willing to defer gratification. Because they do not just live in the moment, they are able to make reasonable preparations for the future. They are less prone to impulsivity.

---

150. For a good discussion of the need for self-awareness, see Benner, *The Gift of Being Yourself: The Sacred Call to Self-Discovery*.

151. Cognitive modesty is a term coined by Belcher, *Deep Church: A Third Way beyond the Emerging*. Cognitive modesty is having the proper confidence that comes from multiperspectivalism. Humility demands that I understand my limitations and finiteness. I do not and cannot have all knowledge on any subject, but merely a perspective, a facet, an angle. See also Poythress, *Symphonic Theology: The Validity of Multiple Perspectives in Theology*.

Edifying Speech

The wise are learning to bridle the tongue, to bring it under the leadership of the Holy Spirit. They are making progress toward the advice of James to be "slow to speak" and "quick to listen" (James 1:19). They are actively seeking to put to death speech patterns that are according to the former self (gossip, slander, etc.) and are seeking to bring edifying speech patterns into their lives on an ever-increasing level (Eph. 4:29). As Proverbs informs us, "the tongue of the wise promotes healing" (12:18; 15:4).

Approval of Others

Wise people, as a result of their godly lifestyle, are often able to secure the favor and approval of others. Joseph conducted himself with wisdom in the prison system of Egypt and was eventually promoted to the direct assistant to Pharaoh. Many people, and especially some in authority, will recognize the prudence in these wise ones and will reward them with greater positions of influence in the lives of others.

Manages Anger

Anger, in itself, is not the problem. We all feel angry and should feel angry at times. Anger, at its most basic level, is an indication that a boundary marker has been crossed. What is key is not the initial anger but what we do with the anger. The wise manage their anger, seeking to pursue the path of wisdom and reconciliation with those who anger them. They direct their anger to positive ends.

Rules over Fools

Several proverbs give the basic principle that the wise will often rule over the fool. This is likely due, in part, to the drastic discipline of the wise contrasted with the slothfulness of the foolish.

Why This Distinction Is Important

If we fail to understand the fundamental difference between these two types of people, our model of conflict resolution will fail to reflect the Bible's wisdom on how to interact with conflict in this two-fold way. Many contemporary Christian models of conciliation do not adequately represent this reality of a dichotomous humanity. Many of the concepts taught in these models are highly useful in the context of believers who are submitted to the Holy Spirit, who will respond ultimately to His Word as their final authority, repent as needed, and resume the task of living at peace with all men (i.e., the wise).

The systems of peacemaking do not work where people persist in foolishness.

The entirety of Scripture certainly lays out not only the path toward wholeness and reconciliation for the wise, but also in a very realistic way, the path toward release to God despite nonresolution in conflicts involving the foolish. The fork in the road is profound. To not see the fork is to miss half the truth in Scripture. Half-truths aren't going to be adequate as a basis for wise living.

Divergent Paths in Conflict

Two roads diverged in a yellow wood . . .[152]

Though many may seek to argue otherwise, there are really only two paths in conflict. For the honest and the broken, there is healing and wholeness. For the dishonest and the unbroken, there is none. Jesus said, "those who are not sick have no need of a physician" (Mark 2:17). So it is with those who refuse to come to the light and to be honest about their brokenness. The greatest tragedy of all can be seen in broken people, hiding in the darkness claiming to be whole.

152. Robert Frost, "The Road Not Taken," in *The Road Not Taken and Other Poems* (Mineola, NY: DoverThrift, 1993), 1.

There are two paths in life. There are two paths in conflict. The question is, "Which path am I on?" One path is much more difficult to remain on than the other. The path of wisdom is the path that goes against our nature. It is unnatural, as children of Adam, to respond in accordance with this path.[153] When we stop actively pursuing this path of wisdom, we revert to the other by default—the path of foolishness. This is consistent with the teaching of Jesus who taught us that the broad way, the one that's easy to follow, leads to destruction, but that the narrow way, the difficult one with few on it, leads to everlasting life (Matt. 7:13–14).

Conflict Resolution above the Line

The line is a metaphor for the division between proper and improper, between truth and falsehood, between wisdom and folly, and between righteousness and sin. A line implies a standard.[154] Though we don't like lines in our current culture of tolerance, it is an important and helpful biblical concept.[155] It provides a readily available manner of assessing our current behavior in the midst of ongoing strife and division.

In the midst of conflict, we can find ourselves in the process above or below the line. In essence, living above the line is what we normally refer to as wisdom, and living below the line is what unfortunately represents foolishness.

---

153. This explains the importance and meaning of the new birth. Our nature is actually changed in relation to our union with Christ by the Spirit.

154. See Sumner, *Leadership above the Line: A Character-Based Leadership Tool That Leads to Success for You and Your Team*.

155. Many would object the notion of a line dividing ethical and unethical behaviors is far too black and white. Instead they would prefer that everything be gray—that there be no line.

							OFFENDED	MUTUAL
	OFFENDER							
		Owning Our Sin					Paying the Price	Ultimate Goal
wisdom		Confession	Repentance	Apology	Restitution	Lifestyle Change	Forgiveness	Reconciliation
folly	Offense	Denial	Hardening	Excusing	No Consequence	Status Quo	Unforgiveness	Estrangement

"the line"

Table 2. Two Paths—Conflict Resolution above and below the Line

Table 2 illustrates the contrast of the two paths available to us. Staying above the line requires effort in reliance on the strength of the Holy Spirit. It is far easier to fall below the line. This explains why so much conflict, even among professing Christians, is not managed through the more arduous path of wisdom illustrated above. Taking the broad and easy way comes naturally for sons and daughters of Adam. It should not be so among those who are united to Christ.

The Path of Fools

Foolishness comes naturally. It is the default response. "Folly is bound up in the heart of a child" (Prov. 22:15a). To be foolish is easy.

The moment we cease to seek wisdom, we are susceptible to foolishness.

At any point in the process, we can easily revert to the path of the fool. To merge onto this path, we need to simply stop making any genuine efforts toward pursuing a transformative relationship with God.[156]

The foolish respond entirely differently than the wise. At times, wise people initially play the fools in a conflict. But ultimately, through the persistent work of the Holy Spirit in the hearts of believers and the authority of the Scripture, the followers of Christ who are wise are brought to a place of honesty and wholeness. Wise people own their sins before God and others, repent, seek forgiveness, and are willing to do whatever it takes, including restitution, to be reconciled to those they have offended. They seek transformation by the power of the Holy Spirit, so those areas of past failure and sin can be remade after the likeness of Christ.

The path of fools is the antithesis of the path of wisdom. Whatever wisdom dictates, fools do the opposite. Fools continue in sinful patterns, do not resist temptation, and if religious, rely on the abundant and free grace of God to continue to cover over their offenses as they pile up. As the foolish continue on their path, their course is eerily predictable. We all act in accordance with our character. Foolishness is a characterological problem. Denial (not confession) characterizes the fools' paths. Denial, a form of falsehood, is consistent with the character and values of fools. Instead of owning their sins, fools are never responsible for what "didn't happen."

Hardening in sin and refusal to take ownership of it (not repentance) characterize the fool's attitude. The sad reality is fools are so hardened to the work of the Holy Spirit; they have moved themselves to a place where repentance may no longer be found (cf. Judges 16:20). Excusing themselves from any responsibility (not apologizing) goes with the paradigm of fools. Fools, by definition, do not receive correction; they are "never wrong." The thought of apologizing is nonsensical to them. Again, "apologize for what?" Fools have no recognition of responsibility (not ever

---

156. We can all, at times, play the "fool." The terms "wise" and "foolish" refer to the overall pattern and trajectory of a life, our overarching character. Each of us has examples of times when we have acted out of character in a given situation. These are exceptions rather than the rule.

thinking of restitution) for what they have done and are doing in the lives of others. They lack empathy in general for others and have a very difficult time connecting their actions with the pain in the lives of others around them.

Status quo living (not a changed lifestyle) is the life of fools. They simply continue in the same patterns that they always have. Change is a foreign concept. Unforgiveness (not a forgiving heart) characterizes their response to perceived slights against them. Though they live freely without the constraint of cumbersome rules, they are quick to lay down the standard for others. Though they give themselves endless grace, for others grace and forgiveness are in short supply. This double standard is characteristic of fools. Because they live in this manner, estrangement from others (not reconciliation) follows them in their relationships. Fools often leave behind them a bloody trail of former relationships, all of which they have used, abused, and then discarded. People have little value to fools, that is, unless the people we are speaking of are them. So it is that fools follow the path that leads to destruction.

Foolishness loves company. People inclined in this direction reinforce each other's behaviors in a reciprocal fashion. There is frequently an unhealthy mutual absolution of one another between them. The unspoken rule is, "I won't hold you accountable if you don't hold me." Thus, both parties drown in a deep cesspool of cheap grace in their shared foolishness. This twisted "love fest," devoid of the qualities that constitute true love (1 Cor. 13), is precisely the concern of Proverbs. This is the destruction connected to ongoing unhealthy relationships with fools. Normally, the wise are the ones who suffer.

The Path of the Wise

The path of the wise, the path of peacemaking, has been made clear in Scripture. It is a path toward the resolution of conflict and the restoration and reconciliation of an erring brother or sister. As illustrated in Table 2, the path of wisdom following the committal of sin begins with honesty.

Confession, repentance, and apology are all aspects of this truthfulness. This path also includes biblically appropriate aspects of restitution and lifestyle change. All of these prepare the way for the offended one to have the best opportunity to offer full forgiveness that opens the door to full reconciliation of the relationship.

The path of wisdom is the narrow path.
It is not the broad way leading to destruction that so many choose to follow.

Folly and Sin, Wisdom and Righteousness

For thee all the follies of sin I resign.[157]

It is not an overstatement to claim that the Hebrew concepts of foolishness and sin, as well as those of wisdom and righteousness, are used synonymously. In the Proverbs, the Hebrew concepts of the wise (*chakam*) and the righteous (*tsaddiq*) are used interchangeably.[158] Further, the opposite principles of foolishness (*ewil*) and its Hebrew synonym laziness (*atsel*) are contrasted alternately with both terms.[159]

> Sin is folly. No matter what images they choose, the Bible writers say this again and again. Sin is missing the target; sin is choosing the wrong target. Sin is wandering from the path or rebelling against someone too strong for us or neglecting a good inheritance. Above all, at its core, sin is offense against God.[160]

As righteousness correlates with wisdom, so sin (unrighteousness) correlates with foolishness. On the one hand, we can see the biblical connection between:

Conflict—Foolishness—Sin

---

157. William R. Featherstone, "My Jesus I Love Thee."

158. E.g., Prov. 9:9; 23:24.

159. E.g., Prov. 10:21; 14:9; 15:19; 21:25–26.

160. Plantinga, *Not the Way*, 123.

On the other hand, we can see the strong biblical and logical connection between:

Shalom—Wisdom—Righteousness

Playing the Fool

Bill has had a long-standing pattern of these kinds of business dealings. Dave and Carol aren't the first former clients in the church to feel that his promises concerning their investments proved to be more than a little misleading. When others confronted Bill in the past, he always maintained his innocence. In fact, he and Jane have already left three other churches over people's overreactions to poorly performing investments. Bill is frustrated with the way people seem to twist the situation to make him seem like the "bad guy."

Bill's behavioral pattern has some troubling tendencies that are becoming clearer to the conciliation team as they continue to gather data. Several other couples have confirmed the pattern of false information and failure to disclose risks related to investments. Bill always assures his clients with,"Trust me." His clients have more often than not taken him up on that promise and have suffered as a result. Most of his clients have not realized anything near the return he promised. His commission structure in most of his deals, however, has made him quite wealthy, even with the significant lack of client retention he has experienced.

Bill is never wrong. Even Jane had to admit to the conciliator that he seldom apologizes for things he has done in their marriage. She feels as if everything is always her fault. She asked him to go to couple's counseling, but he refused and instead told her that she should go to individual counseling to work on her "stuff."

8

The Path of the Wise

It seems so easy. If we would just be honest, admit what we have done, ask for forgiveness, be willing to do whatever we need to do to make things right, everything could be resolved. I so wish we could all do this. This is the path of wisdom. I'm not sure I'm comfortable with applying the term "wise" to myself. That seems like a serious lack of humility, especially considering that I know myself a lot better than anybody else does. I know the inner recesses of my heart and the battles that sometimes rage there. And yet, I really do want to live a life of honesty. I genuinely want to be the type of person, husband, father who says to those I love when I have hurt them, "It was my fault." I don't want to project, to blame shift, to displace. Honesty, though I imperfectly embody it, is my highest personal value.

A good friend of mine and I sometimes commiserate over our common frustration in this area. We are grateful for the way in which we understand one another and yet are cognizant of the way in which this thing we both so highly prize, honesty, is often so unwelcome. She has had her own turn working in a Christian organization and was stumbled, as I have been in the past, at the remarkable lack of honesty, authenticity, congruence, or whatever we want to call it that is lacking in the community that names the name of Christ. How can any of us as professed Christ followers live lives of quiet dishonesty? Perhaps the Bible is right when it informs us that foolishness is bound up in our hearts.

Interestingly, the path of wisdom begins with sin, not the committing of sin, but the honest ownership of our sin that leads to repentance. The difference between the foolish and the wise is never more apparent than after the commitment of sin. Fools hide; the wise come into the light.

Offenses That Come

Where there is no sin (offense), there is no conflict. As conflict has been defined, it cannot exist apart from the presence of sin, the occurrence of actual offenses committed by one party against another or against God. Sin against God and others can be in word, thought, or actions. It can be in things done and things undone (neglect). Here, however, we are focused on the concept of offenses, sins of commission rather than omission, things actually done to others, sins of word and deed.

Jesus once said, "it is inevitable that stumbling blocks come, but woe to that man through whom the stumbling block comes" (Matt. 18:7 NASB). The influence of some Calvinistic theologies for nearly four centuries has resulted in a common understanding of sin as being inevitable in our lives. Scripture seems to say something different, however. Sin is always a bad idea and never something that we had to commit. The apostle John wrote:

> My little children, I am writing these things to you *so that you may not sin*. And if anyone sins, we have an Advocate with the Father, Jesus Christ the righteous; and He Himself is the propitiation for our sins; and not for ours only, but also for those of the whole world. (1 John 2:1–2 NASB; italics added)

John assumed that the believers to whom he wrote did not have to sin. They could walk in the light, even as God is in the light, and not give in to the desires of the flesh, that is, sin.

We don't have to sin.

We don't have to respond to frustrated desires or blocked goals by sinning against others. In fact, this is the goal of the New Testament—for believers to be mature, to resemble Christ who did not return evil for evil and who did not respond sinfully when His desires or goals were not attained. The best place to stop conflict is at the level of the offense. No offense, no conflict. Just as God warned Cain, "Sin is at the door seeking to have you. Resist it!" (Gen. 4:7). The path of wisdom is first a path of prevention and one of keeping short accounts with God and others.

We are not talking here about perceived offenses but actual ones. When there is uncertainty about actual offenses being committed, the answer is not the path described in the chapters that follow. Rather wisdom would dictate clarification of misunderstandings. Though many offenders will claim to be misunderstood, there is a critical difference between real, perceived, and imaginary offenses. Real offenses require a real process that moves toward reconciliation. This is the first step on the path of conflict resolution. Ironically, the offense necessitates the process itself.

The commitment of actual offenses marks the beginning of our deviation from the path of wisdom and back to the path of folly. The wise person yields not to temptation but by the power of the Holy Spirit, resists the impulses of the flesh. When we sin, however, we face the decision about which path to follow.

Ownership of Our Offenses

When we sin, the key for returning to the path is found in owning our offenses. Owning our sins is about honesty and sincerity with ourselves, God, and those we have sinned against. Can we be honest about our sin? Is it important for us to pursue this kind of sincerity? Can anyone fully know himself or herself? Martin Luther took this practice to its literal extreme. He wore out his confessors day and night, rehearsing the iniquity he saw within his heart. His relief came when he realized for the first time that the sacrifice of Christ had created a way for him to be made right with God, justified by faith. Does our justification by faith then render a healthy practice of owning our sin no longer relevant?

If we are honest, we would have to admit there still remains areas of struggle and failure in our lives. There are sins we sincerely repent of that we find ourselves drawn back to again and again. What is our attitude toward these sins? Have we given up and resigned ourselves to simply accept that we are sinners and that we will commit sin or are we striving against the sin that remains in us (Heb. 12:4)?[161]

There is all the difference in the world between someone who lives honestly before themselves, God, and others and people of the lie.[162] If the pattern of our lives is characterized by little to no self-awareness, little to no personal responsibility for our actions, engrained tendencies toward self-deception, and patterns of dishonesty with those around us, we are not people of the truth. Most often those who walk in truth are well aware of their personal struggles and could delineate them upon request. The same is not true of those who do not own their sin. The question for them is, "forgiven from what?"

The degree to which this ownership is present in the offender determines the degree to which full forgiveness or full reconciliation can be realized.

This is not to say perfect ownership is possible.[163] Even David admitted this when he said to the LORD, "Declare me innocent from hidden faults" (Ps. 19:12), from sins outside of his awareness. Healthy ownership of our sin as revealed in Scripture, nonetheless, involves at least five aspects: confession, repentance, apology, restitution, and lifestyle change.

161. The unfortunate influence of antinomianism has made the notion of striving against sin seem like an archaic and irrelevant topic of discussion.

162. See Peck, *The People of the Lie: The Hope for Healing Human Evil.*

163. This is important. Just as Luther almost drove himself and Von Staupitz, his confessor, crazy nearly introspecting to death, so we will not and cannot perfectly own our sin in its entirety, subtlety, and complexity. Though our self-knowledge is imperfect, it is essential for our growth and maturity.

There are ways in which the offended can unilaterally move past the offense committed against them, but the best solution involves interpersonal forgiveness and reconciliation based on the fullest possible ownership of sin. Let's look briefly at these five aspects of the path of wisdom in conflict.

Confession: Being Honest

We have an Advocate with the Father (1 Jn. 2:1). Thus John said, "If we confess our sins, He is faithful and just to forgive us our sins and to cleanse us from all unrighteousness" (1 Jn. 1:9). Confession is the first step toward wholeness when we have sinned.[164] Confession is agreeing with God that our sin is sin. Honesty is required in confession. We need to be honest with God, with ourselves, and with others. True confession means we are not seeking to hide the seriousness of our sins, to deceive others about our sin, or to shift blame somewhere other than our own sinful hearts. This aspect of confession goes against so much in our culture today. Our narcissistic culture says, "It is never our fault." True confession says otherwise. It is our fault. True confession steps up to the plate and owns the responsibility rightfully ours before God, others, and ourselves.

When we have sinned, confession is the beginning of the path of wisdom. It releases us from the prison of denial and frees us to pursue the Lord and those we have sinned against with renewed honesty and integrity. As Dietrich Bonhoeffer commented,

> He who is alone with his sin is utterly alone. . . . It is the grace of the Gospel, which is so hard for the pious to understand, that it confronts us with the truth and says: "You are a sinner, a great, desperate sinner; now come, as the sinner that you are, to God who loves you." . . . This message is liberation through truth. . . . You do not have to go on lying to yourself and your brothers, as if you were without sin; you can dare to be a sinner.[165]

---

164. If we haven't sinned, confession is actually falsehood. We should never confess sins we have not committed. This is dishonest and unhealthy.

165. Dietrich Bonhoeffer, *Life Together*, trans. John W. Doberstein (New York: Harper and Row, 1954), 110–111.

The wise own their sins, accept the consequences, and risk further susceptibility by being entirely honest about what they have done. They put themselves in a position of vulnerability to the mercy of those they have sinned against.

The off-ramp from the way of wisdom at the point of confession is found in denial and covering up. The Bible says clearly, "He who covers his sins will not prosper" (Prov. 28:13). In the place of honesty and self-awareness, the path of folly is a path of dishonesty and self-deception.

Repentance: Changing Our Minds, Feelings, and Behavior

Repentance is quite misunderstood in our generation. Repentance involves a change in our entire disposition toward God and others. It involves our minds, feelings, and wills. It is a turning away from the foolish path we have been traveling and a return to the path of wisdom. It involves a change in our behavior that springs from an inward change at the thinking and affective levels. True repentance sorrows over sin. True repentance hates sin and turns away from it. Nonrepentance robs us of the healing grace that comes to the contrite in heart. It also robs those we have wronged of the ability to be reconciled with us. Reconciliation without repentance is impossible. Therefore, as Dan Allender wrote, "The ultimate betrayal is not merely the harm but the refusal of the one who perpetrated the evil to repent. Repentance is the sole ground for trust or relationship to be restored."[166]

The path of wisdom includes repentance. The hardened refuse to be softened. Just like Pharaoh, the foolish harden themselves under the heat and light of God's revealing Word. Like bricks forged from soft clay, the exposure to heat makes them impenetrable.

---

166. Dan Allender, "The Mark of Evil" in *God and the Victim: Theological Reflections on Evil, Victimization, Justice and Forgiveness*, ed. Lisa Barnes Lampman and Michelle Shattuck (Grand Rapids, MI: Eerdmans Publishing Co., 1999), 49.

Apology: The Key to Forgiveness

Our culture is terrible at making apologies. This much-needed skill that exemplifies wisdom is in short supply. Often we give and receive apologies like the following:

- *If* I did anything to hurt you, I'm sorry.
- I'm sorry that *you thought* what I did was hurtful.
- I'm sorry I hung up on you, *but* you made me mad.
- I'm sorry I didn't handle this in a way you think is biblical.

We're so passive–aggressive as a culture; we don't even realize it anymore. We are masters at shifting the blame away from ourselves and onto others, even the ones whom we have sinned against. Nothing is our fault anymore. We are truly a generation and a nation of narcissists.[167]

True apology avoids terms that negate the apology. It addresses real offenses, confessing they are real offenses. It is nonevasive, not self-protective. It embodies true repentance, a real sense of sorrow over our sins against God and others, not just over getting caught or the consequences. It steps up, takes responsibility for previous sinful actions, and asks for mercy that is not deserved.

The path of wisdom in apology is short-circuited when we make excuses. Excuse making is the return to the path of the fool. If nothing is ever "our fault," those we have sinned against are left without the ability to offer sincere or effective forgiveness. Instead, our victims are left with the inability to be validated in their pain, a pain we have caused.

Restitution: Making Victims Whole

Often overlooked in the contemporary discussion of reconciliation and forgiveness is the inclusion of restitution. The Old Testament clearly required restitution on the part of offenders to maintain justice and order in society. For example, the Mosaic Institution lays out the following requirements:

---

167. See Twenge and Campbell, *The Narcissism Epidemic: Living in the Age of Entitlement.*

> Whoever takes an animal's life shall make it good, life for life. If anyone injures his neighbor, as he has done it shall be done to him, fracture for fracture, eye for eye, tooth for tooth; whatever injury he has given a person shall be given to him. Whoever kills an animal shall make it good, and whoever kills a person shall be put to death. (Lev. 24:18–21)

Often, it was required in making restitution to pay additional penalties to the victim of the offense. Those who were guilty of stealing were required to pay back an additional twenty percent to their victims (Lev. 6:4–5; Num. 5:6–7). Other crimes required four or five times the original sum be paid to those who had been wronged (Exod. 22:1).

The language of restitution is not limited to the Old Testament. One of the most famous children's stories in the New Testament involves a small man who was a tax collector. This "wee little man" named Zacchaeus, desired so to see Jesus, he climbed up a sycamore tree to get a better view of the Master. Jesus discerned his presence and heart condition and drew near to him. Zacchaeus, upon beginning to follow Jesus, restored fourfold those things he had defrauded others of (Luke 19:1–10). Zacchaeus illustrates an important aspect of true repentance, a heartfelt desire to do whatever can be done to make those we have wronged whole.

Restitution is not always possible for various reasons. Whether reparation can be effected or not, the critical aspect of this part of the process is the heart attitude of the offender. The eighth and ninth of the twelve steps of Alcoholics Anonymous say it well:

> Step 8: Made a list of all persons we had harmed and became willing to make amends to them all.
>
> Step 9: Made direct amends to such people wherever possible, except when to do so would injure them or others.

Restitution is an important part of the process both for the offender and the offended.[168] Attempting to restore what was lost in harming others

168. For a good discussion of biblical restitution, see Sande, *The Peacemaker*, Appendix C: Principles of Restitution, 276–278.

gives us the ability to more deeply grasp the impact of our actions on them. This is a great gift to us that will allow us a greater possibility of avoiding those things that have proved so costly to them and us. Where consequences for wrong actions are small, the tendency to reoffend increases. *Recidivism increases where restitution is not practiced.*

Restitution is not only helpful and necessary for the offender but also for the offended. Those who have truly lost in the relationship, whether tangible or intangible losses, are in need of being brought closer to former wholeness. Some damage is irreparable. Some reparations can be made. Substantive damages are the easiest to repay. Money and property can be replaced with interest. Other nonsubstantive damages are more difficult, yet attempts at reparation in these areas will be just as helpful to all parties involved. Where lies, slander, and gossip have been perpetrated, the truth can be told as widely as the falsehood was. Where irreversible losses have occurred (death, permanent disability, job losses, etc.), offenders, in keeping with the spirit of true repentance, should be willing to do anything and everything within their power to ease the suffering and hardship they have imposed onto their victims and their families.

> "Restitution symbolizes a restoration of equity, and it states implicitly that someone else—not the victim—is responsible. *It is a way of denouncing the wrong, absolving the victim, and saying who is responsible.* Accordingly, restitution is about responsibility and meaning as much as or more than actual repayment of losses."[169]

The path of wisdom following our offenses often needs to include some form of restitution, not as penance, but as a healthy outward evidence of true inward repentance. The path of foolishness refuses to take responsibility for actions and its impact on others. The fool wants consequence-free living.

---

169. Howard Zehr, "Restoring Justice," in Lampman and Shattuck, *God and the Victim*, 145. (italics added)

Lifestyle Change: Fruits Consistent with Repentance

Jesus' first word in His public ministry was "repent." Early on in His ministry, Jesus encountered the Pharisees and Sadducees, publicly warning them to "bear fruit in keeping with repentance" (Mark 3:8; Luke 3:8). Throughout His earthly ministry, Jesus emphasized the principle that the validity of faith and repentance could be assessed through the works that flowed from professors. He taught His disciples "a tree is known by its fruit" (Matt. 7:15–20). Paul, later, in explaining the gospel to King Agrippa, commented he had instructed the Gentiles not only to "repent and turn to God" but also to perform "deeds in keeping with repentance" (Acts 26:20). Lifestyle changes consistent with our professed repentance are a critical aspect of the path of wisdom in conflict.

For example, in the case of marital infidelity, it greatly increases the likelihood of full reconciliation if the offending party is accountable for implementing lifestyle changes to assure the wounded spouse the past will not repeat in the future. Without these lifestyle changes, the hurt spouse has little ground on which to hope for future marital security and safety. Outward behaviors showing the reality of inward change are necessary to reestablish trust in relationships. Lifestyle change over time is key not only to the initial process of forgiveness and/or reconciliation but also to its maintenance.

Consider the case of a drunk driver who is responsible for the death of a couple's teenage daughter. Choosing to get behind the wheel of a car, knowing he was unfit to safely drive home, the perpetrator finds himself behind bars and charged with manslaughter. The scene in the courtroom is palpable as from the witness stand, he tells the parents how sorry he is for what he has done. He understands "he is responsible for the death of their daughter and he has no right to being forgiven." What he has done is "unforgivable," he says. Moved by his sincerity, the parents respond. The mother of the teenage girl mouths the words, "We forgive you," to the convicted man. Nothing can bring their daughter back, but upon the confession of his thoughtless act and a request for forgiveness, the mother, at least, offers the gift of forgiveness. The mother knows how much she has been forgiven by God and extends the same to this man who has taken her daughter's life.

Fast-forward this scene from the courtroom. It is now five years later and the drunk driver has served his time. He is released from prison. The parents of the teenage victim are out to dinner at a local restaurant when they hear a ruckus coming from the bar. To their surprise, the loud person is none other than their daughter's accidental killer. The man is highly intoxicated. The couple makes eye contact and to their horror the man says with a hint of sarcasm, "Hey, it's you! So sorry about your daughter." The father enraged lunges at the man. The mother bursts into tears. How will this new data affect the mother's ability to hold her forgiveness for the man? Lifestyle changes over time demonstrate the sincerity of our initial repentance and apology. This, in turn, directly affects the ability of others to forgive or be reconciled to us.

The path of wisdom is a path of an outward lifestyle that reflects inward change. The path of foolishness is a path of the status quo. The fool is highly resistant to change and refuses to be transformed. The fool returns to his folly over and over. "Like a dog that returns to his vomit is a fool who repeats his folly" (Prov. 26:11).

Forgiveness: The Victim Pays the Price

In response to the sincere confession, repentance, and apology of those who have offended us, the child of God is enabled to grant interpersonal forgiveness. The essence of forgiveness involves the victim, in the face of real offenses and harm, absolving the offender of the consequences of those actions. The price is borne by the one who was offended.[170] In this, the forgiving one resembles the Family of which he or she is a part. Even as God forgives sinners, taking their just penalty upon Himself in the work

170. A curious development in modern society involves the supposed granting of forgiveness on the part of others who were not personally offended. As a society, we have become quite comfortable exonerating individuals from natural consequences of their sins (crimes) against others. See Prager's comment in Appendix B.

of the cross, so the believer forgives the worst offenses in and through the power of the Holy Spirit. Forgiveness in the truest sense follows upon confession, repentance, apology, restitution. and lifestyle change. Where these are weak or nonexistent, forgiveness will always be hindered.

The path of wisdom at the point of forgiveness in response to sincere apology often gives way to the foolishness of unforgiveness. The unforgiving person belies a serious condition of the heart. Those who refuse to forgive those who sincerely repent and request forgiveness are in danger of the kind of judgment administered to the unforgiving servant of Matthew 18:23–35. That servant was severely reprimanded by the Master for his wickedness (folly).

Reconciliation: The Ultimate Goal

Reconciliation is relational. We have defined conflict as consisting primarily in a broken relationship due to the presence of unresolved offenses. Therefore, the ultimate goal, the answer to conflict, is found in reconciliation. Reconciliation, the restoration of a right relationship between the conflicting parties is the ultimate end of the biblical path of wisdom. The path of wisdom leads to life. The path of folly leads to death. In this case, foolishness ultimately ends in relational death. The price we bear is a painful estrangement from one another. Foolishness and sin bring relational separation from God and others.

The good news of the gospel is that God was in Christ reconciling the world to Himself. God initiated the process of seeking to draw us back into a right relationship with Him. He so loved us that He was willing to pay the highest possible price for our redemption, the life of His one and only Son. Jesus came as one of us. He lived a sinless life reckoned to us as we are united to Him by faith. He died as our substitute, bearing the full penalty our sins deserved. He rose again for our justification and ever lives to make intercession for us at the right hand of His Father and ours on high. After He ascended, He sent His Holy Spirit, another Comforter just like Himself, to be our constant Guide and Companion. Father, Son, and Holy Spirit, all in perfect agreement concerning their love for us, have conspired to bring us back to Them. We, as believers, have been reconciled to God. We are at peace with Him (Rom. 5). There is no longer separation between us.

Dave and Carol

Dave and Carol have had their share of difficulties. Dave grew up Methodist and Carol is from a Catholic family. When they first married, they were ill prepared to deal with the conflicts that come to newly married couples. Seven years into their marriage, they saw their first marriage counselor who introduced them to completely different ways of dealing with conflict. They learned a new way of being honest with each other, with God, and of working through their disagreements where they actually felt closer after the conflict than before. In the past, they would "sweep everything under the rug," which was the pattern in both of their families while growing up.

They are baffled that Bill and Jane just do not seem to understand the health and wholeness that can come as a result of following this biblical path of wisdom. Though they feel upset toward their "best friends," they are unwilling to just gloss over this situation in a way that would ultimately be detrimental in their lives. They love them too much to just pretend. They are willing and want to forgive their friends, but have felt hindered in doing so by Bill and Jane's constant denial of wrongdoing.

9

Telling the Truth

When I'm honest with myself about myself, there is much that makes me uncomfortable. I, in no way, feel as if I have arrived. I was leading a small group once, and we were discussing the doctrine of sin. We were going around the circle and describing how we personally felt about our sinfulness (this is something Calvinists are prone to do). It was my turn. I went on to describe my connection to Paul's self-description as the "chief of sinners." I knew exactly what he was talking about. It's not hard to convince me of the truth of "total depravity." Since that time I've wondered whether my ease of embracing that doctrine is because of the biblical truth of it or because it resonated with my inner sense of self. Feeling bad about myself has never been hard for me.

So, the circle continued. A few people later, one member of the group shared her sense of self. "I'm a pretty good person. I don't understand this inner sense of feeling bad about yourself. I know I'm a 'sinner,' but I'm not a bad person." "What?" I thought, trying not to show my surprise. "Are you kidding?" I still don't know what that person was describing. I can't know it, at least experientially. When I look in the mirror, I'm confronted with the glaring reality of who I am. My comfort is in how the Bible connects this honest self-assessment with the way to salvation. I'm fully aware I am one in need of the Great Physician, which means I'm sick.

"The truth? You can't handle the truth."[171] Truth is at the very heart of the process of real conflict resolution. The key is not truth, in the sense of doctrinal precept, but rather truth, in the sense of honesty and personal integrity. In this chapter, we want to take a closer look at three aspects of our "above-the-line" path in conflict. These all connect intimately with the importance of truth. It is likely we see so few examples of true reconciliation because we have a huge societal problem with simply being honest, even within evangelicalism. It all hinges on telling the truth.

Owning Our Sins

It is in the aftermath of our sin where our true character is most often revealed. The question is not simply, "Do we sin?" Instead the question is, "What do we do when and if we sin?" The believer following sin is moved back onto the path of righteousness in a specific way under the conviction and leading of the Spirit. The path of wisdom begins with owning our sin, opening up the possibility for forgiveness and reconciliation with God and others. We often expend much energy, however, trying to hide our sin. Proverbs is clear, "Whoever conceals his transgressions will not prosper, but he who confesses and forsakes them will obtain mercy" (Prov. 28:13). Covering our sins is natural according to the flesh. However, as David Benner wrote,

> As long as we try to pretend that things are not as they are, we choose falsity. *The first step out of the bushes is always, then a step toward honesty with our self.* We all tend to fashion a god who fits our falsity. . . . Having first created a self in the image of our own making, we then set out to create the sort of a god who might in fact create us. Such is the perversity of the false self.[172]

Coming to the light, which includes the exposure of our sins, in contrast, is supernatural. By the grace and power of God, we are enabled to be

171. Jack Nicholson as Col. Nathan R. Jessup in *A Few Good Men*, 1992.

172. David G. Benner, *The Gift of Being Yourself: The Sacred Call to Self-Discovery* (Downer's Grove, IL: Intervarsity Press, 2004), 88–89 (italics added).

honest about ourselves. This is the first step toward the kingdom as John Wesley pointed out, "All of you: know now the first step in repentance, prior to faith. It is conviction, or *self-understanding*."[173] Grace assures us if we are honest before a holy God, He will not cast us away but rather receive us and forgive us all our transgressions.

These three, confession, repentance, and apology, are three (of five) facets of owning our sins.

Confession: Telling the Truth to God, Others, and Ourselves[174]

Someone recently said, "Confessing when the light turns on in the kitchen and you've got your hand in the cookie jar isn't hard." The point being that confession is the easy part in contrast to the difficult work of true repentance, restitution, and so forth. But here's the mystery about confession. Sometimes, despite the obviousness of our hand in the cookie jar, we find ways to deny the plain truth in front of us. "What cookie jar?" "That's not 'my' hand in the cookie jar." We all agonized as former President Clinton worked so hard to redefine "is." He looked into the camera and assured us all that he did not have "sexual relations" with that woman.

When truth is obscured, confession becomes impossible.

We always break the tenth commandment concurrent with the breaking of any of the other nine. Desire, as we have seen, is always on the path toward transgression. This is evident in the Garden. The woman desired the fruit and then proceeded to transgress against God's command. In a

173. Wesley, *Standard Sermons*, 1:132.

174. This section is focused on the beauty of sincere confession and concerned first about the problem of nonconfession or underconfession. It should be noted, at times, believers are pressured to overconfess, to own things as wrong that are not wrong or they have not committed. We should never confess things we have not done, nor things not sinful. It is not the intent of this section to prey upon the overly active consciences of some of those who have been wounded and struggle with overly frequent feelings of guilt.

similar way, we also frequently break the ninth commandment in conjunction with other transgressions. We lie to ourselves, others, or God about the reality of our sins forbidden in the first eight commandments. Falsehood, the very thing forbidden in the ninth commandment, is almost always present in conjunction with our other struggles. So not only do we commit sin, we lie about it, robbing ourselves of the blessing found in true confession.

The Gift of Confession

We frequently find ourselves in conflicts that go unresolved, sometimes for many years. The person who has seriously hurt us in the conflict for many years maintains their innocence. In a way, we feel trapped by our feelings of hurt so deeply connected to a series of incidents said to have "never happened." "Am I crazy?" we ask ourselves. "Did I imagine the whole thing?" Or worse yet, as is often implied to victims of serious offenses, "Was I just being oversensitive?" The situation continues to ache.

Relief is nowhere to be found. We seek various means of easing the pain—from personal counseling to prayer. Prayers seem to be in vain. Many well-meaning people close to us counsel us to unilaterally forgive the offenses. It is so hard though to forgive what is not acknowledged to have happened. How do we do it? If we try to express forgiveness to the offender, we will likely exacerbate the problem. Now the offender is offended that we would have the audacity to suggest they have sinned against us. We try to move on. We practice the things outlined in chapter six of this book. We've already tried, numerous times, to lovingly confront offenses too serious to overlook. But still things are not really resolved. It's as if the need to prove the validity of our pain leaves us in a place of needing to continue at some level to prosecute our case. When we are honest about how we feel, many Christians are more than willing to charge us with the sister sins of unforgiveness and bitterness.

Confession is a gift given by the offender to the one they have offended.

Then it comes, a confession that names some of the specific offenses. Those things that have been denied are now owned right in front of us, and in writing. We're not crazy. Those things actually happened. What a gift! What an answer to prayer! This is the gift of confession. It validates that the offense occurred; the hurt experienced is a real reaction to real events.

I'm aware of a situation that is still, to my knowledge, unresolved. A friend of mine has recently begun in his middle age to unpack the pain connected to childhood sexual abuse in his "Christian" family of origin. So many well-meaning but irritating Christians don't understand the pain of such things is not so easily "forgiven and forgotten," nor should it be. He has begun to courageously face the abuse that occurred. He has begun to feel the anger against this violation of his body, against the conspiracy of his family of origin who for so long has kept this sin a secret. Such is the nature of dysfunctional families, Christian or otherwise. You see, because this sin is not acknowledged, it cannot be dealt with. This is the beauty of confession and why it is, in fact, one of the greatest gifts we can give and receive.

To confess is to "agree that it is so." We agree, first and foremost, with God who ultimately defines what "sin" is. This is the beauty of the well-known passage in first John:

> This is the message we have heard from him and proclaim to you, that God is light, and in him is no darkness at all. If we say we have fellowship with him while we walk in darkness, we lie and do not practice the truth. But if we walk in the light, as he is in the light, we have fellowship with one another, and the blood of Jesus his Son cleanses us from all sin. If we say we have no sin, we deceive ourselves, and the truth is not in us. If we *confess* our sins, he is faithful and just to forgive us our sins and to cleanse us from all unrighteousness. If we say we have not sinned, we make him a liar, and his word is not in us. (1 John 1:5–10; italics added)

We have two options: to confess our sins in the presence of God, who was there and saw exactly what we did or to pretend we have not sinned, effectively making God a liar. God can't lie, as we've seen previously. He only has one version of what happened—the truth. Confession is aligning our story with His story to the best of our ability.

The Risk of Confession

Confession is risky business. To confess is to come clean about the actual fact of our sin. To be honest about our guilt is to be vulnerable. This *vulnerability is likely the main hindrance to more honest confessions.* It is commonly known in the judicial system that more confessions are not given because attorneys are seeking to minimize the legal exposure of their clients. When we confess, we own what we have done in all its disgrace and shame. Those we have offended could well use this confession against us. The heart of the gospel, however, is that God, who is well aware of whom we are and what we have done, promises never to use that knowledge against us, but instead has fully paid the penalty of those things in His Son's death on the cross. So it is with followers of Christ; when they receive honest confessions of sin from others who have offended them, they quickly realize the grace they have received and extend similar grace to others.

The Essence of Confession

Confession in the New Testament (*homologeo*) means to "say the same thing" (cf. 1 John 1:9). Confession in the Old Testament (*yada*) means to "know" our sin (cf. Ps. 32:5). When we confess our sins to God, we say the same thing about them as He does, namely, that they are sins. We know and acknowledge our sins before Him as ours. The essence of confession involves honesty. The excuses are gone. The ifs, ands, and buts are no longer in play, just the stark reality of our transgressions against God for which we have no excuse. So in the vertical dimension, confession is our honest owning of sin before the presence of God. We call it what it is. We name it specifically and claim it as no one's fault but our own.

In the horizontal dimension, confession is similar. With God, all things are open and naked. He sees our hearts and hears our confession, which often includes not only owning the acts of sin we have committed, but the inward motives of the heart that are connected. When we practice interpersonal confession, we are not required to confess, nor should we, sins that never progress beyond the level of the heart. For example, we don't go to a coworker and confess lusting after her in our heart. That is a sin that is dealt with before God. We don't tell someone at church we have been struggling with envy regarding their position over us in the youth ministry.

With others, we confess those sins moved beyond inclinations of the heart and into actions. We confess sins of word and deed to those against whom we have sinned. We don't confess our sins beyond the appropriate circle of those directly affected by our sins. When we confess our sins to others, we agree with them and with God the things we have done are, indeed, sinful. Agreement with God's standard, His definition, His label on our actions—this is the essence of confession. Confession is intimately related to the second principle of these three, repentance.

Repentance: Getting Back onto the Path of Righteousness

When we are honest with God and ourselves about our sin through the blessing of confession, we can then practice repentance from a sinful path. To sin is to stray from the path of righteousness. To repent is to return. When we see how we have strayed, repentance allows us to not only turn around, but to return to the point on the path where our deviation began.

The Gift of Specific Repentance

Repentance is the gift of God given to us that allows us to turn from our sins and return to the path of obedience. Once we have come clean through the power of confession, we see our sins for what they are. We are no longer able to deny the existence of our sin nor to ignore the seriousness of it. The Greek word for repentance (*metanoia*) is literally a "change of mind." This points to the cognitive component. It is, however, more than just cognitive. It includes the whole person. Repentance includes several key ingredients. To borrow from Thomas Watson, there are at least six: "sight of sin, sorrow for sin, confession of sin, shame for sin, hatred for sin, turning from sin."[175] Having already addressed seeing our sin and being honest about our sin under the heading of confession, the remaining elements of repentance include emotional and behavioral aspects.

To repent, in general, falls short of true repentance. This is nothing more than admitting the obvious that one is a sinner. True repentance requires ownership of our sins in their specifics. The Westminster Confession describes this principle, "Men ought not to content themselves with a general repentance, but it is every man's duty to endeavor to *repent of his particular sins, particularly*."[176] Often, this specificity is missing from the peacemaking process.

Godly and Worldly Sorrow

True repentance includes godly sorrow as opposed to its worldly alternative. The apostle Paul writing to the church at Corinth described the difference between the two:

> For though I caused you sorrow by my letter, I do not regret it; though I did regret it—for I see that that letter caused you sorrow, though only for a while— I now rejoice, not that you were made sorrowful, but that you were made sorrowful to the point of repentance; for you were made sorrowful according to the will of God, so that you might not suffer loss in anything through us. For the *sorrow that is according to the will of God produces a repentance without regret*, leading to salva-

175. Thomas Watson, *The Doctrine of Repentance* (Carlisle, PA: Banner of Truth Trust, 1987), 18.

176. *Westminster Confession of Faith* (Norcross, GA: Great Commissions Publications, 1993), 13 (italics added).

> tion, but the *sorrow of the world produces death.* (2 Cor. 7:8–10 NASB; italics added)

Godly sorrow produces repentance without regret. This constructive sorrow given by God leads to repentance and salvation. It is not regretted because it arises from deep heart-felt conviction. This is the sorrow that marks the difference between genuine repentance and its counterfeit. This sorrow is not merely psychological guilt but a "love motivated emotion that is the biblical alternative. . . . it is a love-motivated desire to change rooted in concern for the offended person and one's relationship to God."[177]

Worldly sorrow does not lead to life through honesty and repentance but instead leads to death. It leads to death because it short-circuits the sorrow of the Lord that leads us to repentance and true change. Therefore, false sorrow thwarts deep change, rendering those who are under its sway confirmed in their impenitence and on the path that leads finally to death.

> Many Christians go through repeated cycles of sin, guilt, feelings, confession, temporary relief, and more sin. The confession was not accompanied by true repentance or remorse. It was designed to give them a bit of inner peace until they sinned again—a rather selfish motivation! . . . We fail to change because we didn't experience constructive sorrow.[178]

Worldly sorrow is insincere. It is not according to truth but instead is driven merely by human regret. It is sorrow, not over the depth of sins committed against God or others, but over the temporal consequences that naturally flow from offenses. It weeps not for the way God and others have been offended but only for itself.

King Saul is a classic example of this worldly sorrow. At the key moment in his life, he professed repentance (1 Sam. 15:24, 30) only to con-

177. S. Bruce Narramore, *No Condemnation: Rethinking Guilt Motivation in Counseling, Preaching and Parenting* (Eugene, OR: Wipf and Stock Publishers, 1984), 152.

178. Narramore, *No Condemnation*, 155.

tinue on the path of disobedience before the LORD. Esau is another tragic example. After he sold his birthright for a bowl of stew, "he found no chance to repent, though he sought it with tears" (Heb. 12:17). It is for this reason the writer of Hebrews used Esau as an example of a "profane man" (v. 16), who did not possess the "holiness without which no one will see the LORD" (v. 14). Worldly sorrow is not holy sorrow. It is not genuine sorrow. It is sorrow without repentance. It is not the sorrow God graciously allows His own children to feel as they consider the weight of their sin.

Changed Behavior

True repentance includes not only changed feelings but also changed behaviors. Repentance, true repentance, includes not only cognitive aspects (*metanoia*), agreement regarding the truth; affective aspects, godly sorrow and all it entails; but also behavioral aspects. To truly repent is to seek behavioral change. The person who "repents" only to run out and immediately do the same thing is missing the point of repentance. True repentance involves hard work. It would be far easier for us to continue to do as we have done in the past. That will come quite naturally for each of us. Repentance drives us to seek deep change to be reflected in our daily living. True repentance is never cheap and it is never easy.[179]

Apology: Requesting Forgiveness without Demand

When we acknowledge our sins through confession and resolve to turn from them to the path of righteousness through repentance, we will by the same graces of the Holy Spirit be led to seek the forgiveness not just of God but of those we have sinned against.

True apology is requesting, not demanding, forgiveness.

---

179. I have a friend who takes this point, to her credit, quite seriously. She actually writes out a repentance plan that details the specific ways she plans, by God's strength, to implement change in her life. This may sound radical to our ears because we are an evangelical culture of complacency.

When we have sinned against others, we have forfeited our right to be demanding. By honestly owning our sin, we recognize that we have no right whatsoever to demand anything of the one against whom we have sinned. Apology, therefore, is a humble request that the one we have sinned against would bear the weight of our sin in themselves. Through restitution, we can sometimes, repair some of the damage we have done. Apology undemandingly asks the offended person to bear whatever cannot be restored.

The Essence of Apology

Apology is closely related to confession and repentance. Often, however, an apology is attempted without either. A mother tells her child, "Now, tell him you're sorry." The child responds with an unfeeling, "Sorry!" Saying, "I'm sorry," is not an apology. Saying, "I'm sorry," is a statement about how we are feeling. It is short for, "I am feeling sorrowful about this matter." True sorrow of heart, godly sorrow, is certainly an important part of true apology. It is not, in itself, an apology.

The Elements of an Apology

Apologies that are thorough enough to begin to open the door to reconciliation through interpersonal forgiveness contain certain key elements. As a culture, we are highly unpracticed in the skill of healthy apologizing. Many of us have never conducted ourselves in this manner. We are habituated to minimizing our responsibilities in regard to the manifold ways in which we hurt each other. Therefore, the list that follows is an entirely new skill set for us to integrate into our personal lives while interacting with one another.

Agree with the one offended about the offense(s).

Call it what it is. Don't minimize the truth about what you have done. If it is adultery, call it adultery. If it is slander, call it slander. The more you and the one you have offended agree about the nature of the offense, the more likely it is that real reconciliation can take place. It is also extremely helpful to use biblical terminology, if both you and the one you have offended are believers. This validates a common point of reference, further promoting mutual understanding.

For example, "*I slandered your reputation when I told Sally that you were sleeping with Tom.*"

Not, "*I might have hinted to Sally that you might be behaving inappropriately with Tom.*"

Tell the right people.

Don't tell everybody. Don't tell people who don't need to know. But tell everybody who needs to know about what you have done. In some cases, it may be appropriate to tell the whole church body. In most, it is not necessary. But in every case, make sure you are addressing everyone who is involved in what happened. Be careful in telling about your sin, you don't "accidentally" tell about sins you feel were committed against you. Be especially careful, if children, mentally challenged people, or elderly people are involved. Consider age and aptitude-appropriateness in determining whom to tell.

Keep the circle of apology the right size and the level of each person in the circle appropriate. The circle of those needing to be addressed will vary from situation to situation. Keep the circle as small as possible for as long as possible. Don't tell the wrong people, the people who have no need to know about the situation. Apologize to those who need to know at the right time in the overall process.

Tell the truth without excuses.

Ken Sande wisely said that proper apologies avoid "if, but, and maybe."[180] Rarely do we see or hear in our culture examples of proper apologies. Many of us did not have this modeled for us in our families growing up either. This is a skill well worth learning, even though it involves breaking many persistent bad habits. When you apologize, avoid

180. Sande, *The Peacemaker*, 127–128.

making excuses for your sin or blame shifting the responsibility for your sin onto others. Own what is yours, clearly and unequivocally.

For example, *"I sinned against you when I spoke ill of you to Sally."*

Not *"If I said something to Sally about you, I'm sorry. I didn't mean to say anything that she would take as negative about you, but I was just upset."*

Tell the whole truth.

It is possible to lie by omission. We can make true statements that will actually work to conceal key aspects of the situation to others. We can commit falsehood by both what we say and what we do not say. Omitting information and allowing people to jump to false conclusions are in essence lying. Leaving out key details of the situation that reflect poorly on us is misleading to the hearer. Speak as the oath in court binds us to "tell the truth, *the whole truth*, and nothing but the truth, so help you God."

For example, "*We are ashamed of our behavior. It was wrong for us to mistreat the pastor when we spoke harshly to him that day. He was simply asking us to consider our actions and to prayerfully consider them before God.*"

Not, "*He told us that we ought to be ashamed of our behavior. We don't have any idea why he would tell us to be ashamed.*"

Own the impact.

Our sins always impact others. We may never completely be able to understand the full impact our actions have had on others. Nonetheless, to the extent we are able, it is critical for us to own and acknowledge how our sins have caused others pain. We are responsible not only for the sin itself but also for its consequences in the lives of those we've sinned against. Part of owning the impact might involve some form of restitution as appropriate to the situation.

For example, "*My sin of adultery against you has caused you great pain. You have every right to feel betrayed. I don't know how you will ever trust me again.*"

Not, "*I'm sorry if it hurt you, but I was in a lot of pain at the time as well.*"

Feel the impact.

Empathy is critical to future healing of the relationship. Empathy is the ability to not only own the impact of our actions on others, but to actually feel their pain. We are able to enter into their place in the conflict and step into their shoes. When we allow our heart to be broken in connection to the hurt they have felt, we can weep with those who weep, even over things we have caused in their lives. Most empathic responses in these situations will not be verbalized.

For example, *looking into the eyes of the person we have hurt, with sincere tears, feeling the impact on them.*

Not, *looking away from the other person who weeps in light of the pain we have caused.*

Accept the consequences.

When we sincerely apologize to others, we accept the consequences of our actions. The contract may be lost. The dating relationship may be over. Membership in the church may not be restored. The other person is not required to remove all the consequences of our actions. When we truly apologize, it will be evident we have come to a place of accepting the things that flow from our sin.

For example, "*I understand that we will no longer date and this is my fault.*"

Not, "*Now that we've covered this, we will still date, right?*"

Ask for forgiveness.

We need to actually ask for forgiveness from the other person. We don't demand it. We don't threaten them with God's judgment if they cannot forgive us. This goes far beyond, "I'm sorry." When we ask for forgiveness, we are asking for the other person to bear in themselves what we cannot pay or repair. We acknowledge an unpayable debt that has no remedy aside from them simply absorbing the balance owed.

For example, "*I have done all I can think of to undo the damage I have caused with my sinful speech to others about you. I will continue to seek ways to repair your reputation in any way I can in the future. I realize, even after all these attempts, there are some with whom I have irreparably damaged your reputation. I am asking that you would please forgive me for this damaging sin I have committed against you.*"

Not, "*I said I was sorry. How much more do you want me to do? As a Christian, you need to forgive me and move on.*"

Final Thoughts on Ownership

The key aspect that seems to differentiate the foolish from the wise is this principle of ownership. Perhaps the reason we so seldom see true restoration of interpersonal relationships is due to rarely owning our sin.

Where there is little or no ownership of our sins against God and one another, we will inevitably experience little to no reconciliation.

God help us to be honest, to simply tell the truth.

What Sin?

Bill has a hard time owning anything he has done wrong. This pattern has always been present in his marriage to Jane, with their children, with his former bosses, and now for the last several years, with his clients. He is bothered by the implication in the pastor's sermons that all people are sinners. He considers himself to be a pretty good guy. He never intentionally hurts anyone and feels deeply misunderstood by everyone, including Jane.

This situation with Dave is all too familiar for Bill, though he tries hard not to connect the dots between similar experiences. For some reason, unbeknownst to him, people seem to always falsely accuse him of things. "Bill just doesn't ever receive correction. He gets mad when I suggest things he needs to change," explained Jane to the marriage counselor.

Several years ago, Dave felt he had offended Bill over a situation with their two sons. Dave had said things about Bill's son, Corey, and he knew had deeply hurt Bill. Dave admitted specifically what he had said and explicitly asked for Bill's forgiveness. Bill forgave him but thought he was making a big deal out of nothing. He felt it was odd that Dave insisted on apologizing. He just couldn't understand why Dave was so serious about making things right.

10

Forgive as the LORD Forgave You

Jesus, just prior to His ascension said, "It was written that this message would be proclaimed in the authority of His name to all nations, beginning at Jerusalem: "*There is forgiveness of sins for all who repent*" (Luke 24:47 NLT; italics added). These are among the very last words of instruction from Jesus to the disciples. William Booth, founder of the Salvation Army, made the following prophetic statement in 1912:

> The chief danger that confronts the coming century will be religion without the Holy Ghost, Christianity without Christ, *forgiveness without repentance*, salvation without regeneration, politics without God, heaven without hell. (italics added)

Look how far we've come! The measure of our collective drifting can be seen in the extent to which Booth's fears have been realized at the beginning of the twenty-first century. The notion that forgiveness would be considered without repentance one hundred years ago was unheard of. Today, this is the dominant position among evangelicals.[181]

Misunderstanding of the biblical teaching concerning forgiveness runs rampant in the church today. For the sake of so many who have been revictimized by the church following serious sins committed against them,

181. See Appendix A: An Analysis of Therapeutic Forgiveness. Therapeutic forgiveness is the dominant view in our culture, Christian and secular, at the beginning of the twenty-first century.

we need to review the biblical data. For many people inside and outside of the church, forgiveness has become an obscene word. It is carelessly tossed about and prescribed as a simple and quick fix. The impact of this on those who have felt the deep sting of betrayals and oppression is often seen in a recoiling at the mere mention of the word. It shocks their sensibilities and evokes a deep response. It seems profane. It seems immoral, and rightly so, that they are asked of God to "just forgive" their offender in such a way that their offender "just gets away with it." Due to the inept way many in the Christian community have misrepresented the biblical teaching, the true blessing from the practice of biblical forgiveness is missed. The church has often blamed victims, has lacked compassion for them, and has condemned them to supposed lives apart from God for eternity. The church has grossly misrepresented the heart of God for those who are victimized.

Important Aspects of Biblical Forgiveness

These are the "givens" of forgiveness, the principles central to understanding its true contours. Without this conceptual underpinning, forgiveness will be free to float according to the culture around us. In this area of forgiveness, we see again the tremendous need for biblical mooring lest we drift away from the truth.

God Is the Forgiver

If it is true all sin is first and foremost committed against God, it then follows that God is the One who first and foremost has the right to forgive those sins committed against Him. All sin is personal. It is all personally offensive to the One who has made us, the One who owns us. We do not belong to ourselves. So, in a very real sense, only God can forgive sin.[182] God has never given this divine prerogative away to any individual or to the state (Rom. 13:1–7). We do not, as individuals, have the authority to

182. This was reflected in the shock of those offended when they heard Jesus forgive sin. They rightly observed that "only God can forgive sin" and caught the implication Jesus intended. Jesus was saying in effect, "I am God and I therefore do forgive sin." (cf. Mk. 2:7)

pronounce the absolution of sin and the cancellation of its debt. We don't forgive others in that sense. Only God can and does do that.

Even the church of Jesus Christ, as His representative on earth, has only the authority to make temporal pronouncements or rather to provide earthly interpretations of biblical requirements. Jesus instructed His disciples, "whatever you bind on earth shall be bound in heaven, and whatever you loose on earth shall be loosed in heaven" (Matt. 18:18). Earlier He told Peter, "I will give you the keys of the kingdom of heaven, and whatever you bind on earth shall be bound in heaven, and whatever you loose on earth shall be loosed in heaven" (Matt. 16:19). Jesus, therefore, gave to the apostles the ability to bind and loose on earth through the use of the keys of the kingdom of heaven.[183] Though the Church of Rome and even Martin Luther thought of this as giving the church the power to forgive sin and retaining or loosing a person's guilt, most evangelicals would disagree.

Binding and loosing is most likely a reference to a rabbinic practice. The rabbis would bind or loose by interpreting and applying the extent of the believer's requisite obedience to the commands of Scripture. The rabbis sought to carefully apply the commandments to specific situations of daily life. Jesus seems to be doing just this in the Sermon on the Mount.[184] The church does not forgive sin. Individual believers do not forgive sin in the ultimate sense. God alone has this prerogative. He, therefore, is the only true and ultimate Forgiver.

---

183. This authority was given to all of the apostles, not only to Peter. In chapter 16, the language is second person singular, but in chapter 18, it is second person plural. All of the apostles were given this commission collectively.

184. Keith Drury, "Who Says What the Bible Says? The Keys to Kingdom, Binding and Loosing," accessed April 15, 2013, www.drurywriting.com/keith/wesley.quadrilateral.community.htm. Drury showed how Wesley and the early Methodists applied this practice through the use of small groups (class meetings), conferences, and through the application of Wesley's doctrine that became known as the quadrilateral.

Forgiven and Forgiving

"Those who have been forgiven much, love much" (Luke 7:47). Where would we be without the forgiving love of God toward us? The Psalmist said it well,

> If you, O LORD, should mark iniquities,
> O Lord, who could stand?
> But *with you there is forgiveness,*
> *That you may be feared.* (Ps. 130:3–4; italics added)

We, above all else, are a forgiven people. He has forgiven us an unpayable debt.[185] If He were not a forgiving God, we would justly have no hope. But because He is a God who forgives us, a God of relentless *hesed,* of steadfast love, we can now live in a relationship of holy fear with Him. Forgiveness is at the heart of the gospel. Without forgiveness freely given to us, we would bear the weight of our sin debt before a holy God. "Our sin, not in part, but the whole, is nailed to the cross and we bear it no more."[186]

We have experienced love beyond degree in and through the forgiveness secured in the cross of Christ. This experience of being forgiven is connected to our interpersonal forgiveness of others. The disciples' model prayer includes an important principle. He told them to pray, including the petition, "forgive us our debts as we forgive our debtors" (Matt. 6:12). Just as we seek God's ongoing forgiveness of our sins, we also seek to practice that same forgiveness horizontally with those who have sinned against us. We receive His forgiveness, the cancellation of the debt we owe Him, even as we forgive our debtors, those who owe us. John Wesley remarked that,

185. Just like the servant in the parable, we have a debt that can never be paid back through our own effort. In Matthew 18:24, Jesus described the man's debt as "ten thousand talents." This is an unpayable debt, which is why the servant's statement he would "pay it all back" (v. 26) belied the heart condition of the servant. He failed to realize his utter inability to take care of this problem himself. His only appeal was to the mercy of the King.

186. Horatio Spafford, "It Is Well With My Soul."

> God forgives our trespasses and sins if we forgive others, and as we forgive them . . . God forgives us in the same way that we forgive others. . . . To the extent that we do not forgive, we are not forgiven.[187]

The two transactions are integrally connected. The parable of the unforgiving servant rightly shocks our sensibilities.[188] How can one who has been forgiven such a great debt refuse to forgive such less significant things committed against them?

The Christian is a forgiven and a forgiving person.

Forgiveness Acknowledges the Reality of the Offense

By definition, *to forgive is to acknowledge the existence of an offense.* This is an inherent assumption in any form of forgiveness with God or others. If this is not the case, it is a misnomer to speak of forgiveness. *Where there is no actual offense, forgiveness has no place.* Forgiveness inherently involves the bearing of a cost, a debt incurred in and through an offense committed. In some cases, then, we should speak of clarifying misunderstandings instead of forgiveness. This is often the reality: A perceived offense can readily disappear in the light of additional information that explains the true nature of the action.[189]

Sins committed against God and others always require some process of working through the offense to renewed relationship. It takes additional effort to restore the relationship to a place of honesty. Owning our sin is the beginning of health. As C. S. Lewis pointed out,

---

187. Wesley, *Standard Sermons*, vol. 2:166.

188. The parable of the unforgiving servant is told in Matt. 18:21–35. The servant who was forgiven an unpayable debt by his Master promptly went out of the throne room to collect on an insignificant debt he was owed by another. His failure to connect the mercy he had received with the extension of mercy to others angered his Master. It ought to shock our sensibilities to see how readily we can move from the experience of God's mercy in forgiving us to promptly and severely exacting justice from our fellow man.

189. Caution, however, is to be exercised. It is common for offenders to maintain the matter is all a "misunderstanding." The facts of the case must determine the reality, whether a misunderstanding or actual offenses.

> "Real forgiveness means looking steadily at the sin, the sin that is left over without any excuse, after all allowances have been made, and seeing it in all its horror, dirt, meanness, and malice, and nevertheless being wholly reconciled to the man who has done it."[190]

It is fascinating what we as fallen human beings are capable of. Human beings have an uncanny ability to twist and distort reality, to deny the existence of problems in plain view of those same difficulties. We have our hand in the cookie jar and still seek to question the reality of the jar, the cookies, and our own existence in the kitchen. Forgiveness doesn't do this. Forgiveness looks the vilest offense squarely in the face and owns it in all its gory details. Forgiveness is based on honesty.

Acknowledging our offenses and their impact on those we have offended is an indispensable part of the biblical act of forgiveness.

Forgiveness is Costly, Never Cheap

Forgiveness is always at a cost. The deepest forgiveness, being made right with God, came at the highest price, the life of His only begotten Son. The most precious commodity in the universe is not silver or gold but the precious blood of the Lamb that takes away the sin of the world (1 Pet. 1:18). The price of our redemption is the measure of God's love for us. He demonstrated we were worth a Son to Him when He allowed His own Son to be wounded for our transgressions. Forgiveness is never cheap. Grace, though freely given, is extremely costly.

Just as forgiveness with God is costly, interpersonal forgiveness likewise comes at a high price. The forgiver pays the price in offering forgiveness. Ultimately, only God forgives sin. But on the human level in the horizontal aspect of forgiveness, we bear the price in ourselves when we forgive. We look squarely at the offense and our offender, and by the strength only God provides, we make a decision to bear the cost of forgiving them.

---

190. Lewis, *Weight of Glory*. 181.

Much of what we are asked to forgive is irreparable damage. We have often been deeply impacted, perhaps forever altered, by things done to us. We choose to forgive those who have sinned against us, bearing the cost within ourselves.

Forgiveness Follows Repentance

Is forgiveness conditional or unconditional? How is repentance related to forgiveness? We've come a long way in the evangelical community under the influence of a new paradigm. The therapeutic model has essentially reshaped the contours of forgiveness for many in the Christian community.[191] We've moved into an understanding of unconditional love, acceptance, and forgiveness that bears little resemblance to the Bible at all.

A key passage clearly referencing the terms of forgiveness includes language that demonstrates the conditionality of Christian forgiveness.

> And he said to his disciples, "Temptations to sin are sure to come, but woe to the one through whom they come! It would be better for him if a millstone were hung around his neck and he were cast into the sea than that he should cause one of these little ones to sin. Pay attention to yourselves! If your brother sins, rebuke him, and *if he repents, forgive him*, and if he sins against you seven times in the day, and turns to you seven times, *saying, 'I repent,' you must forgive him*." (Luke 17:1–4; italics added)

Jesus clearly said that the principle of forgiving seven times a day, *unlimited forgiveness*, is directly connected to the presence of repentance and a request for forgiveness. The word "if" clearly makes the entire statement conditional. "*If* he repents, *if* he returns to you saying, 'I repent, *then* you *must* forgive him." Even if this same process happens seven times in the same day, each time someone sins against us and comes in true ownership of their sin, repentantly asking for our forgiveness, we must forgive

191. See Appendix A for a comparison of therapeutic and biblical concepts of forgiveness.

them.[192] So, *forgiveness is both unlimited in scope and conditional in practice.* There is no sin which cannot be forgiven, which ought not to be forgiven, *if* the sinner comes clean before God and those they have sinned against, owning their sin and humbly requesting forgiveness from both.[193]

Forgiveness Is Not Reconciliation

While forgiveness involves the release of the consequences resulting from an offense committed, reconciliation is a relational term.[194] Forgiveness leads to reconciliation. Clearing the offense between us, in our sin, and those we've sinned against, releases us from the legal liabilities of our actions. In forgiveness, the offended give up their rights and agree to bear the cost of the matter in themselves. This legal transaction paves the way for the possibility of a relational restoration.

Forgiveness and reconciliation, though intrinsically related, are not identical.

It is possible, however, to transact forgiveness and yet fail to achieve full reconciliation. For various reasons, the fullness of reconciliation and restoration of the way things were is no longer possible. Consider the case of a marriage that ends as a result of infidelity. If the wronged party in the divorce chooses to remarry, he or she is acting within biblical rights to do so. If the former spouse comes later in repentance and sincerity, asking for forgiveness for the adultery committed, he or she can and should forgive. However, full reconciliation may no longer be possible in the sense of the

192. For a thorough unpacking of the conditionality of forgiveness, see Brauns, *Unpacking Forgiveness: Biblical Answers for Complex Questions and Deep Wounds.*

193. For additional quotations regarding the conditionality of forgiveness, see Appendix B: Conditional Forgiveness Quotations.

194. To forgive (*aphiemi*) is to "release, send off, and let go" of the consequences of an action that has damaged another. It is, therefore a legal concept s the concept of reconciliation, a relational concept. Forgiveness removes the legal barrier so the broken relationship can be reestablished. The legal precedes the relational aspect, but the relational aspect is the ultimate end. Forgiveness is the penultimate goal. Reconciliation is the ultimate.

restoration of the marital relationship. Some damage, it seems, on the horizontal level is irreparable.

Think of the case of a pastor who is wrongfully terminated from his charge due to sinful gossip, slander, and undermining by members of his congregation. Years later, those members may come and seek his forgiveness for their sin against him. He may then, in his new charge, forgive them but will not be reunited to them as their pastor. Things have been altered. Actions have consequences. He can, in that case, fully release any residual feelings connected to the past event, but he may or may not choose to reenter those previously close relationships. This is the fundamental difference between forgiveness and reconciliation.

Forgiveness Is Not Forgetfulness

Sadly, with the help of popular authors, Christians have glommed on to this slogan and connected various passages (Heb. 8:12; Ps. 103:12; Mic. 7:19) to suggest God has literally *forgotten* our sins.[195]

Forgive and forget. This is one of the most unhelpful, erroneous, and unbiblical statements ever uttered.

God informs us that He chooses to never bring up our sins against us judicially again because of Christ and our union with Him. He will not use them as the grounds of our condemnation. However, He does not have amnesia. In His omniscience, He has a perfect memory of all past events, including our sinful acts.

Part of our fear may arise from bizarre pictures of judgment day for the believer.[196] We have likely been mistaught concerning the nature of final judgment, with visions of God displaying our indiscretions on a huge

195. This unfortunate phrase was given validation in the Christian community by Lewis B. Smedes in *Forgive and Forget: Healing the Hurts We don't Deserve* .

196. For me, this goes back to a Jack Chick tract that I used to read during church as a young boy. The tract pictured judgment day as including the showing of a movie of my entire life for the viewing pleasure of everyone else—my most shameful and embarrassing acts played publicly before all people. What a nightmare! I would much prefer the forgetful God to this horror.

screen for all to see. The atonement of Jesus Christ has effected a real forgiveness of our sins, such that the believer will never experience judgment (John 5:24) or condemnation (Rom. 8:1) in association with our sins. However, neither we, nor God, nor those we have sinned against, will necessarily forget what we have done, nor should they. The memory of past sins can actually serve as a motivation to further future godliness in our lives.

God doesn't forget. We don't forget. Why should those we have sinned against be told to forget? Incidentally, forgetfulness is a passive process. Try to forget something that has deeply impacted you. There is simply no support in Scripture for this common myth. We are called to forgive in accordance with God's commands and conditions. *We are never commanded to forget.*

Vertical and Horizontal Forgiveness

Vertical forgiveness is God's forgiveness of us. Horizontal forgiveness is our forgiveness of others. These two dimensions of forgiveness are interrelated and interconnected in the language of Scripture. For example, the Disciple's Prayer[197] includes the line, "Forgive us our debts *as* we forgive our debtors" (Matt. 6:12; italics added). In this model prayer, Jesus connected horizontal forgiveness (our forgiveness of others) with vertical forgiveness (God's forgiveness of us) by using the word *as*.[198] He was saying these two things are comparable in nature. The Apostle Paul used similar language when he told the Ephesians to "be kind to one another, tenderhearted, forgiving each other, *just as* God in Christ also has forgiven you" (Eph. 4:32 NASB; italics added).[199] So, Paul connected the two dimen-

197. The Lord's Prayer, Jesus's prayer, is actually found in John 17. The prayer we commonly call the Lord's Prayer is a model prayer Jesus gave the disciples to pray to the Father.

198. Luke's version used the Greek word *gar* here, which can be translated "because." Matthew used *hos*, normally translated "as."

199. Paul used *kathos*, an even stronger term that combines *kata* (according to) and *hos* (as) to result in a term that refers literally to these two forgivenesses being "just as, exactly as, in direct proportion to, corresponding fully" to one another.

sions of forgiveness by telling the Ephesians they were to forgive others in the same way God forgave them. This language is representative of the general thrust of Scripture.[200] These two dimensions are highly similar, if not congruent. The two dimensions could be drawn like this:

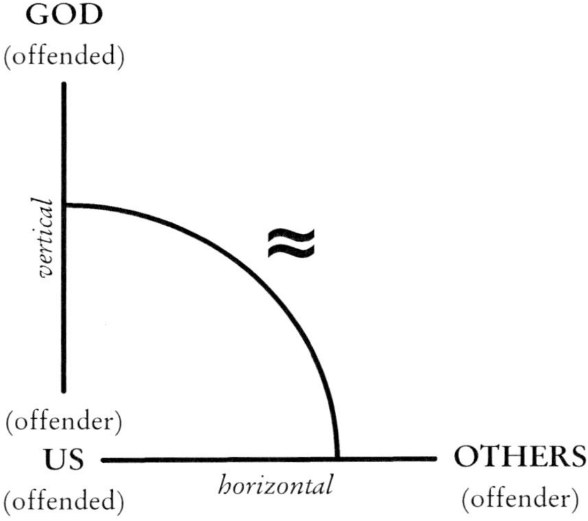

Figure 5.1. The Two Dimensions of Forgiveness

The diagram above indicates vertical forgiveness and horizontal forgiveness are highly similar.[201] Next, we need to consider the direction forgiveness flows.

Forgiveness is always directional.

---

200. This use of the comparative term "as" is common in Scripture when comparing God's manner of dealing with us and our manner of dealing with others. Colossians 3:13 is a direct parallel to the passage in Ephesians 4.

201. Much contemporary literature, including Christian authors, would take issue with this point. Among those who write about therapeutic forgiveness, many would seek to say God's forgiveness and our forgiveness of others are actually very different. See Appendix A.

It always flows from the offended (the one sinned against, whether God or others) to the offender. Forgiveness never goes in the reverse direction.[202] We never forgive God because He has never sinned against us.

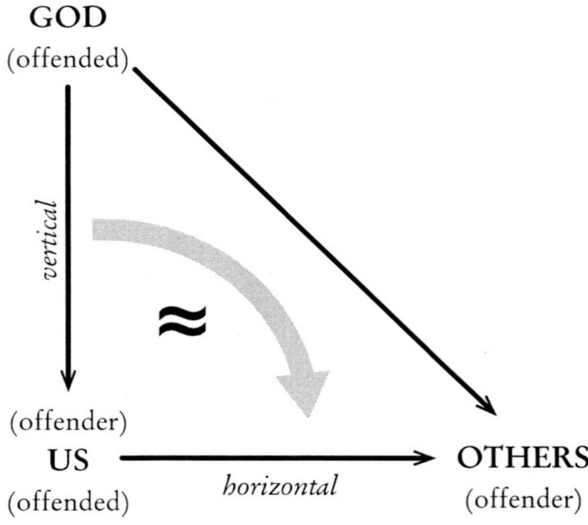

Figure 5.2. The Direction of Vertical and Horizontal Forgiveness

Several passages in Scripture show the seriousness of this connection between these two dimensions. The parable in Matthew 18 of the unforgiving servant stands as a fearful warning to those who would ignore the horizontal dimension of forgiveness (Matt. 18:23–35). This isn't the only passage that evokes fear in those who refuse to forgive. To refuse to forgive those who have come in sincere repentance seeking our forgiveness can actually put us in jeopardy with the Lord Himself. The Scripture repeatedly cautions us that the unforgiving are in danger of becoming the unforgiven.[203]

These two dimensions of forgiveness exist and are interconnected according to Scripture. C. S. Lewis agreed.

202. Therapeutic forgiveness confuses this point. It claims forgiveness is primarily for the benefit of the offended party. That would make God, in vertical forgiveness, the main benefactor from His act of forgiveness. As you can see, this gets things a bit backwards.

203. See also Matt. 6:14–15; 18:34–35; Luke 6:37; 2 Cor. 2:10–11; Heb. 12:15.

> We believe that God forgives our sins; but also that He will not do so unless we forgive other people their sins against us. . . . It is in the Lord's Prayer, it was emphatically stated by our Lord. If you don't forgive, you will not be forgiven."[204]

But which dimension is the more powerful. Does one dimension determine the other? Are we forgiven by God *because* we forgive others? That would seem to be justification not by grace alone through faith alone but somehow justification by the work of forgiving others. Do these passages imply that unless we absolutely forgive everyone who has ever sinned against us, we are in jeopardy of forfeiting our own salvation? In other words, is the horizontal dimension of forgiveness stronger than the vertical and does it determine the existence of the vertical dimension? Or have we gotten things backwards?

Certainly forgiven people ought to be forgiving. However, this does not negate the point that God's forgiveness, just like ours, is in response to the repentance of the offender and the sincere request for forgiveness.[205] Certainly, we are not asking God to forgive us our sins of which we have not repented. Neither is He asking us to forgive the sins of those who've sinned against us and have not repented. Christians are to be like God, rich in forgiveness toward those who come in repentance.

The Bible consistently says that ultimately, all sin is first and foremost against God Himself. Look, for example at David's sin in the Bathsheba incident. He certainly sinned against his other wives, against Bathsheba, against her husband Uriah, and even against the nation. But David had the boldness to say that all these other levels of his sin paled in comparison to his sin against God. Notice how he prayed:

> For I know my transgressions, and my sin is ever before me. *Against you, you only, have I sinned* and done what is evil in your sight. (Ps. 51:3–4; italics added)

---

204. Lewis, *Weight of Glory* 178.

205. Notice in the parable of the unforgiving servant (Matt. 18:21–35), both servants acknowledged their debt to their debtor and that each accordingly pleaded for mercy. This is the assumption underlying both Wesley and Lewis' comments. To refuse forgiveness after sincere pleading on the part of the offender is a serious matter and worthy of our attention.

David at least seemed to understand the vertical dimension of his sin to be more significant than the horizontal. He owned both, but he clearly had them in that order.

Another example might help. When Jesus forgave the notoriously sinful woman, the Jewish crowd was rightfully shocked, asking the question of Jesus, "Who are you to think that you can forgive sins?"[206] They understood from Sabbath school only God forgave sin in the ultimate sense. In our culture today, have we drifted into thinking we have the power to forgive sins? But the Bible is clear, *only God, ultimately, forgives sins*. When we take to ourselves the power to absolve someone else of his or her sins, we are playing God. Our forgiveness of others (horizontal forgiveness) never absolves them of their responsibility before God as the ultimate Forgiver. Instead of the horizontal aspect being primary, the vertical aspect is primary in terms of forgiveness.

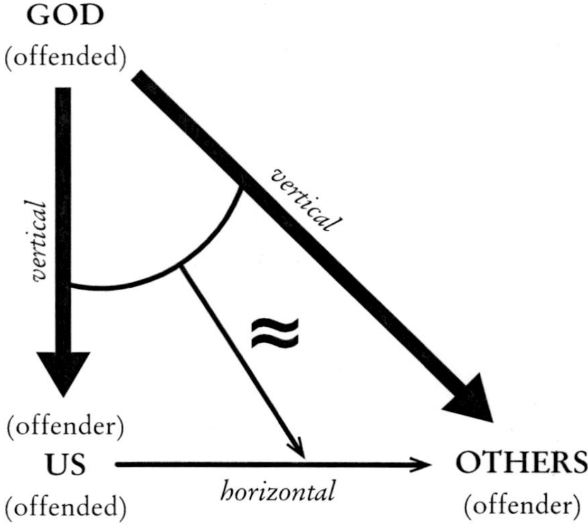

Figure 5.3. Forgiving As We Have Been Forgiven by God

206. Cf. Luke 7:36–50.

Now that we have a framework to work within, we can begin to discuss vertical forgiveness and then horizontal forgiveness. The order in which they will be discussed is the same order of priority found in Scripture.

Vertical Forgiveness (God Forgives Us)

God's forgiveness of us as sinners in need of forgiveness is ultimate and primary. God's forgiveness, obviously, is eternally significant. It is the difference between eternal life and eternal death. There is nothing more important to us than being forgiven by God. But how does God's forgiveness work? Are there important principles involved in His forgiveness of us that we can apply or better that Scripture applies to the topic of horizontal forgiveness? Let's begin by asking and answering some questions about God's forgiveness.

We all have "sinned and fallen short" (Rom. 3:23). Scripture throughout informs us that we are, by nature and by default, a fallen and depraved people in need of forgiveness. Without forgiveness, we will perish eternally. To grant us forgiveness, the Son became flesh, dwelt among us, died in our place, was raised the third day, and ascended to the right hand of the Father. Now, by faith we are united to Him and receive all the blessings that come from this union. Chief among these blessings is forgiveness of sins. So, for all those who are "in Christ," forgiveness is theirs.

The first obvious question is, "Are all in Christ?" In some sectors of the church, the old lie of universalism is coming back into favor.[207] The Bible seems clear on this. There are many who on that day will hear the fearful response, "I never knew you" (Matt. 7:23). Jesus said, "Broad is the way that leads to destruction, and narrow is the way that leads to everlasting life" (Matt. 7:13–14). His meaning is not hard to grasp. Many (most) will follow the broad way.[208] Few will follow the narrow way that leads to salvation and forgiveness. The question remains, "Is God's forgiveness universal or limited?" Notice the question was not whether His love was universal

---

207. Rob Bell's recent book, *Love Wins*, is an example of this recent trend.

208. The Greek here is *polloi* which suggests not only "many" or "much" but even the "majority."

or limited but rather His forgiveness. Most evangelicals would see clearly in Scripture the principle that *God loves all*, but would *not* see in Scripture that *God forgives all.* So the first question must be answered "no." *God does not universally forgive everyone.*

The second question involves the "how" of God's forgiving. For those He does forgive, how or when does He forgive them? In other words, is God's forgiveness of us conditioned on anything, and if so, what are the conditions of His forgiveness of us? We are all born sinners under the just penalty of sin and separated from God. This is the default position of *unforgiven.*[209] So how do we get from the default position of *unforgiven* to the wonderful position of *forgiven*? The Bible tells us. Forgiveness comes to us as a result of agreeing with God that we are sinners (confession), turning from our sinful ways (repentance), trusting in God's provision for us in Christ (faith), and making Him Lord of our lives (submission).[210] Does God forgive anyone without confession, repentance, faith, and following? The Bible says "no." Therefore, *forgiveness with God is conditional.* In regard to time, His forgiveness follows after our confession and repentance and not before. This seems to be what the Bible itself says.

> *If* we confess our sins, he is faithful and just to forgive us our sins and to cleanse us from all unrighteousness." (1 John 1:9; italics added)

Forgiveness is not automatic. This is the historic teaching of the Christian church. In addressing Exodus 34:6–7, the puritan Thomas Watson wrote concerning God's nature:

---

209. It is difficult to apply aspects of this statement, as in the case of the mentally impaired, infants who die, or aborted babies, to name a few. It is, however, a true statement that even these are born or conceived in sin, but the grace of God to receive and save these who are incapable of ever choosing Him seems consistent with His nature. For most of us who are capable of responding to the call of God to receive Him and His forgiveness, this is the starting point biblically. This is why Christians are so adamant on the need for evangelism. Without hearing and responding to the gospel of Christ, people are lost. At least, we used to believe they were.

210. We make Jesus Lord (*kurios*) of our lives, not just Savior. The most basic primitive confession of faith is "Jesus is Lord," not merely "Jesus saves."

> Though God is more full of mercy than the sun is of light, yet he will not forgive a sinner while he goes on in his guilt: "he will by no means clear the guilty"! The pure nature of God denies communion with an impenitent creature. Till the sinner repents, God and he cannot be friends. . . . *If God should be at peace with a sinner before he repents, God would seem to like and approve all that he has done. He would go against His own holiness.*[211]

God forgives us conditionally. He forgives us on the basis of our repentance and faith and never before or without either. Both faith and repentance are preconditions of God's forgiveness. This is common ground to historic Reformed and Arminian theologies.

> The gospel is not only that by grace are we saved through faith but it is also the gospel of repentance. . . . the emphasis which the Scripture places upon faith as the condition of salvation is not to be construed as if faith were the only condition . . . True faith is suffused with penitence. And just as faith is not only a momentary act but also an abiding attitude of trust and confidence directed to the Savior, so repentance results in constant contrition. . . . The way of sanctification is the way of contrition for the sin of the past and of the present.[212]

Horizontal Forgiveness (We Forgive Others)

Now that we've looked at vertical forgiveness, we're ready to unpack horizontal forgiveness. Vertical forgiveness precedes horizontal, not the opposite. If our forgiveness of others is to reflect God's forgiveness of us, what does that imply? The first obvious thing it implies is that *our forgiveness of others is not greater than God's forgiveness.* God would never create a situation in which He asks us to do what He hasn't done or isn't going to do. Does God expect more of us than He practices Himself? The answer is clearly "no." God asks us to be like Him in every way, to imitate Him,

211. Watson, *The Doctrine of Repentance*, 59–60, (italics added).

212. John Murray, *Redemption Accomplished and Applied* (Grand Rapids: Eerdmans, 1955), 115–116.

to reflect a Family resemblance. So, let's look at God's forgiveness and see how horizontal forgiveness lines up.

God's forgiveness of individuals is not universal, and He does not say we must be more forgiving than He is. God does not universally forgive all people, so neither may we forgive everyone universally. Sometimes the question comes up at this point, "What about Jesus on the cross?" "Didn't He forgive everyone, even His crucifiers?" His cry to the Father from the cross was not the pronouncement of absolution of their sins but rather a prayer for His enemies. [213] In this He was modeling what He asks us to do as we pray for those who spitefully use us. *Praying for enemies is not the same as forgiving them.* Many of those enemies for whom He prayed were forgiven fifty days later on the Day of Pentecost when Peter's sermon, by the power of the Holy Spirit, "cut them to the heart" (Acts 2:27). We can see, then, that *horizontal forgiveness, like vertical, is not universal.*

Second, we need to ask the question, "Is horizontal forgiveness conditional or unconditional?" The overwhelming consensus among contemporary evangelicals is our forgiveness of others is *unconditional.* But what is the Bible's teaching on this matter? Some of the passages state conditions for forgiveness and some do not. We have already noted the key text in Luke 17. Why did Jesus specifically include the qualifier, "if he repents?" If He meant for us to forgive unconditionally, this passage is confusing. Are there other passages containing conditional forgiveness?

One of the most often referenced passages in terms of forgiveness is the Parable of the Lost Son as told by Jesus (Luke 15:11–32). The parable displays the amazing love and grace of the Father who welcomed the prodigal back, bearing the shame of His son's covenant breaking in Himself. The wayward son was brought to real repentance in the acceptance and embrace of the father. *The story would read entirely differently if the son continued in prodigal living and the father blessed him anyway and moved into the*

213. We'll return to this critical passage in chapter 14 as we discuss prayer for enemies. This prayer from the cross is the exemplar of enemy prayers. It is not, however, an absolution of the sins of those who crucified Jesus. For further discussion, see Sande, *The Peacemaker*, 210–211.

Gentile city to be with him in his prodigal lifestyle. This is some evangelicals' conception of the grace of God. He loves us no matter what we do and accepts us as we are, period.

The penitence of the prodigal is key. His father's kindness and willingness to meet him at the outskirts of the city, bearing the shame his son deserved, were instrumental in bringing him to repentance. His father's public acceptance of him and restoration to the family makes no sense without it. In this story, as in life, the Father is the Initiator. The son, however, responded in true repentance resulting in full forgiveness. It seems then horizontal forgiveness, which is patterned after vertical forgiveness, is neither universal nor unconditional. We forgive others as God has forgiven us. This is the clear teaching throughout Scripture.

Conclusions about Forgiveness

Let's summarize our findings regarding biblical forgiveness:

- God is the ultimate and exclusive Forgiver of sins.
- God's forgiveness of us (vertical forgiveness) and our forgiveness of others (horizontal forgiveness) are analogous to one another.
- God's forgiveness of us follows our sincere confession, repentance, and apology (as well as restitution and lifestyle changes).
- Our forgiveness of others follows their sincere confession, repentance, and apology (as well as restitution and lifestyle changes).
- Neither God's forgiveness of human beings nor our forgiveness of others is universal or unconditional.
- We are to follow God's example in forgiving all those who come in sincere repentance seeking forgiveness.
- Forgiveness is the legal releasing of debt. It opens the door for the restoration of the relationship (reconciliation).
- Forgiveness is not forgetfulness.
- Forgiveness always includes truth, an acknowledgment by both parties, the offender and the offended, that what happened, happened.
- Forgiveness is never easy; it is never cheap.

Forgive or You Will Not Be Forgiven

The pastor read the text for the morning sermon. The text was from Luke 6. The pastor read, "forgive and you will be forgiven." Dave worried about his own forgiveness from God. He had been struggling for over six months, trying to unilaterally forgive Bill and Jane for all the ways they had hurt Carol and him, but in his heart he knew he had not really forgiven Bill or Jane. It hadn't helped him that both Bill and Jane denied any wrongdoing and instead had twisted the story to others to make them the victims of Dave and Carol.

The text really got to Dave. He and Carol talked about it in the car the whole way home. "If we don't forgive them, will God forgive us?" they questioned. They just wished Bill or Jane would be honest about what had transpired, so they could forgive them, but Bill and Jane showed no sign of softening. They appeared to be resolute in their claim to have done nothing wrong. They thought about trying to offer them forgiveness anyway, to write them a letter telling them they had forgiven them for everything. But then they thought, "They'll be offended at the implication that there is something they need forgiveness for." They were stymied and could not think of a way to proceed. Many well-meaning friends who did not understand the depth of the hurt involved told them all sorts of Christian platitudes. None of them helped. All of them just added to their pain.

11

Reconciliation, the Ultimate Goal

It's all about relationships! But what kind of relationships are we talking about? I'm an introvert, a label I'm just recently becoming comfortable accepting.[214] What that means is I'm wired for having fewer, deeper relationships constructed on a foundation of honesty and vulnerability. The problem with this desire on my part is how frequently it sets me up for disappointment and heartache. To have this kind of relationship, it requires mutual safety. When we refuse to reconcile, really work through things honestly with one another, the residual lack of safety is a relationship killer.

For me, when serious things have transpired in a relationship, it is rarely an option to "just get over it." I probably have a higher need than lots of people to talk through the problem, hear one another, and find our way back to a relationship where trust is possible. I know I'm not alone in this disposition. The situations in my life that remain unresolved are the source of much pain and ongoing concern. It seems impossible for me to just let go of people who matter to me and move on. And yet, at the same time, I cannot bear the thought of simply going back to the way things were, pretending like

214. For greater understanding of the impact of introversion on American Christians, see Cain, *Quiet: The Power of Introverts in a World That Can't Stop Talking* and McHugh, *Introverts in the Church: Finding Our Place in an Extroverted Culture*. Some have seen an anecdotal correlation between introversion and susceptibility to greater vulnerability or less resilience in response to mistreatment and abuse.

what happened never happened. This is my personal quandary. Would that God would bring these impossible situations, these broken relationships in my life, to a place of true heartfelt reconciliation.

The ultimate goal in the entire process on the path of wisdom is reconciliation. As we will see, interpersonal reconciliation is patterned after and is a response to God's reconciling us to Himself. Apart from the grace of God in this way, we would be left estranged from Him and without hope.

Reconciliation is the reestablishment of a broken relationship to its former status on the basis of forgiving the offenses that caused the breach.

God reconciles us to Himself. Reconciliation is the heart of the gospel. Justification by faith alone through grace alone is critical to the content of the gospel but in itself is not the gospel. God did not merely justify us in a legal sense so that we could be freed from a guilty verdict before His justice. He justified us so we could have a restored relationship with Him. God initially justifies us and continues to sanctify us so He can have a relationship with us. Legal aspects of salvation necessarily precede relational aspects. But, *the relational aspect of salvation is superior to the legal aspect.* Justification is unto reconciliation. Restored relationship is the ultimate goal. What God really wanted was a restored bond. He made this possible through the atonement of the cross of Christ. Though we had offended Him, He pursued us. God is the Reconciler.

For God, reconciliation, the removal of enmity that separates us from Him relationally, is the ultimate goal. God reconciled us to Himself in and through the person and work of the Lord Jesus Christ. Notice Paul's argument:

> From now on, therefore, we regard no one according to the flesh. Even though we once regarded Christ according to the flesh, we regard him thus no longer. Therefore, if anyone is in Christ, he is a new creation. *The old has passed away*; behold, *the new has come*. All this is from *God,*

> *who through Christ reconciled us to himself* and gave us the ministry of reconciliation; that is, *in Christ God was reconciling the world to himself*, not counting their trespasses against them, and entrusting to us the message of reconciliation. (2 Cor. 5:16–19; italics added)

Notice the emphasis in Paul's description of the new perspective that comes with reconciliation. In and through reconciliation, we are able to be regarded and to regard others as new people. Because sins, which were legally counted against us, are paid for in full through the blood of Christ, we are now able to enter into a new relationship with God. The enmity that was has given way to unfettered access and peace. God is no longer our enemy, but rather, now He is our friend. We have been brought near. He is not far off; neither are we.

In the case of vertical reconciliation, God clearly initiates the process. He is the offended One, the aggrieved Party. The offended One initiated a process of reconciliation by sending His own Son and allowing Him to suffer the just penalty for our sins. God pursues His enemies with love and grace. His love for us preceded the giving up of His Son on Calvary. He loved us when we were His enemies. God drew us to Himself, reconciling us to Him. He is the great Initiator.

Reconciliation is Relational

Reconciliation is a term derived from the Latin *re-concilliare, concilliare* meaning "to bring together." So we have reconciliation, meaning "to bring together again." The term presupposes a former friendship. That relationship which was lost is being restored. Our friendship with God lost in the first Adam is restored in and through the Second Adam. As we have seen, our peacemaking is to imitate God's. His children ought to bear a family resemblance. This should be evident in how we are able to live lives of reconciled relationships. Like Father, like son or daughter.

When God forgives us in response to our honest confession and repentance, we move back into a restored relationship with Him. There is no hesitation, no standoffishness in God. He doesn't remain arm's length from us. When sin is removed through the transaction of forgiveness, there no longer remains any obstacle to fellowship with God. He thoroughly removes the relational consequence of our sins or as the Scripture says, "He remembers them no more" (Isa. 43:25; Heb. 8:12). The gospel tells us God chooses not to remember or more accurately chooses not to allow those past forgiven offenses to cause a barrier in His relationship with us. So it is with reconciliation in general. It signifies a change of relationship, "an exchange of antagonism for amity, a turning of enmity into friendship." J. I. Packer continued,

> To reconcile means to bring together again persons who had previously fallen out; to replace alienation, hostility and opposition by a new relationship of favour, goodwill and peace; and so to transform the attitude of the persons reconciled towards each other and to set their subsequent mutual dealings on a wholly new footing.[215]

Reconciliation, then, is the restoration of a relationship to its former state. With God, it appears He is willing and able to resume an intimate relationship with us the moment we come clean with Him. He trusts us, drawing near to us again, with full awareness we will likely betray that trust again.

Relationships Are Built on Trust and Honesty

Trust is the air relationships breathe. Our relationship with God at its core is one of active trust (*pistis*). Trust is built on our history of finding the other to be reliable. With God, this is not difficult. We trust Him readily knowing He is fully trustworthy and always honest with us. We may be faithless or unfaithful at times, but His faithfulness is sure. Trust moving in this direction, from us to God, from offender to Offended, is not difficult to comprehend. If God held our past sins against us as reasons for Him to discontinue the relationship, what would become of us? We could

215. J. I. Packer, *God's Words: Studies of Key Bible Themes* (Grand Rapids, MI: 1981), 121–122.

not survive this situation. As the Psalmist commented, "there is forgiveness with You, so that You may be feared" (Ps. 130:4).

What of interpersonal relationships? Consider the difficult case of marital reconciliation after adultery. The offended party, in the case of adultery committed by the spouse, has grounds for divorce. However, he or she is not *required* to divorce the unfaithful partner. In fact, the emphasis in Scripture would encourage, even in the case of adultery, to instead pursue reconciliation. How does a spouse trust again after such intimate betrayal? If trust is not restored, the marriage is effectively over anyway.

Reconciliation is based on renewed trust. Renewed trust is only possible in the presence of honesty. Perhaps we do not experience reconciliation at the conclusion of our processes because *we are not truly being honest with one another*. It is very hard to completely forgive something that is inadequately owned. Full ownership of our sins should include not only honest confession, but also sincere repentance, willing restitution, and sincere efforts at lifestyle alteration. Where these are incomplete or inadequate, we will be hard-pressed to see anything near full reconciliation.

The Offended Trusts Again

As we have seen in our relationship with God, immediately upon repentance and confession, God not only forgives us our sins but also restores us relationally to Him. He does not legally forgive us and keep us in the relational doghouse. He does not forgive us and wait to see if we continue to bring forth fruits to demonstrate the sincerity of our repentance before He draws near. God readily puts Himself back fully into the relationship the moment forgiveness is transacted. In other words, *with God, it is nonsensical to speak of His child being forgiven but not reconciled to Himself.* Does God, however, forgive us and reconcile us to close relationship on the basis of a merely mechanical request for forgiveness? If He knows we are not truly repentant, is He bound to forgive us anyway on the basis of a contractual obligation? When God reads our hearts and the words we say don't match our true heart condition, which one does He respond to?

How is this principle applied on an interpersonal level? How can we trust again after serious betrayal? As we have seen, the resumption of trust is critical to reestablishing any relationship. *The key to trusting again, if any, may be found in the sincerity of the penitent.* Perhaps Fanny Crosby was right when she said, "the vilest offender who *truly* believes, that moment from Jesus forgiveness receives. (italics added)"[216] This small five-letter word, "truly," may hold the key to this process. With God, our hearts are open books. He readily restores us to full relationship with Him following our sincere repentance. It is easy for Him to read the heart condition we bring. Do we think for a moment we can somehow be really restored to a right relationship with God by fooling Him with counterfeit repentance? So it is with interpersonal relationships. The authenticity and sincerity of our ownership of our sin and its consequences are the only foundation upon which future reconciliation can be erected. Perhaps we do not see more reconciliation because true repentance and real honesty are so rare.

Forgiveness and Reconciliation

Forgiveness is the legal removal of the penalty of the offense that has caused the relational breach. Reconciliation is the restoration of the relationship itself. These two are different but highly interconnected. Allender and Longman explained,

> Reconciliation is not to be withheld when repentance—that is, deep, heart-changing acknowledgement of sin and a radical redirection of life—takes place in the one being rebuked. Nor is reconciliation (the offer of restoration and peace) to be extended to someone who has not repented. *Forgiveness involves a heart that cancels the debt but does not lend new money until repentance occurs.*[217]

216. Fanny Crosby, "Praise the Lord."

217. Allender and Longman, *Bold Love,* 162.

True forgiveness, on the basis of sincere repentance, necessarily leads to reconciliation. Logically, there is no ground to stop the flow of the process at forgiveness. If there is *true repentance*, which we have already shown is the basis for biblical forgiveness, then reconciliation needs to follow.

We often hear people say, "I forgive him, but I want nothing further to do with him." "I forgive her, but after what she did, I can never trust her again." Is God's forgiveness of us like this? If we are correct in concluding we are to imitate God's dealings with us in our relationships with others, what do we do with statements such as these? Is not true biblical forgiveness an invitation back into relationship? Notice, again, how these two principles are connected:

> Biblical forgiveness is never unconditional and one-sided. It is not letting others go off scot-free, "forgiven," and enabled to do harm without any consequence. Instead, forgiveness is an *invitation* to reconciliation, not the blind, cheap granting of it.[218]

In God's forgiveness, the entire penalty connected to our offense is removed from us. If the penalty, the "remembrance" of our sin, is no more, no barrier to future friendship with God remains. This is the core meaning of reconciliation. To be reconciled with God or others is to be restored to a right relationship on the basis of a sincere heart.

Limits of Reconciliation

With God, there do not appear to be limits to His ability to fully reconcile us to Himself. Yet, we hesitate to consider fully reconciling with those who have grievously sinned against us. David Augsburger went so far as to say that forgiveness must result in reconciliation. He explained that

> Authentic forgiveness is the mutual recognition that *repentance is genuine* and right relationships are achieved. Forgiving requires the grace to accept the other as an equal partner in the search for reconciliation and

218. Ibid.

> the genuineness to give repentance or to respond to another's repentance with full trust and respect. . . . Forgiveness is not finally complete until the severed friendship is mended. [219]

Responding to those who have hurt us, even to their repentance, with "full trust and respect" is a daunting proposition. As C. S. Lewis reminded us,

> To love at all is to be vulnerable. Love anything, and your heart will certainly be wrung and possibly broken. If you want to make sure of keeping it intact, you must give your heart to no one, not even to an animal. Wrap it carefully round with hobbies and little luxuries, avoid all entanglements; lock it up safe in the casket or coffin of your selfishness. But in that casket,—safe, dark, motionless, airless—it will change. It will not be broken; it will become unbreakable, impenetrable, irredeemable. . . . The only place outside Heaven where you can be perfectly safe from all the dangers . . . of love . . . is Hell.[220]

In situations involving serious sin, mistreatment, or abuse, being vulnerable again appears impossible. It is certainly inadvisable in the absence of whole-souled repentance and a safe support system.

Reconciliation, however, becomes impossible when the offender refuses to change. Refusal to be transformed is the heart of foolishness. God is not calling us into a repeating cycle of abuse and maltreatment. In some cases, full reconciliation is neither possible nor advisable.

> In the case of the deep physical, emotional, and psychological trauma of abuse, the abused may not and often should not return to relationship with the abuser. . . . If a woman is in a marriage or family where there is physical or psychological abuse, counsel that in the name of spirituality recommends forgiveness, denies the violence being done, and overlooks the exploitation being endured, is actually spiritual abuse.[221]

---

219. David Augsburger, *The New Freedom of Forgiveness*, 3rd ed. (Chicago: Moody Press, 2000), 32.

220. C. S. Lewis, *The Four Loves* (Orlando: Harcourt Brace, 1960), 169.

221. Augsburger, *New Freedom*, 42.

Sometimes for various reasons, psychological, spiritual, and ethical, people cannot and will not deal honestly with their issues. They refuse to face with integrity the manifold ways they have hurt others in their relational sphere. Without self-awareness and the resultant humility and repentance that follow, people are highly likely to repeat the same offenses. True reconciliation is not pretending this is not so. True reconciliation is a lofty goal. It is God's ultimate end for our relationship with Him and with others. However, its full realization with our fellows is often limited by the presence of sin and foolishness among us.

We can't be reconciled because the requisite ownership of sin is not present. Our forgiveness in such cases will be less than the biblical picture. True forgiveness is the release of the debt incurred as a result of the offense. To release the debt is to remove the barrier to restored relationship. Just as it is with God, so it should be with one another. Vertical reconciliation is our pattern for horizontal reconciliation. Our inability to be honest, really honest with God, ourselves, and others is robbing us of the possibility to be fully restored to relational wholeness.

Modern-day Americans are not good at repentance. Because deep repentance is such a rare occurrence, we frequently practice a form of forgiveness that does not lead to reconciliation. We are likely afraid of the personal consequences of not forgiving, and therefore, we claim to have forgiven and in the next breath say, "but I want nothing further to do with that person." Where would we be if God's reconciliation of us were like our nonreconciliation of others? Perhaps it is worth the effort and cost involved in seeking after true biblical forgiveness so that true reconciliation can follow.

Real reconciliation requires a great deal of effort. It neither cheapens grace and forgiveness nor creates mechanical results that do not lead to restored relationship. Citizens of the heavenly kingdom, on orders of the King, seek something far greater and much more substantial than these earthly substitutes.

> One insufficient version of Christian mission is reconciliation without memory, jumping over the past too quickly by offering cheap grace to those who have done wrong and never repented. But the other extreme is to create sophisticated initiatives that speak of redressing the structural results of historical injustices yet do not cast the vision of a new future of community and friendship between historic enemies. We call this "justice without communion." A future of shared life with enemies requires a long journey of persuasion and transformation of hearts, minds, and desires.[222]

This kind of transformation is only possible on the path of wisdom with the empowering of the Holy Spirit. True reconciliation is possible. We know the way and we have the power required to get the task completed. Why then do we so seldom see full reconciliation in this life? The next chapter seeks to answer this question.

Broken Relationships Hurt

Dave and Carol poured out their hearts in the pastor's office. They were heartbroken over the loss of their best friends. They longed for the possibility of actually restoring the relationship and putting the things that separated them behind them. "How can we fix this?" Carol asked. "There has to be a way to repair this," Dave added. The pain of a broken relationship is deep. The closer the relationship, the deeper the pain. The problem with Dave and Carol is that although they were willing to reconcile, Bill and Jane wouldn't admit there was anything to reconcile. They were blocked from working through things by the inability of Bill and Jane to honestly own their contribution to the breakdown of the relationship. Sadly, this is often the case.

---

222. Emmanuel Katongole and Chris Rice, *Reconciling All Things: A Christian Vision for Justice, Peace and Healing* (Downer's Grove, IL: InterVarsity Press, 2008), 33.

12

Why Can't We All Just Get Along?

A key part of my personality, the "S" steadiness part on the DISC, is all about everybody getting along, everybody, especially family, being together.[223] *For this reason, I instinctively hate conflict and in my natural state always tend to set aside my preferences for the greater good of everybody "getting along." This strategy worked for the better part of my life. I am a master at yielding to the preferences of others for the sake of unity. I naturally don't like to stir things up, don't like people to be upset. So, some of the outcomes of my attempts to follow what I thought was the path of biblical peacemaking have left me with deep confusion. "Lord, if I have followed the instructions You gave us, why aren't things resolved? Don't You want us all to dwell together in unity? Wasn't that Your prayer the night You were betrayed?"*

People not getting along will never feel right to me. Nor should it. Things aren't the way they are supposed to be. Sin has come and with it conflict and broken relationships. I feel this reality deeply and due in large part to the personal pain involved with this understanding; I long for the day when

---

223. The DISC model is a trait-based description of four behavioral styles into which individual's typical actions fall. It was originally developed by psychologist William Marston. His original system has gone through many subsequent generations of refinement and is now widely used and accepted as a way of understanding human behavior. Its four continuums are: D (Dominance), I (Influence), S (Steadiness), and C (Compliance).

things will be as they should be. I wish it were the case that we could just get along, but the cost of "just getting along" for me, carries its own sense of loss.

> People, I just want to say, you know, can we all get along? Can we get along? Can we stop making it, making it horrible for the older people and the kids? . . . It's just not right. It's not right. It's not, it's not going to change anything. We'll, we'll get our justice . . . Please, we can get along here. We all can get along. I mean, we're all stuck here for a while. Let's try to work it out. Let's try to beat it. Let's try to beat it. Let's try to work it out.[224]

The situation in which Rodney King made these comments was quite serious. We can readily appreciate his appeal to stop the onslaught of violence that erupted after the verdict in his police brutality trial. Rodney's comments attempted to quell the outrage, appealing to the principle that violence was not the answer; if people just try harder they can work it out.

Rodney's situation is similar to situations that occur in our daily interpersonal relationships. The word of the day in our culture is tolerance. Bumper stickers proclaim the ideal that we can all peaceably "coexist." Truth has moved from absolute to relative, not just in the area of theology but also in the area of ethics. What is right for me may or may not be right for you. Our ethic is highly individualized today. This is the cultural context we find ourselves in.

In the Christian community, we find similar thoughts and sentiments. When two believers end up separated as a result of serious and meaningful offenses, it makes us uncomfortable. In our zeal to repair the rupture, we move toward one or both parties, urging restoration and reconciliation. We question, "How can it be that two Christian people cannot be restored to each other? How can two Christians continue to be estranged? Is there anything so serious that it cannot simply be forgiven and forgotten?" The heart of this ideal resonates among us. "Can't we all just get along?" We

224. Writequotes.com, accessed April 13, 2013, www.writequotes.com/rodney-king/78078/.

push both parties to drop their issues, to come to the table, to "kiss and make up."

This well-meaning, yet naive, attempt is often grounded in a theological construct of universal forgiveness. In this view, the call to the Christian is to love all people, especially brothers or sisters, without distinction and in a nonjudgmental way. This "loving" includes overlooking offenses (regardless of the severity) and granting unilateral forgiveness (with or without repentance or restitution). This is all part of the supposed unconditional love we are called to have toward one another. In effect, we have no enemies because Christ gives us the ability to be friends with all people. True Christian charity in this view includes continuing normal loving relationships with unrepentant individuals grounded in the truth that Christ has forgiven us our own sins, which are many.

In this view, holding on to previous offenses is the height of intolerance, lacks love, and is indicative of a lack of maturity in anyone who cannot just "get over it." If this were the Christian ethic (unilateral forgiveness of all offenses and continued normal relationship regardless of prior history), we would expect to see this principle born out in the Scripture. Is this what we see?

The Myth of Utopia: The Not Yet in the Now

The Bible portrays God's clear desire for shalom. God's people, who reflect His holy character, also long for things to be as they ought to be. We long for the day when love will reign supreme, when not merely peace but shalom in all its facets will characterize our existence. This deep longing is a healthy desire and a natural part of our vital connection to the heart of God. We can, however, with the best of intentions mixed with our impatience, seek to bring these longings to fruition through earthly means.

We rightly understand that Christ's first advent began the conquest of the kingdom of darkness by the kingdom of light. Further, we correctly understand that Jesus Himself has given us His Spirit so we can be salt and light in the world presently. We should exert a shaping, preserving, and restraining influence in society as sons and daughters of the kingdom to come.

Since the turn of the nineteenth century, the church has been influenced by the thought that redeemed humanity on earth could usher in the kingdom.[225] Though this optimism suffered the loss of many adherents following two world wars and a number of additional international conflicts, today it is experiencing a resurgence of sorts. We so deeply desire the end of sin and its effects in society, we are at times tempted to think we can presently bring an end to the chaos. Dallas Willard called this "forcing 'Jerusalem' to happen." He commented,

> The greatest temptation to evil that humanity ever suffers is the temptation to make a "Jerusalem" happen by human means. . . . We are supposed to act, and our actions are to count. But there is a limit on what human arrangements can accomplish. They alone cannot change the heart and spirit of the human being.[226]

All of redemptive history is moving toward this eventual restoration to the way things should be. Though creation itself groans in anticipation of the final redemption and manifestation of the sons and daughters of God, the birth has not yet come (Rom. 8:18–25). We don't yet see all things "under the feet of Jesus."[227] Though the triumph of Christ and his ultimate defeat of all His enemies are certain, the final unveiling in its entire splendor remains for the final consummation. Though the end is a prophetic certainty, the Lord Jesus, will historically bring it to pass in His personal return.

---

225. Classic postmillennialism teaches the kingdom of God, which came in the first advent of Christ, His ascension, and sending of the Holy Spirit, will be more and more brought to fruition, ushered in by the work of the Holy Spirit in and through the church. The missional church of today embodies similar thoughts, with or without a direct or intentional connection to the postmillennialists of the past.

226. Dallas Willard, *The Divine Conspiracy: Rediscovering Our Hidden Life in God* (New York: Harper Collins, 1997), 380.

227. Cf. 1 Cor. 15:27; Eph. 1:22; Heb. 2:8.

We see the Christian ideal as portrayed in the New Testament and wish it could be so. And it will be. Just not yet. The New Testament gives us a realistic assessment of our present place in redemptive history. God knows one day He will make all things right. Meanwhile, as children of the living God we do all we can to live out of our Family values, knowing that we are children of light among a crooked and twisted generation.

A Biblical View of Conflict–Why We Can't All Just Get Along

As we've seen, the story of human history, as told by secular historians as well as biblical writers, is a story of ongoing conflict. From shortly after the beginning, people have experienced the consequences of the great tragedy of Eden. The first couple didn't "just get along" when they were confronted by God after disobeying His command. The first brothers didn't "just get along." The planet was flooded as a result of humanity's determination to continually do evil in God's sight. They weren't "just getting along." Civilization tried to get along in building a tower to reach the heavens. God came and disrupted their ability to work together on inappropriate projects by confounding their languages. In one sense, the remainder of the biblical record is a story of ongoing conflict. Even after the first coming of Christ and the sending of the Spirit, apparently we're not "just getting along."

The Possible Path of Reconciliation

In a fallen world of fallen people, it is inevitable that we will offend one another. Sin is a part of our current reality. There is a day coming when the offenses that divide us will be a thing of the past. The Bible outlines the path toward reconciliation for those who are wise. When pieces that need to be there aren't, the full process leading toward reconciliation is short-circuited.

In situations where the path toward reconciliation is not possible, isn't it still the case that we should all get along? It may surprise some of us to learn the biblical answer to this question. Looking at the example of Jesus and of the apostles, we observe lives not marked by an absence of conflict or by peace with all men at all costs. Instead, we see, much to our surprise, individuals whose lives seem to be marked with disagreements and conflicts. Strife with various parties over issues too serious to overlook seems normative. There is an antithesis between darkness and light, between evil and good, between the Seed of the woman and the seed of the serpent. The Bible, as God's inspired instructions for life, not only reveals that not all conflicts will be resolved, but actually goes on to describe situations and ways in which believers are called to separate from the impenitent. So, the Bible says we can't all just get along and we shouldn't all just get along.

Biblical Passages That Discuss Legitimate Reasons to Separate

While the overriding thrust of the gospel is Jesus Christ has come to reconcile us to God and one another, the Scripture provides a realistic approach to the possibility of relationships in this present world remaining broken for necessary reasons. Consider the following passages (italics added):

Proverbs (Various Passages)

> Do not enter the path of the wicked, and do not walk in the way of the evil. *Avoid it*; do not go on it; *turn away from it and pass on.* (4:14–15)
>
> Whoever walks with the wise becomes wise, but *the companion of fools will suffer harm.* (13:20)
>
> *Leave the presence of a fool*, for there you do not meet words of knowledge. (14:7)
>
> Whoever goes about slandering reveals secrets; therefore *do not associate with a simple babbler.* (20:19)
>
> *Make no friendship with a man given to anger, nor go with a wrathful man*, lest you learn his ways and entangle yourself in a snare. (22:24–25)

> My son, fear the LORD and the king, and *do not join with those who do otherwise.* (24:21)

This representative selection of passages from Proverbs shows that the principle of nonassociation with fools is a key aspect of biblical wisdom. The Proverbs warn of the harm that will come to those who continue in relationship with fools. Therefore, the wise person does not get entangled with the folly of those who refuse to be transformed.

1 Samuel 15:34-35

> Then Samuel went to Ramah, and Saul went up to his house in Gibeah of Saul. And *Samuel did not see Saul again* until the day of his death, but Samuel grieved over Saul. And the LORD regretted that he had made Saul king over Israel. (italics added)

Saul had been given many opportunities by the Lord to truly change. The incident with the Amalekites appears to have been the final straw (1 Sam. 15:1–33). Samuel announced God's rejection of Saul to him. After informing Saul, Samuel went home to Ramah and Saul to Gibeah. These two towns were just a few miles apart. Samuel and Saul were neighbors. Samuel, however, never saw Saul again though he grieved over him. This is an example of Samuel refusing to maintain a relationship as usual with the impenitent and forsaken former king of Israel. This separation between the prophet and the king was brought about after Saul repeatedly refused to do the right thing. *Samuel was not corrected by the Lord for disassociating with Saul.* He was, however, encouraged to complete his grieving over Saul and get on with the task of anointing the new king (1 Sam. 16:1).

Matthew 10:11-14

> And whatever town or village you enter, find out who is worthy in it and stay there until you depart. As you enter the house, greet it. And if the house is worthy, let your peace come upon it, but if it is not worthy, *let your peace return to you.* And if anyone will not receive you or listen

> to your words, *shake off the dust* from your feet when you leave that house or town. (italics added)

Jesus called the twelve into ministry and gave them specific instructions for reaching out to the "lost sheep of Israel" (Matt. 10:6). As part of their instructions, he told them how to assess the current spiritual condition of a given town or city. When they entered, they were to greet the people and if the people were worthy, they were to pronounce peace upon the people. If not, *they were not to pronounce peace upon them*, but rather, to shake the dust off of their feet, as a sign of contempt and move on. Notice how Eugene Peterson interpreted this section:

> When you knock on a door, be courteous in your greeting. If they welcome you, be gentle in your conversation. If they don't welcome you, *quietly withdraw*. Don't make a scene. Shrug your shoulders and be on your way. You can be sure that on Judgment Day they'll be mighty sorry—but it's no concern of yours now.[228]

The initial reception of the disciples was determinative of the disciples' response to each community. They were not called to endless patience with those who would not hear their words or receive the One who had sent them.

Matthew 18:15-17

> If your brother sins against you, go and tell him his fault, between you and him alone. If he listens to you, you have gained your brother. But *if he does not listen*, take one or two others along with you, that every charge may be established by the evidence of two or three witnesses. *If he refuses to listen to them*, tell it to the church. And *if he refuses to listen even to the church*, let him be to you as a Gentile and a tax collector. (italics added)

---

228. Eugene H. Peterson, *The Message: The New Testament, Psalms and Proverbs in Contemporary Language* (Colorado Springs: Navpress, 1993), 31.

The teaching of Jesus in Matthew 18 outlines a process by which believers may be restored to one another and to the fellowship of the church. The sobering result of a process that does not result in restoration is found in Jesus' words, "treat that person as a pagan or a corrupt tax collector" (Matt. 18:17 NLT).[229] This does at least imply that a relationship as normal is inappropriate in such cases. The person who conducts themselves without regard for the warning of the Christian community is to be evangelized. A person who continues in willful and continual sin is a not to be a part of the community of the faithful.

The entire process outlined in Matthew 18 is conditioned by three levels of a person not listening, not receiving correction, and refusing to be transformed. This, as we have seen, is foolishness in action. If a person persists in impenitence, there is a point at which we no longer maintain relationship with them. When we practice this difficult separation, we have the assurance Jesus is with the two or three of us in the process of discipline.[230]

Romans 12:18

> *If possible, so far as it depends on you,* live peaceably with all. (italics added)

Today's culture says, "Live at peace with everybody." Paul said, "*If possible, so far as it depends on you, live peaceably with all.*" Paul qualified the limits of the Christian's ethical duty. The Christian is responsible to do

229. The Anabaptist practice of shunning is a misapplication of this passage.

230. This is the context of the often quoted, "where two or three" passage. What Jesus means in context is when we do the difficult thing of seeking the restoration of someone in serious sin through a process similar to the one He is describing in Matthew 18, He is with us. We have his support. The two or three in His name are the witnesses required in a courtroom to establish the factual basis for the case. This passage is often quoted out of its original context. When we get together as believers in a group of two or three, Jesus is certainly there in the midst of us. It is just as true, however, when I am alone, I am never truly alone, He is ever-present with me by the indwelling presence of His Holy Spirit.

what is possible to live in peace with others from his or her side of the equation.

Romans 16:17-18

> I appeal to you, brothers, to watch out for those who cause divisions and create obstacles contrary to the doctrine that you have been taught; *avoid them*. For such persons do not serve our Lord Christ, but their own appetites, and by smooth talk and flattery they deceive the hearts of the naive. (italics added)

Here is perhaps one of the clearest passages that does not fit with the contemporary mind-set. Paul had the nerve to command the Romans to "*note those who cause divisions and offenses contrary to the doctrine which you learned, and avoid them.*" How can someone adhere to this commandment in today's culture of "Christian forgiveness"? Paul outlined a two-fold strategy for dealing with fools here. He described their lack of character in clear terms. He reminded the Roman believers these people who appear to serve Christ, in actuality serve their own appetites. They are smooth-talkers and use flattery to deceive simple people in their relational sphere.

Once these individuals were known as such, Paul's advice was to avoid them. Avoidance of such people was part of what Paul called remaining innocent concerning that which is evil. The believers were to have nothing to do with such people, because to continue in relationship with such would inevitably have a negative impact on them.

1 Corinthians 5:5, 9-13

> You are to *deliver this man to Satan* for the destruction of the flesh, so that his spirit may be saved in the day of the Lord. . . . I wrote to you in my letter *not to associate* with sexually immoral people—not at all meaning the sexually immoral of this world, or the greedy and swindlers, or idolaters, since then you would need to go out of the world. But now I am writing to you *not to associate with anyone who bears the name of brother* if he is guilty of sexual immorality or greed, or is an

> idolater, reviler, drunkard, or swindler—*not even to eat with such a one.* For what have I to do with judging outsiders? *Is it not those inside the church whom you are to judge*? God judges those outside. "*Purge the evil person from among you.*" (italics added)

This man in Corinth who was having a sexual relationship with his father's wife was being treated normally within the community of believers. They were all "just getting along." This was precisely what Paul needed to correct. This pretense was killing the body and was detrimental to the man in need of repentance and restoration. *Peacefaking kills everybody.* Paul informed them that the man needed to be given over to Satan and disfellowshipped from the church *so that his soul may ultimately be saved.* The man should have been treated differently, not so that he could be done away with, but ultimately, so he could be restored to health and usefulness.

The Corinthians were not to keep company with or conduct normal relationships with people who were continuing in an unrepentant pattern of willful sin. This principle pertains to professing believers who are living contrary to their profession, not to unbelievers. We can receive unbelievers as they are. We have no reasonable expectation of godly living from them. But among believers, there is (or should be) a difference. With such people who profess faith in Christ, who nonetheless continue in unrepentant patterns of sin, we are to alter our relationship. We are not to keep company with them or even eat with them, indications of normal relationship. For us to spend time with erring brothers or sisters, sharing meals together, having relationships as normal, is to send them a message that "all is well."

1 Corinthians 15:33

> Do not be deceived: "Bad company ruins good morals."

This saying is derived from a Greek comedy written by Menander (342–292 BC).[231] Bad company, those who refuse to repent, those "who do not have the knowledge of God" (15:34), will have a corrupting influence

231. R. C. Sproul, ed., *New Geneva Study Bible* (Nashville: Thomas Nelson, 1995), 1822.

on the godly. Therefore, as Paul had already informed the Corinthians, such are to be avoided (1 Cor. 5:11). This contradicts the relationship-as-usual paradigm, which so many believers feel compelled to practice and advocate.

Ephesians 5:11

> Take no part in the unfruitful works of darkness, but instead expose them.

The King James Version translates this verse, "have no fellowship." In other words, the believer here is to have no normal contact with shameful and sinful behaviors that are "not fitting for saints" (v. 3). A two-fold admonition is given: (1) don't maintain relationships as usual with such people, and (2) expose the works of darkness practiced among them.

2 Thessalonians 3:14-15

> If anyone does not obey what we say in this letter, *take note of that person*, and *have nothing to do with him*, that he may be ashamed. Do not regard him as an enemy, but warn him as a brother. (italics added)

Paul was dealing with a group of idle believers in Thessalonica. Some, believing that the Lord Jesus' return was imminent, had stopped working and were living off of the charity of others in the body. With all the time they used to spend being productive now on their hands, they were drifting into becoming busybodies (v. 11). They were acting in a disorderly manner (v. 10). Paul specifically told the Thessalonian believers to not only *note* such individuals but also to *not keep company with them*. This disassociation from them was intended to bring healthy shame on them, so they would realize the error of their way and repent. To admonish was to put them in mind of their current behavior. It is the polar opposite of denial and pretense.

2 Timothy 3:1-7

> But understand this, that in the last days there will come times of difficulty. For people will be lovers of self, lovers of money, proud, arrogant, abusive, disobedient to their parents, ungrateful, unholy, heartless, unappeasable, slanderous, without self-control, brutal, not loving good, treacherous, reckless, swollen with conceit, lovers of pleasure rather than lovers of God, *having the appearance of godliness, but denying its power. Avoid such people.* For among them are those who creep into households and capture weak women, burdened with sins and led astray by various passions, always learning and never able to arrive at a knowledge of the truth. (italics added)

These false believers will become apparent in the last days.[232] They will have fatal character flaws, just like Jannes and Jambres who opposed Moses (Exod. 7:10–12). It is important to note that these ones will have an appearance of godliness. They will be within the visible body of believers. They will have a type of godliness that is not genuine, but it will fool many, especially gullible and vulnerable people who will be influenced by them.[233] Paul's advice was clear and consistent with his advice to the other churches: *avoid them*!

Titus 1:10-11, 13-14, 16

> For there are many who are insubordinate, empty talkers and deceivers, especially those of the circumcision party. *They must be silenced*, since they are upsetting whole families by teaching for shameful gain what they ought not to teach. . . . Therefore rebuke them sharply, that they may be sound in the faith, not devoting themselves to Jewish myths and the commands of people who turn away from the truth. . . . *They*

---

232. These are clearly *false believers.* They do not have genuine godliness, nor the power from which it derives (the Holy Spirit). They are unable to arrive at the knowledge of the truth. They are "corrupted in their minds" and "disqualified concerning the faith." These are tares among the wheat (Matt. 13:24–30, 36–43).

233. Some of these individuals are predatory. They will take advantage of the weak, infirmed, ignorant, and vulnerable ones in the congregation.

> *profess to know God, but they deny him by their works.* They are detestable, disobedient, unfit for any good work. (italics added)

Paul gave quite specific instructions regarding the treatment of professing believers in the church at Crete. Paul commanded Titus to "*rebuke them sharply.*" He called into question their profession of faith, pointing at the lack of good works as evidence. He didn't simply grant them a charitable judgment. Titus was not just to "get along" with them, but rather, to "silence" them. Their influence in the body was to be stopped, and it was Titus's job as the leader appointed by Paul to see this was done. There was no room in this situation for pastoral passivity or covering over offenses. This required swift and specific action. This approach does not fit with the current cultural context of universal forgiveness and charity so prevalent in the evangelical church today.

Titus 3:9-11

> But avoid foolish controversies, genealogies, dissensions, and quarrels about the law, for they are unprofitable and worthless. As for a person who stirs up division, after warning him once and then twice, *have nothing more to do with him*, knowing that such a person is warped and sinful; he is self-condemned. (italics added)

Later in the letter to Titus, Paul urged Titus to "*reject*" divisive men after a first and second warning, knowing that further interaction with such is futile.[234] The verb used by Paul (*paraitou*) can be translated as "refuse" or "avoid," including the idea of legitimately ceasing relationship with someone. Calvin understood this avoidance as "cutting off the handle for fighting which they are eager to find."[235] Whatever this means, it does not fit with the idea that we ought never to separate from or avoid another individual in the church.

---

234. The English Standard Version translates this verb as "have nothing to do with." It is translated in several older translations as "reject."

235. John Calvin, *Commentary on the Epistle to Titus,* of Calvin's Commentaries, trans. William Pringle (Grand Rapids, MI: Baker, 1996), 21:341.

Notice the reference to this person's character or lack thereof. They were warped and sinful, entrenched in a lifestyle of sin that had altered their character. This is the problem of foolishness. People whose lives are marked by the presence of ongoing controversies, dissensions, and quarrels (i.e., conflict for which they are catalysts) are to be rejected after two warnings. The speed with which Titus was urged by Paul to move on these cases is also interesting. Such people are not to be incessantly warned. After the first and second warning, they are to be considered divisive people. Divisiveness is like cancer in a body. Leadership must act quickly to limit the leavening effect within "the whole lump" (1 Cor. 5:6). Titus, as for himself, needed to avoid these kinds of strivings, but he also needed to make sure that the body was kept free from these corrupting influences.

Other Evidence

Paul warned Timothy on two occasions about Alexander, the coppersmith in Ephesus, likely a professing believer (1 Tim.1:20), telling Timothy that Alexander had "*done him much harm*" (2 Tim. 4:14; italics added). Today's church would have gotten after Paul for his lack of forgiveness toward Alexander. Paul had the nerve to write that his desire was "the Lord would repay Alexander according to his deeds." We don't know what to do with such a statement today. Many would say Paul was sinning when he stated that. Was it wrong for Paul to desire that Alexander be justly judged?

Think about Jesus. He told us in the Sermon on the Mount to "*love our enemies*" (Matt. 5:44). The obvious point in his statement is we are able to identify our enemies as enemies, yet to love them with enemy love. If we have no "enemies" because we live at peace with all men, the Lord's words have no application in our lives.[236]

These passages and others contradict the notion that Christian duty involves universal forgiveness and an overlooking and forbearance of all

236. The common proverb is true. A friend to all is a friend to none. True friendship involves loyalty. It is therefore impossible to, in the truest sense, be everyone's friend.

offenses. Instead they seem to validate the idea that there are legitimate reasons for the good of both parties not to carry on business as usual. The biblical answer to the question, "Are we required to universally maintain normal relationships with everyone, regardless of prior history?" seems to be a resounding "no."

The Cost of Persisting in Our Delusion

These passages shatter the illusions of the romantic Christian who longs for "peace on earth and good will to all men" (Luke 2:14) in their day.[237] The only answer to getting along in this life with others is found in the gospel of Jesus Christ. Through the gospel, we learn the good news of God's love for sinners who see their need for a Savior. People who recognize their need for new life in Christ are, by the exercise of faith and repentance, brought into a new relationship with Him. It is this sentimental gospel that lies at the root of our inability to understand and work through conflict biblically. We have deluded ourselves into thinking we can all "just get along," sin is not a real problem, and grace and forgiveness are cheap. If we persist in our delusion, there is a high cost in the body of Christ for this wishful thinking.

The Reality of Sin and Ongoing Consequences

Notice in each of the previous passages, the individual from whom the Christian is to withdraw is continuing in a pattern of sin. If the sin is owned, confessed, repented of, and appropriate restitution made, the offense can be worked through to some level. Reconciliation can come. This is the end sought for the ultimate good of both the offender and the aggrieved party. If not forsaken, sin remains and causes the breach in relationship.

Sin is not a popular term in our culture. It is highly likely that the current advocacy of universal forgiveness and tolerance is rooted in a down-

237. These passages only shatter our paradigm if we allow them to speak. Through the use of suppression and denial, we can so easily discount and ignore such passages, which don't fit our preferred understanding of the way things ought to be.

grading of the biblical concept of sin. We are sinners by nature and we commit sin, before and after conversion. Notice in the examples above, it is most often professing Christians who have committed sin (actual offenses), creating the need for separation from them. *Actual sin has actual consequences, even for the believer* (Gal. 6:7).

The reason we do not yet have the ability to live at peace with all people in an absolute sense is that sin has not yet been eradicated from the people of God or others in society. In the consummation of all things, perfect unity and harmony are realized because righteousness reigns in the kingdom. There is nothing there that "defiles or causes an abomination or a lie," a.k.a. "sin" (Rev. 21:27). On that day, all will be made right; God's people will be made perfectly righteous and unable to offend one another any longer. Many in the church, in accordance with this ideal however, seek to bring this reality of perfect love and harmony to pass today. This romantic attempt to bring the *not yet* into the *here and now* is not without consequences.

Lack of Personal Accountability—Not Loving the Offender

Because the offense that might otherwise result in interpersonal relationship damage is glossed over in the name of love, the person who commits serious offenses is robbed of the blessing of accountability and potential for growth and recovery. The erring brother or sister is enabled in his or her sin. We, at some level, become culpable for enabling them. Paul rebuked the Corinthians for not doing something, for being unaffected by the sin among them, for not mourning over it (1 Cor. 5:2). In the name of love, we assist people to remain in patterns that bring death instead of life.

When we create consequence-free living, we rob offenders of the accountability that may bring them back to a right and honest relationship with God and those they have sinned against.

We rob them of the chance to be turned back to the Lord. Even as James wrote, "My brothers, if anyone among you wanders from the truth and someone brings him back, let him know that whoever brings back a sinner from his wandering will save his soul from death and will cover a multitude of sins" (James 5:19–20). Notice that the sins are covered after the erring brother or sister is returned from wandering, not before. The cost for our delusion is most acute in the person who stands in need of correction. Love corrects. True love does not rejoice in falsehood and deceit. The person who has sinned, if truly loved, will be given the grace of accountability until such time as they repent and are restored.

Secondary Victimization—Blaming the Victim

Secular literature recognizes a phenomenon called *secondary victimization*, where those who have been previously traumatized are *revictimized* by being blamed for the original trauma and for their inability to transcend their own hurt. The classic example used in this discussion is the proverbial rape victim. Rape is a heinous crime against another human being. It is a violation of everything in the victim that relates to a person's dignity and worth as the image of God. Rape is a violent act of dehumanizing another person.

Nonetheless, we commonly hear ignorant people discussing the ways in which the victim was partially responsible for the act perpetrated against her. She did not dress modestly enough. She should not have been out at that time of night. She should not have been alone. She should not have been drinking. All of these wrongly seek to distribute blame from the perpetrator to the victim. The fact remains. Nothing on the part of the victim in any way makes her responsible in part for the perpetration of such an inhumane act against her.

The church is famous for secondary wounding. We blame abused spouses for their abuse, telling them to be more submissive. We blame abused and mistreated children in the name of "children obey your parents" (Eph. 6:1). We blame pastors for the abuse they suffer at times, telling them that they need to suffer like Jesus suffered. We blame victims of pastoral misuse of authority under the guise of their need to honor those in authority. The list goes on.

Though the psalms give expression, over and over, to the pain brought about by the sins committed against us by others, especially those of the household of faith, many who subscribe to this simplistic theology place this additional burden on those who have already been wounded.[238] Someone once said, "The church is the only army that shoots its own wounded." The pain expressed throughout the psalter is exacerbated by the lack of a just response among the people of faith. For some reason, believers often have a difficult time showing compassion to victims of mistreatment and abuse. We don't very well or very readily "weep with those who weep" (Rom. 12:15). It is far easier for us to distance ourselves from the plight of others, telling ourselves that *they* somehow deserved what happened to *them*.[239] Is this our way of defending ourselves from the uncertainty and unpredictability of the world, by telling ourselves such things could never happen to *us*? Whatever the twisted reasoning is in our heads, the way in which we blame victims (something that is always based on flawed thinking), which flows from this sentimental theology, is reprehensible.

Misrepresenting the Character of God

This is the third leg of the stool. When we persist in our delusion, we not only hurt the offender and the offended, but we also misrepresent the nature of God Himself. "God is love" (1 John 4:8). In the current evangelical culture, one would think that this is His only attribute. Though few

238. In the midst of a painful abusive situation in which I experienced deep hurt, I had someone seeking to help in an authoritative position claim that, "All hurt is sin." This is certainly an example of bad theology run amok. Hurt is the natural response we feel when we are sinned against by someone who matters to us. The Holy Spirit who loves us feels grief when we sin. If He grieves when we sin, why would we not experience feelings of hurt in response to the sins of others against us?

239. This is frequently referred to in philosophical and psychological literature as "just-world theory."

follow out their presuppositions to their logical conclusions, a God who is only all loving is not a God who would ever send anyone to hell (Does this sound like tolerance again?). The fact of the matter is God is love, God is just, God is holy, God is omnipotent, and so forth. If we are being changed into the image of Christ (Rom. 8:29) who is the "image of the invisible God" (Col. 1:15), we ought not be surprised to see in our lives an ever-increasing expression of all of God's communicable attributes, which include both the presence of love and a desire for justice in the world.

When we live lives free from all discernment and only express love and acceptance toward others, we invite an interesting comparison with God. If we are to conduct ourselves in this way, is this because our Father in heaven is like this? As we have seen, the character of God is often altered to fit our understanding of what a loving God should be. However, if we allow God to be whom He says He is in Scripture, we will see a God who is a holy and just Judge. Will we then somehow exalt in the knowledge that we have been more loving than God? We have tolerated what He cannot tolerate. We have blessed what He cannot bless. We have blessed things He is compelled to curse. We can readily see the damage done to the biblical revelation of God's holy character as a direct result of our refusal to submit to the entirety of the Scripture.

Enough is Enough

As we have seen, there is ample biblical evidence for the right and even the duty to separate from the foolish people in our lives. We separate not because we hate them, but because we love them too much to allow them to continue as they are. By definition, fools will refuse our best efforts at confrontation and correction. We are still responsible before God, to wisely and lovingly seek to restore those caught in sin (Gal. 6:1). We won't know people have become entrapped in foolishness until we confront their behavior. We enter tentatively into situations where loving rebuke is indicated, hoping for the best, granting charitable judgments, praying for repentance and softening of hearts. However, what we sometimes realize in the process of doing all we can—to live at peace with all men as much as it depends upon us and is in our power—is even our best efforts cannot bring the restoration of the shalom we hope for.

We can't always get along. Sometimes, withdrawals and avoidance are necessary, and healthy solutions to conflict cannot be applied due to unrepentant hearts. Not only are these responses allowed in Scripture, but in their appropriate context, they are commanded. If at the end of all our efforts at lovingly confronting a fool, we still find no change, no movement toward the path of wisdom, our final gift to them is the grace of excommunication, suspending the relationship. Dan Allender and Tremper Longman wisely stated that "at some point, it is not loving to continue an evil relationship with a person who consistently and perniciously sins against you without some sign of repentance and change."[240] This breaks our hearts. It is so difficult to give someone we love and care deeply for over to God, asking that He would work in their lives with and even through our disassociation with them. This, however, is a part of the path of wisdom laid out for us in Scripture.

Rodney King's appeal is admirable but naive. The interracial tensions that initially broke out in downtown Los Angeles began to quickly spread to neighborhoods throughout southern California. Those were tense days. So much historical harm done to African–Americans has never been owned by much of white America. When unresolved conflicts sit just under the surface, it takes little to stir the flames anew. Rodney's request that we all get along is a noble one. However, *just getting along at all costs is not the best means of healthy relationships.* The Bible soberly sees this getting along as the ultimate end of the return of Christ. When He returns, all things will be put to right. Until then, we will not be able to eradicate the presence of broken relationships. May God help us to faithfully serve Him as stewards of conflict situations until that Day.

---

240. Allender and Longman, *Bold Love*, 252.

Is That in the Bible?

Dave puzzled as the pastor explained the Bible's recommendations in dealing with people who refuse to own their sin. The passages used by the conciliation team were ones Dave was just not familiar with, and frankly, they didn't seem to fit with most of what he had been taught all of his life. This was the reasoning behind meeting with the pastor for clarification. He was comforted that the Bible seemed to validate his sense of not being able to resolve things. He took note of the language used in the Bible that included the possibility of moving away from relationships with destructive people. He still had a hard time thinking of Christian people not being able to get along.

The pastor reviewed the passages Dave had received from the conciliators and had to confess that these were not passages he referred to often nor were ones he had preached from. As the two of them looked over the verses, they seemed a bit surprised the biblical principles were as clear as they now seemed to be. The pastor wondered why he had never covered this topic in seminary.

13

Dealing with Fools

Wouldn't it be great if we could all just sit down with each other, be honest, talk it all through, own our offenses, find real forgiveness, and experience the blessing of complete reconciliation in our interpersonal relationships? The Bible seems to me to clearly lay out the path toward these very things. And yet, in some of the most significant relationships in my life, I have not yet experienced this end. Though I have, for my part, tried to embody the values I have described as constituting the path of wisdom, in some key relationships, the longed-for results have not come. I have been forced to face the sobering reality that I can only control and be responsible for my own behavior.

The church doesn't know what to do with people like me. It has no patience for those of us who have reached the end of our efforts at reconciliation to find the other party is unwilling to reciprocate our efforts. It shames us for our failure to resolve the unresolvable. A comment between services reminds us of our unrelenting "guilt," "What are you doing about the situation?" Or, the always popular, "Just go fix the situation." What those unsolicited advice-givers don't realize is that you've done all you can do and will continue to do. You would like nothing more than a resolution to the situation. You are, however, unwilling to bring peace at all costs. You're not willing to be part of an unhealthy cover up in the name of grace.

When I've sought to resolve key conflicts in my life, I have frequently been shocked and surprised by the way those I've sought to talk things through with have behaved. I'm keenly aware that I have, in the past, been guilty of believing the fallacy that if I treated others with respect and honesty, it would be reciprocated. This has not proven to be the case. I am less shocked than I used to be when I observe the concrete ways in which those who are choosing to remain foolish behave. Choices have consequences. Choosing to remain on the path of foolishness has real-life implications for our interpersonal relationships.

The path of wisdom involves truthful ownership of sins committed against one another. Where this honesty is present as evidence of a vital relationship with God through the active indwelling of the Holy Spirit, we have hope for reconciliation of relationships that have suffered even the most serious offenses. This, however, is not always present. In many cases, we can't just ignore the problems and simply get along. The Bible gives us clear directions regarding the need to break off normal relations with those who persist in patterns of destruction and foolishness. *We do not have to continue to suffer harm.*[241] In such situations, the Lord provides us a *way of release.*

We Can't Get Along with Fools

There are two biblical paths from which to choose: the path of wisdom leads to life and healthy relationships; the path of foolishness leads to death of all sorts, most notably relational death. Foolishness kills relationships. Wise people know by experience the beauty of repentance and confession of their sins as the only way out of broken relationships. Fools don't understand.

Frequently, the believer will be involved with someone who appears to be a fool, whose behavior is characteristically foolish. Though the be-

241. Continuing to suffer harm can often be seen as the Christian's duty in such situations. The Scripture does call us to suffer with Christ is some ways. However, in many of these ongoing conflicts with foolish individuals, our suffering becomes an unhealthy *martyr complex.*

liever initially grants charitable judgments, it becomes apparent over time that some individuals insist on the way of foolishness. These individuals, knowingly or unknowingly, are often used by the enemy to bring discouragement and despair into the lives of the faithful. This is a pattern as old as the Psalms. Repeatedly, the writers of the Psalms revealed their struggle with enemies was a struggle with fools.

Those who recognize they are in conflict with a fool need to realize the way this critical observation will change their approach to conflict. Fools are not always easy to spot, and it is inconsistent with the biblical call to love and patience to hastily label people with whom we conflict as "fools." However, there comes a time, when with reasonable certainty and the wise counsel of others to confirm our suspicions, we need to conclude that our opponent appears to be a fool. With people seeking to be on the path of wisdom, there is hope of correction, of repentance, of confession, of change. With fools, by virtue of the nature of foolishness, these things are not found.

We cannot engage with fools in the same way as with other people. Fools do not fight fair. The following aspects of foolishness make the process fail before it begins. Fools do not:

- *Ever own their sins.* They deny, deny, deny.
- *Speak the truth.* Fools do not fear the consequences of lying. Therefore, they are more than willing and able to simply fabricate untruths and to obscure the truth.
- *Keep confidences.* Fools will take things shared in confidence and tell them to others in an effort to secure their base. This normally happens in conjunction with not speaking the truth so that not only gossip but also slander is common.
- *Receive correction.* Nothing is ever their fault. They are defensive from the start and are masters at the unhealthy skill of projecting onto others.
- *Are angry and disrespectful of others.* This will often come out in attempts to seek conciliation with fools. They use angry outbursts, insults, threats, and other forms of intimidation.

- *Don't hear others and don't care about them (lack empathy).* Active listening is usually a key part of the process. Empathy is a key to rebuilding the relational bridge. These two things will often be sadly lacking when dealing with fools.
- *Don't submit to God or other authorities.* Fools, as we have seen, are autonomous. They don't fear God and won't submit to Him or anyone else in authority. Therefore, most third-party mediators have no authority to use to solve the conflicts at hand.
- *Don't have or yield to the Holy Spirit.* For Christians, the ultimate Confronter is the Holy Spirit inside of us. He convicts of us sin, moves us by His kindness to repentance, and allows us to experience and give grace to others. Fools either do not have the Holy Spirit or have so quenched and grieved Him in their lives, they no longer hear His voice.[242]

The Psalms: A Paradigm for Conflict

The psalms provide a paradigm for viewing conflict in the lives of God's people. The pattern is informative to us today. Throughout Israel's history, the righteous lament the presence of enemies. God's people find themselves in distress due to the attacks of others. Those who make God's people so miserable are most often called fools. Though these individuals are often religious and a part of the community of faith, they are nonetheless fools. It is in their opposition to the righteous where they show their true colors. They make the lives of those they target a living hell. Listen to the effect of fools through the laments of the Psalmists:

> I am a worm and not a man. Scorned by mankind and despised by the people. *All who see me mock me*; *they make mouths at me*; *they wag their heads*. . . . I am poured out like water, and all my bones are out of joint; my heart is like wax; it is melted within my breast; my strength is dried

242. Jan Silvious answers the question, "Can a fool be saved?" in her book *Foolproofing Your Life*. She looked to no avail for evidence of the fool being a "backslidden believer," but concludes, "I am convinced by my study of the Word, however, that even if this person is the biggest churchgoer in town, if he repeatedly displays the classic foolish thinking and behavior patterns described in this book, then the person can't be a believer who is 'born again,'" 206.

> up like a potsherd, and my tongue sticks to my jaws, You lay me in the dust of death. (Ps. 22:6–7, 14–15; italics added)

> I am in distress; my eye is wasted from grief; my soul and my body also. For my life is spent with sorrow, and my years with sighing. (Ps. 31:9–10)

> I am restless in my complaint and I moan. Because of *the noise of the enemy*, because of *the oppression of the wicked* . . . My heart is in anguish within me; the terrors of death have fallen upon me. Fear and trembling come upon me, and horror overwhelms me. And I say, "Oh, that I had wings like a dove! I would fly away and be at rest; yes, I would wander far away; I would lodge in the wilderness; I would hurry to find a shelter from the raging wind and tempest." (Ps. 55:2–8; italics added)

Fools affect us. The anguish expressed above is representative of much pain throughout the centuries among God's people in conflict with the wicked.

The Effect of Fools: Fretting

Psalm 37 is representative of this pattern. It begins with the simple admonition, "Don't fret!" We are told by the Psalmist not to "*fret* because of evildoers (fools)" (Ps. 37:1; italics added). This word in Hebrew for fret is instructive. *Charah* means "to glow warm" or "the burning or kindling of anger."[243] Other scholars describe *charah* as "a mixture of anxiety, resentment, and irritation."[244] Fear and anger share some territory in our brains. They are both distress signals, telling us something is wrong that needs our attention. They signal that a boundary important to us and to our safety has been crossed. Often, anger protects us from the more vulnerable emotion of fear. Fretting is a combination of these traits.

Many of us woke up the morning of 9/11/2001 to see the horror of a jumbo jet being flown directly into the World Trade Center. In a mo-

243. W. E. Vine, Merrill Unger, and William White, *Vine's Expository Dictionary of Biblical Words: A Complete Expository Dictionary of the Old and New Testaments in One Volume* (Nashville: Thomas Nelson, 1985), 5.

244. John W. Baigent and Leslie C. Allen, "The Psalms," *The International Bible Commentary with the New International Version*, ed. F. F. Bruce (Grand Rapids, MI: Zondervan, 1986), 581.

ment, as we began to be aware that individuals were willfully perpetrating this evil against innocent civilians, our world changed. As we watched the news coverage, the level of anxiety grew. We watched as a second plane hit the second tower. Then we saw the president excuse himself from an elementary school presentation and move to an undisclosed location. We saw another plane hit the Pentagon. We heard about flight 93 crashing into a field in Pennsylvania. The towers in New York City collapsed. The world as we knew it, our assumptive world, was gone in that moment. Our safety we had always taken for granted was no more. As we watched in horror, we began to fret. We began to fret because of evildoers. We weren't safe and we knew it. We felt a mixture of outrage at the injustice of these evil acts and anxiety for our national security. Anger and fear all mixed together—this is what we feel when we fret!

Many Christians aren't particularly comfortable with either emotion of fear or anger. We have been warned so many times about the sins of fear and anger to the point we naturally suppress both. However, neither fear nor anger is automatically or necessarily an issue of sin. The Bible is very clear that anger is not simply sin. Paul warned the Ephesians not to sin in their anger (Eph. 4:26).[245] Clearly, then, anger is not inherently sinful.

> The capacity for anger is one of God's gifts. We often misuse and pervert it, of course, but anger is a gift nonetheless. Our misuse does not change the fact that its purpose is positive: to serve as an alarm signal that warns us when our self is endangered and to prepare us for defending our selfhood, which is precious to the Creator.[246]

Look at the example of Jesus' anger against the money changers who had turned the house of prayer for the nations into a den of thieves (John 2:13–22). Jesus was clearly angry, advocating for the nations and their access to the Father's house, yet without sin. Lester commented,

---

245. Ephesians 4:26 shows us Paul distinguished anger and sinfulness. He made it clear that anger itself is not inherently sinful when he stated that "in our anger" we can avoid "sinning."

246. Andrew D. Lester, *The Angry Christian: A Theology of Care and Counseling* (Louisville, KY: Westminster John Knox Press, 2003), 175.

> To model Christian living after the example of Jesus demands that we be advocates willing to courageously confront those who would overlook any person and deny them their rightful place in the human community. To be an advocate is to become indignant, even angry, on their behalf; to fight for their rights; and to be in defense of, and to campaign for, their well-being. . . . *If we are to love as Jesus loved, then we must be angry as Jesus was angry—when the values of the gospel are violated.*[247]

What about anxiety? For some believers, to admit anxiety is tantamount to an admission of unbelief. Notice that although the Bible and the Lord Jesus Himself repeatedly tell us not to fear, it is rarely in a context of rebuke.[248] Rather, He tells us with great compassion our worrying is pointless. Instead, He says we need to know how deeply loved and cared for we are by the Father (Matt. 6:25–34). He does not shame us in our fear but calms our fears through gentle reassurance and reminders that we have a good Father in heaven who has not forgotten any of His children. If we see fear and anger as inherently sinful, we will be hindered from the practice of the psalmists, the "lost language of lament."[249] It is these laments that characterize the response of the righteous to opposition from fools.

Four Responses to Fretting

When we encounter opposition that creates inward pain, we have limited options available to resolve the pain coming from our circumstances. The first three options will likely result in becoming stuck in a situation. They will not bring us to a place of healing.

Despair is a common response to ongoing opposition and prolonged conflict. We can easily lose sight of God who seems remarkably absent in the midst of the situation. Just like Job, in the midst of the trial, we can be led to the brink of despair and disillusionment. As we will see,

---

247. Lester, *The Angry Christian*, 168.

248. It has been reported the Bible tells us 365 times not to fear. That means for each day of the year we have an encouragement not to fear. Fear, in other words, is a daily reality. God does not merely rebuke us for our fear but as a loving Father comforts us when we are afraid.

249. See Card, *A Sacred Sorrow: Reaching Out to God in the Lost Language of Lament*.

> "Lament and despair are polar opposites. Lament is the deepest, most costly demonstration of belief in God. Despair is the ultimate manifestation of the total denial that he exists."[250]

Denial is suppressing our true feelings and what we know to be true. Denial is the enemy of healthy relationships. If healthy relationships are built on trust, denial is the removal of the ground for future trust. Things not owned cannot be dealt with. Unconfessed sins remain unforgiven. The path of wholeness and healing is a path of honesty, not covering up.

If we do not deny the reality of those things done to us nor allow those things to drive us to despair we can still face a third unhealthy option. Seeing the injustice for what it is and seeing God for whom He is, we are still capable of erring by allowing the situation to cause bitterness in our hearts. *Bitterness* holds on to the claim for justice and longs for vengeance, for righting the wrong in the punishment of the perpetrator. It has no room or patience for mercy.

Bitterness is holding tightly to our claim for justice, so tightly that we begin to play God.

Thankfully, there is a fourth option available to us. We do not have to give in to despair, to pretend things are fine, or allow the situation to make us bitter. The healthy option always before us when dealing with fools and the strife they bring is to process the pain, releasing the matter into the care of our Loving Father. This process is called lamentation. *Lamentation* is a healthy reaction to opposition from the wicked.

A Healthy Process of Release

The heart of the biblical process of working through conflicts with our enemies who refuse to be corrected is a process of release. This release is more than just a catharsis but includes a significant validation of our emotional responses to the conflicts that beset us. It reveals afresh a God who cares deeply about those things we have suffered.

250. Michael Card, *A Sacred Sorrow: Reaching Out to God in the Lost Language of Lament* (Colorado Springs: NavPress, 2005), 55.

Lamentation

As one author wrote, "lament is a precondition for healing."[251] This is a controversial statement in the evangelical church today. Many believers have been persuaded that the expression of deep emotions, especially negative emotions, such as fear, anger, or sadness, are inappropriate in the prayer life of the faithful. To have faith, we are told, is not to feel or express fear, anger, or sadness. This claim is entirely inconsistent with the language of Psalms. The 150 psalms reflect a recurring pattern of God's people in history working through their struggles in an attitude of prayer with incredible honesty. Often in the midst of interpersonal struggles, we find ourselves experiencing deep emotions. We can go to God with these emotions. He invites us to come.

Lament is not a sign of rebellion and faithlessness but rather a pattern of the language of faith revealed to us in Scripture. The psalms of lament are an inspired communication pattern with God.

> Prayers of complaint can still be prayers of faith. They represent the last refusal to let go of the God who may seem to be absent or worse—uncaring. If this is true, then lament expresses one of the most intimate moments of faith—not a denial of it.[252]

Lament is real pain expressed toward God. Notice the language of Psalm 6:2–7:

> Be gracious to me, O LORD, for I am languishing;
> Heal me, O LORD, for my bones are troubled.
> My soul also is greatly troubled.
> But you, O LORD—how long?
>
> Turn, O LORD, deliver my life;
> Save me for the sake of your steadfast love.
> For in death there is no remembrance of you;
> In Sheol who will give you praise?

---

251. Zehr, in Lampman and Shattuck, *God and the Victim*, 153.

252. Card, *Sacred Sorrow*, 30.

I am weary with my moaning;
Every night I flood my bed with tears;
I drench my couch with my weeping.
My eye wastes away because of grief;
It grows weak because of all my foes.

Pleading

As the psalmist lamented before God, he allowed himself to feel what he felt. Part of what we often feel in the midst of mistreatment and injustice is a desire for vindication or deliverance. Sometimes, we are falsely charged in the midst of a conflict. We long to have our names cleared from these false accusations. We cry out to God for His intervention. Notice this second aspect of the pattern as evident in Psalm 25:19–22:

Consider how many are my foes,
And with what violent hatred they hate me.
Oh, guard my soul, and deliver me!
Let me not be put to shame, for I take refuge in you.
May integrity and uprightness preserve me,
For I wait for you.

Redeem Israel, O God,
Out of all his troubles.

The believer pleaded with God, expressing a real desire for justice.[253] This desire for wrongs to be made right is consistent with the faithful's understanding of God's nature. God is ultimately the Judge of all the earth before whom all are accountable.

---

253. Some of the psalms move even deeper into this desire for vindication. The imprecatory psalms portray a desire for God's destruction of the wicked, calling down curses upon them. The imprecatory psalms are as follows: 5, 6, 11, 12, 35, 37, 40, 52, 54, 56, 58, 69, 79, 83, 137, 139, 143. New Testament examples of imprecations are: Matt. 23:13; 26:23–24; 1 Cor. 16:22; Gal. 1:8–9; 5:12; 2 Tim. 4:14; Rev. 6:10 indicating this sentiment is not necessarily limited to the old covenant.

Praise

Then the unexpected appears. A miraculous change occurs following the honest expression of lament and our desire for God's vindication. By focusing our desire on God in our prayers, our prayers naturally incline toward praise.

Praise ironically often follows the honest expression of pain.

Perhaps, our dishonesty about our pain has inhibited our ability to praise. Notice the shift in Psalm 31:14–21a from honest expression of pain to faith in God and praise for His faithfulness:

> But I trust in you, O LORD;
> I say, "You are my God."
> My times are in your hand;
> Rescue me from the hand of my enemies and from my persecutors!
> Make your face shine on your servant;
> Save me in your steadfast love!
>
> O LORD, let me not be put to shame,
> For I call upon you;
> Let the wicked be put to shame;
> Let them go silently to Sheol.
> Let the lying lips be mute,
> Which speak insolently against the righteous
> In pride and contempt.
>
> Oh, how abundant is your goodness,
> Which you have stored up for those who fear you
> And worked for those who take refuge in you,
> In the sight of the children of mankind!
> In the cover of your presence you hide them
> From the plots of men;
> You store them in your shelter
> From the strife of tongues.

Blessed be the LORD,
For he has wondrously shown his steadfast love to me.

New Revelation of God

A new revelation of God is what we need to counter lies and deception. One of the greatest effects the wicked have upon us is the alteration of our vision of whom God is. By listening to repeated false claims about God and His connection to our circumstances, we have begun to question His care for us and for our plight. As we begin to praise Him, we open ourselves to the possibility of a fresh revelation of Him. We begin to see Him as He is, the God who cares about our situation:

> But *You do see,* for *You note* mischief and vexation, that You may take it into Your hands; to You the helpless commits himself; You have been the Helper of the fatherless. . . . O LORD, *You hear* the desire of the afflicted; You will strengthen their heart; You will incline Your ear to do justice to the fatherless and the oppressed, so that man who is of the earth may strike terror no more. (Ps. 10:14, 17–18; italics added)

Not only does He care, God promises to make everything right. Notice this pattern as part of a refreshed picture of His character:

But the Lord just laughs,
For he sees their day of judgment coming.
The wicked draw their swords
And string their bows
To kill the poor and the oppressed,
To slaughter those who do right. . . .
For the LORD loves justice,
And he will never abandon the godly.
He will keep them safe forever,
But the children of the wicked will die. (Ps. 37:13–14, 28)

End the evil of those who are wicked,
And defend the righteous.
For you look deep within the mind and heart,

O righteous God.
God is my shield,
Saving those whose hearts are true and right.
God is an honest judge.
He is angry with the wicked every day. (Ps. 7:9–11)

We begin to see Him again as the God who cares, the God whose love for us is a protective love. This fresh reminder of God's true nature is what we need to be able to release the matter of our enemy and our cause to Him. God cares and He is just. We can trust Him to do what is right on our behalf and on behalf of those who oppose us, our enemies. It is only in light of this new revelation we can finish the work of release.

Ultimately, God is a God who will defend the oppressed. The believer comforts himself or herself in the righteousness of God. Notice the shift in Asaph's attitude as he remembered the holiness of God. In Psalm 73, he lamented the prosperity (shalom) of the wicked. He was tempted to consider his lifetime of piety as for naught. He was in great inward despair until He went into the sanctuary and there saw a fresh revelation of God.

Then I discerned their end.
Truly you set them in slippery places;
You make them fall to ruin.
How they are destroyed in a moment,
Swept away utterly by terrors.
For behold, those who are far from you shall perish. (Ps. 73:17b
–19, 27a)

Oppressed ones find comfort in the future justice of God. Their vision of God rightly and necessarily includes His protectiveness of them. A nineteenth-century Anglican poet beautifully described this sentiment:

O Lord, strengthen and support, I entreat Thee, all persons unjustly accused or underrated. Comfort them by the ever-present thought that Thou knowest the whole truth, and wilt in Thine own good time make

> their righteousness as clear as the light. Give them grace to pray for such as do them wrong, and hear and bless them when they pray—Amen.[254]

Release

Knowing afresh whom God is, we can release the matter to Him. We can commit our way to Him, leaving our reputation and vindication in His hands. In the language of Psalm 37, we can:

> Commit everything you do to the LORD.
> Trust him, and he will help you.
> *He will make your innocence radiate like the dawn,*
> *And the justice of your cause will shine like the noonday sun.*
> Be still in the presence of the LORD,
> And wait patiently for him to act. (Ps. 37:5–7a; italics added)

Ultimately, our lives are in His hand. Our innocence is not forgotten by Him. He will eventually, in this life or in eternity, make the justice of our cause evident to all. We can then be still, waiting for Him to act on our behalf because we have this confidence in Him. By this principle, we are freed from the temptation to act for ourselves. God has our back. He is our loving and protective Father:

> This is evidence of the righteous judgment of God, that you may be considered worthy of the kingdom of God, for which you are also suffering—since indeed *God considers it just to repay with affliction those who afflict you,* and to grant relief to you who are afflicted as well as to us, when the Lord Jesus is revealed from heaven with his mighty angels in flaming fire, inflicting vengeance on those who do not know God and on those who do not obey the gospel of our Lord Jesus. They will suffer the punishment of eternal destruction, away from the presence of the Lord and from the glory of his might, when he comes on that day to be glorified in his saints, and to be marveled at among all who have believed, because our testimony to you was believed. (2 Thess. 1:5–10; italics added)

---

254. Christina Rosetti in Edward Pell, comp., *Prayers We Love to Pray: Including the World's Greatest Prayers Suitable for Private Devotion* (Richmond, VA: Robert Harding Co., 1909), 48.

Putting all five elements together, we can begin to see the biblical cycle of release. This is a way we can process through unowned offenses committed against us that would otherwise cause us to become stuck in despair, bitterness, or denial.

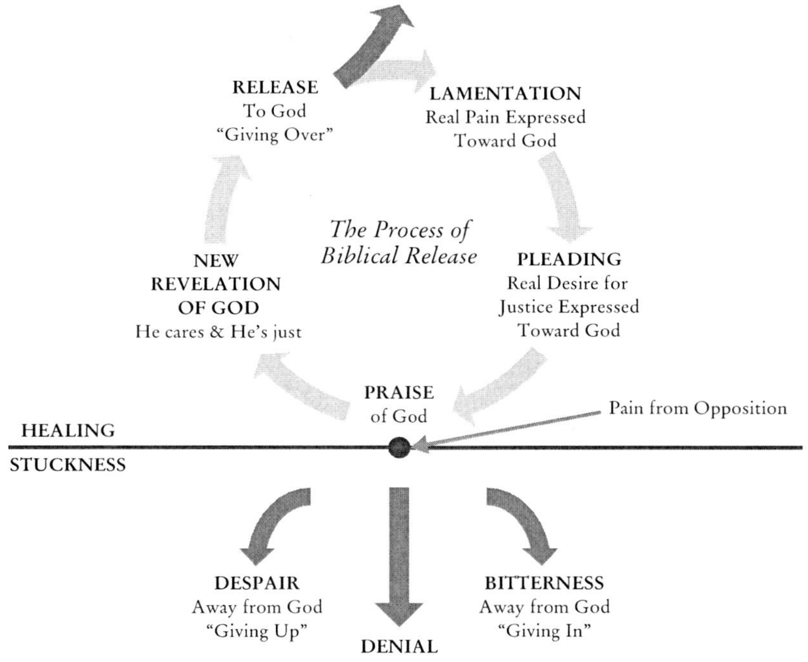

Figure 6. The Process of Biblical Release

Know Your Limits

One of the most helpful verses in the Bible in dealing with fools is found in Romans 12:18. Those two small phrases, "if it is possible" and "as much as it depends upon you" qualify the command to live at peace with "all" men. The Christian ideal is one of peace to the fullest extent possible in this present life under the sun with all these current limitations. Knowing our limits will free us from unhealthy paradigms that promote peace where there is no peace. Thomas à Kempis advised us to pursue wisdom in the following way:

> If anyone, once or twice admonished, doth not comply, contend not with him; but *leave it all to God*, that His will may be done, who knoweth how to turn evil into good, and that He may be honored in all His servants."[255]

This is healthy, God-centered, release of the situation.

We can't all just get along. We will experience opposition, some of which will be unresolvable in this life. We do, however, have a place to go and a means by which we can release the matter. "God is our refuge and strength, a very present help in time of trouble" (Ps. 46:1). By giving the matter into His loving, protective hands, we can move toward healing.

Releasing Bill and Jane

Dave and Carol learned a lot from the entire peacemaking process with the team. The conciliators helped them understand they had exhausted all efforts at trying to help Bill and Jane understand how they had offended them. The passages from the Psalms felt like healing salve pouring over their wounds from the broken relationships. As they learned about the process of lamenting, they were able to express with great honesty the pain they felt to God, who they were learning cared deeply about their feelings. They were able to entrust themselves and the situation to the God who cared so deeply about both them and Bill and Jane. They were able to let go of their desire to play God and to avenge themselves, and instead they put God in His rightful place in their lives and over their situation and reputations.

As Dave and Carol released their cares into the mighty hand of God, they began to feel the burden lifting. The weight seemed to be shifting from them to God. It didn't feel quite so heavy. Their feelings of anger and desire for revenge began to slowly lessen. They knew they were on the path toward healing. They never stopped praying for Bill and Jane, though they never saw them again after the intervention.

---

255. Thomas à Kempis, *The Imitation of Christ* (Grand Rapids, MI: Zondervan, 1983), 28 (italics added).

14

When Conflict Goes Unresolved

"Just let it go. Move on." These well-meaning attempts to help me lay aside the pain connected to the reality of unresolved situations haven't proved to be effective. I feel as if I cannot and should not "let go." One counselor suggested the metaphor of a ski boat with a rope I was clinging to while being dragged all around the lake. He rightly perceived that I was taking on quite a bit of water and was showing signs of emotionally drowning. So he suggested, "Let go of the rope." The opposite of love is not hate, but apathy. I have never been able to be indifferent but continue to hope for a future day of reconciliation. This hope is the essence of my prayers.

Prayer for me, often with tears, has been the most effective means of neither letting go nor holding on so tightly that I'm taken under myself. By giving those I love and long for restored relationships with back to God in prayer, I am not giving up. Prayer for me is "doing something about the situation." I'm pleading with the God of the universe on behalf of those I care deeply about. And yet, by casting my cares onto Him, the weight of the burden for the moment is shifted heavenward. Please don't write off those who desperately need your intercession. God is able to do the impossible.

Many books on the subject of conflict resolution lay out resolution strategies in the hope that the issues dividing us may all be resolved. The sad reality, in this life however, is *many conflicts will not be brought to a sense of conclusion.* As we've seen, the Scripture presents us with specific directions that include disassociation with others who refuse to follow the path of wisdom. It is important we recognize the likelihood of unresolved conflict in our relational networks in this world of tolerance at all costs.

Why Conflicts Don't Resolve

Some conflicts are unresolvable. There are limitations to all attempts at biblical conflict resolution. Consider the account of the Lord Jesus entering the city of Jerusalem on Holy Week. None of his followers, save Mary who had anointed him with precious oil for burial, understood the path to Calvary He was following. As He crested the hill from Bethany coming into Jerusalem, He saw the Temple Mount and began to weep:

> And when he drew near and saw the city, he wept over it, saying, "Would that you, even you, had known on this day the things that make for peace! But now they are hidden from your eyes. For the days will come upon you, when your enemies will set up a barricade around you and surround you and hem you in on every side and tear you down to the ground, you and your children within you. And they will not leave one stone upon another in you, because you did not know the time of your visitation." (Luke 19:41–44)

Jesus saw the impending destruction. He felt deep compassion on the nation that was lost and blind. And yet, He did not do anything further to make peace. He wished they had known the things that would have made for their peace, which would have prevented the coming calamity. Nonetheless, he lamented because their fate was now sure. The Temple that He so revered, the House of Prayer for all the nations, would be leveled in thirty-five years. With prophetic clarity, Jesus saw the future and wept for the nation. Jesus knew the conflict with the Jewish people would not be resolved.

Conflicts do not resolve for a number of reasons. As we've seen, the healthy process (the path of wisdom) that results in reconciliation between conflicting parties involves several aspects. At any and all points in that process, an individual can simply step off of the path of wisdom. This stepping off of the path can be done in ignorance or in willful hardening against the work of the Holy Spirit.

Ignorance of the Process of Reconciliation

There is widespread ignorance in the body of Christ today pertaining to biblical peacemaking and conflict resolution. Though many helpful books have been written and many consultants exist to educate the church in this area, the average churchgoer has not been taught well. Seminaries don't teach about conflict resolution. Young pastors are often shocked in their first assignment when they run head-on into a church that has been mired in conflict for many years. We need more books, more articles, more sermons on this topic to better educate and inform the body of Christ. Many conflicts don't resolve due to this ignorance. This ignorance often is not willful; it just is. Not understanding the way out can leave some conflicts hopelessly unresolved.

Refusal to Act Wisely

At any point along the path, any party can simply refuse to walk wisely. This is a more willful ignorance or pretended ignorance of the process. The default for all of us is foolishness. It comes naturally!

The moment we stop pursuing wisdom in a given situation, we will default to folly.

It is unconscious and automatic to do so. This is what makes the successful resolution of conflict so miraculous. Walking in wisdom is hard work and requires not only self-discipline but also a healthy dose of self-awareness and humility. Many professing believers are simply in short supply of both. Instead of pursuing the path that leads to shalom, they are content to live life "as they see fit." The end of this refusal sadly is often a trail of broken relationships behind them—a wake of sadness, anger, and skepticism.

A Hardening Process

Many people, some of whom are professing believers, seem to simply have become hardened in their refusal to live wisely. The poster boy for this principle is King Saul. Despite repeated attempts by Samuel and the Lord to bring him to a place of real repentance and change, he apparently never did. He was the master of outward showy repentance. In the next breath, however, we observe him right back in the same sinful practices. He just didn't seem to get it.

Pharaoh is another example. Despite the increasing pain and discomfort of the plagues against him and the nation of Egypt, he repeatedly hardened himself against the Lord God of Israel and His servant Moses. He foolishly refused to the end to let God's people go. His foolishness proved very costly for him and for Egypt. An entire generation of firstborn sons was a high price to pay for being a fool. Nonetheless, some people like Saul or Pharaoh simply refuse to be humbled and instead become hardened in their obstinance and defiance of the Lord and His wisdom. Where there is a hardened person, there is no current hope for real reconciliation. *Softening of heart always precedes real change.* For these and other reasons, conflicts don't always resolve.

What Not to Do

When conflicts prolong and go unresolved, it is appropriate to reassess our part, not only in the conflict, but also in all attempts to resolve it. Pressure can grow within us and among those affected by the unresolved conflict to pursue unbiblical ends to the problem. Often, it is just as important to know what not to do, as it is to know what to do. Here are three unbiblical solutions to protracted and prolonged conflict that seems hopelessly unresolved.

Sentimental Forgiveness

We grow weary in well doing. The biblical work of conflict resolution for all involved is hard work. It is understandable we would seek a short cut to resolution. The problem is that most of our shortcuts have another set of problems connected to them. We just trade problems rather than solve them.

Think about the solution of sentimental forgiveness. Sentimental forgiveness is based on the romantic myth of relationships. It is the common concept of evangelical forgiveness that we have been lamenting. We approach life with a "love means never having to say you're sorry" sentimentality.[256] Romantic forgiveness is not true forgiveness. Sentimental forgiveness attempts to cover over serious offenses, to sweep them under the rug, only to hurt the offender and offendee in the long run. This kind of forgiveness is not our solution.

Perpetuating Injustice and Abuse

When we look for less-than-biblical answers to situations the Bible instructs us about, we inherently create a whole other set of problems. This is the case with serious situations of injustice and abuse. When we, due to fatigue, cease holding perpetrators accountable, we inevitably open the door to further abuse and injustice. Abusers abuse. Bullies bully. Ignoring ongoing mistreatment and abuse allows it to continue. There is no neutrality here. To not side with the victims, the downtrodden, the oppressed is by default to side with the oppressors. One thing we cannot do as followers of Christ is to remain a part of the perpetration of injustice and abuse.[257] We cannot in the name of "peace" fail to advocate for the oppressed and misused. There is nothing less Christlike.

---

256. This is "Love Story" theology.

257. Look again at Jesus' job description (Isa. 61:1, 2), which He calls us to partner with Him in fulfilling.

Vigilantism: Taking Matters into Your Own Hands

Regardless of our level of frustration at the way things are, we are not given authority to right all wrongs. The groaning of the creation, in anticipation of the coming re-creation, is echoed in our hearts. We long for the day when children in the womb will be safe. We yearn for the time when small children will never again be victimized at the hands of pedophiles.

In light of this frustration, some have taken justice into their own hands. Professing Christians have blown up abortion clinics and murdered abortionists. Vigilantism fails to see the God who will in the end bring justice and equity to bear in all situations. It is a form of God-playing. We cannot take the matter into our own hands but must rather entrust ourselves and our cause to the sovereign and loving oversight of God.

Guarding Your Heart against Idolatry: What We Can Do

When conflicts go unresolved, our innate desire for justice, vindication, and resolution is blocked. It is natural for us to fall into the unbiblical patterns we have described, to seek shortcuts to shalom, creating false versions of forgiveness that don't heal the real wound. God knows us. He understands the depth of the pain we feel in the midst of the initial offenses committed against us, as well as in the wake of our failed attempts to resolve the problem in a biblical way. He sees us. Our efforts are not in vain in the Lord. Finally, He gives us specific instructions to guard our hearts against additional damage. God calls us to partner with Him on the path of enemy love.

God's Love for His Enemies

God loves His enemies. Were this not the case, He would not ask us to love ours.

God never asks us to do something He Himself is unwilling or unable to do.

However, in the very command of God to love enemies, there is a recognition that we have enemies. Some Christians attempt to live as if they have no enemies. Unfortunately, we all have enemies, our adversary, the devil, being chief among them.

God has myriad enemies. We were once numbered among them. All who are opposed to His rule and reign over them are by definition His enemies. If God has enemies, how can a Christian expect to live life enemy free? If Jesus, the God–man, had enemies, how do we expect to avoid having them? It is the height of arrogance to imply we are somehow able to live life at a higher level than Christ or we are able to do what God is not. We, like God, have enemies. In fact, Jesus told us to expect this. He said, "If they hated me, they'll hate you too" (Matt. 10:22; John 15:18). The question then is how does God treat His enemies?

We remember Jesus' comment about enemy love from the Sermon on the Mount. God loves those who oppose Him, doing them good, sending rain on the unjust as well as the just. God is benevolent toward them, even in their opposition to Him. Likewise, God commands us to love our enemies. In doing this, we demonstrate our true sonship. But does loving our enemy mean unilaterally or universally overlooking their sins? If we love our enemies in this way, how can we also love the victims of our enemies? God loves His enemies, somehow holding in tension His love and His recognition of their accountability before Him. Because He loves all, God is not neutral in battle. God is for the oppressed and the downtrodden, the victims who have suffered at the hands of fools. His ears are uniquely and especially open to their cries. In our love of enemies, we can neglect to love their victims well.

> To identify Hitler or Osama bin Laden or Pol Pot with the "enemy" to be loved, without consideration of these related questions [Is just war theory valid? How do we love not only enemies, but victims?], is to fall into the pacifist error . . . focusing on the enemy and forgetting the victims is a typically sentimental, liberal–humanist error.[258]

258. Carson, *Love in Hard Places*, 114.

God never does this. He never forgets the victim. His ears are always open to their cry.

Our Love for Enemies: An Exposition of Romans 12:12–21

What does enemy love look like? Paul, writing to the church at Rome, discussed enemy love:

> Bless those who persecute you; bless and do not curse them. Rejoice with those who rejoice, weep with those who weep. Live in harmony with one another. Do not be haughty, but associate with the lowly. Never be wise in your own sight. Repay no one evil for evil, but give thought to do what is honorable in the sight of all. If possible, so far as it depends on you, live peaceably with all. Beloved, *never avenge yourselves*, but *leave it to the wrath of God*, for it is written, "Vengeance is mine, I will repay, says the Lord." To the contrary, "if your enemy is hungry, feed him; if he is thirsty, give him something to drink; for by so doing you will heap burning coals on his head." *Do not be overcome by evil, but overcome evil with good.* (italics added)

Overall Context

The epistle to the church at Rome was Paul's response to division between Jewish and Gentile believers in the congregation. Paul reminded them that the same gospel applied to both groups (Rom. 1:16). Paul, in the first eight chapters of the letter, described the way the gospel brings both Jews and Greeks from their unique problem of sin into a relationship together with the one true God by the Spirit and in Christ. He then devoted three chapters (9–11) to discuss the relationship of Israel to the promises of God. Chapter 12 marks the transition in the letter to practical theology. Paul began to discuss Christian living under the metaphor of sacrifice, life lived in response to the mercies of God. The cost is great, however. The believer is called to die to the old self and to find new life in and through Christ. Love (in general) and love for those who oppose us (in particular) are the backdrops of this passage.

Romans 12:12–21 is perhaps the key passage in the New Testament dealing with Christian living in the context of unresolved conflicts with others.[259] This section (verses 12–21) occurs within the overall practical section beginning with the overarching command in 12:2 to be not conformed to this world, but to be transformed by the renewing of our minds. In other words, this section describes otherworldly, supernatural living as opposed to life lived naturally. Christians are to live counterculturally. Nowhere is this more evident than in the area of enemy love.

Christian Love Defined

Paul made several key statements just prior to verse 12 as he described the nature of true Christian love. He said love is to be "without hypocrisy" (v. 9a). In other words, true love, even for an enemy is to be genuine, authentic, and transparent. Paul left no room for pretense and falsehood.

Love is to be honest and true.

In loving others, we are to "abhor what is evil" and to "cling to what it good" (v. 9b). Love, according to Paul, involves *hating evil and holding to that which is the ultimate good for the other.* True love does not enable destructive patterns of sin but seeks rather to see the other restored to health and usefulness. Love, in general, and enemy love, in particular, are unwilling to accept counterfeits. Love has no patience for hypocrisy, hates the evil that underlies the hypocrisy, and seeks the ultimate good of enemies.

Our Response to Persecution

The response commanded by Paul is counterintuitive. Notice what Paul didn't say. He nowhere here implied we should deny the severity of the offenses committed against us. By calling it "evil," he validated the seriousness of the situation. Remember, just a few verses prior, Paul gave the general command to hate what is "evil." The right response toward the

259. This section in Romans, along with the understanding of the path toward release we have observed in the Psalms, most clearly delineates the path for the wise when they are threatened with becoming mired in conflict with foolish enemies.

oppression is hatred. In our response, however, we are to show ourselves to be related to the Family of the Trinity.

Our Family is deeply empathetic to the plight of the oppressed. We are to respond appropriately to both those who weep under the weight of oppression and suffering and to rejoice with those who rejoice, experiencing the blessing of God. Empathy is the direct opposite of envy. Envy inverts our response; it weeps when others rejoice, envying their blessing, and rejoices when others weep, feeling satisfied in the suffering of others.

Limitations on Peacemaking

Peace is not always possible. At some level, bringing things to a successful resolution and peace is beyond our control. If we have stewarded our part in the conflict faithfully, we have done all that is required. We can do what we can in obedience to God's commands and in reliance on the Holy Spirit. We cannot, however, be held responsible for things outside of our control (i.e., the response of others to the Lord and the process).

Paul clearly understood these limitations on our peacemaking task. Thus, the believer is not required to do the impossible. This is not a requirement for peace at all costs. Hendriksen commented, "If the maintenance of peace means the sacrifice of truth and/or honor, then peace must be abandoned."[260] Hodge agreed, "The cause of the conflict must not arise from you. . . . Paul's own example shows that he was far from thinking that either truth or principle was to be sacrificed for the preservation of peace."[261] We are commanded to do what we can. However, we are not responsible for the ultimate outcome.

Don't Avenge Yourselves

We are never to avenge ourselves. We are never to pay back evil for evil to "anyone" (1 Pet. 3:9). Retaliation, or even pronouncing a verdict

260. William Hendriksen, *Exposition of Paul's Epistle to the Romans*, New Testament Commentary (Grand Rapids, MI: Baker, 1981), 421.

261. Charles Hodge, *Commentary on the Epistle to the Romans* (Grand Rapids, MI: Eerdmans Publishing Co, 1886), 400.

of judgment over our enemies, is not ours to do.[262] Taking vengeance to ourselves is tantamount to playing God! We cannot step into the place that belongs only to Him, the Judge of all the earth. Ironically, to do so is to make ourselves guilty of idolatry and God-playing and to provoke His wrath toward our sinfulness. Instead we follow the wisdom of Proverbs, waiting for "God to handle the matter" (Prov. 20:22 NLT).

While we are not responsible to bring about peace in every case, we are responsible to let go of our desire for vengeance.

Leave It to the Wrath of God

Paul wrote, rather than taking things into our own hands, "playing God," we ought to give the matter over to God and to His wrath. We need to leave room for the wrath of God and for His vengeance according to His infinite justice. To the ears of many contemporary evangelicals, this sounds foreign. We hear little of Jesus' mission culminating in "the day of vengeance of our God," or as the NLT translates, "the day of God's anger against their enemies" (Isa. 61:26).[263] We are not comfortable with this biblical language today. Paul grounded his thought in the language of the Old Testament (Lev. 19:18; Deut. 32:35). God's judgment will always be just. Our judgment will often be flawed. Therefore, we are to defer the matter to the heavenly court. This is similar to the Psalmists' attitude (Ps. 37:5–6; 73:17–20). Thomas Schreiner commented:

> Believers will not be able to conquer feelings of revenge unless we know that *ultimately there is justice*, that *God will set all accounts right*. . . . Believers are liberated from taking justice into their own hands and are

---

262. We, as finite, fallen human beings, cannot make the ultimate pronouncement that someone is a "fool." Our conclusions must always be tentative in accordance with our finiteness. God alone knows the state of every human heart.

263. We typically stop reading after verse 2a in Isa. 61. Jesus, at Nazareth, stopped reading at that place because the final aspect of His mission, bringing judgment to all God's enemies, was not part of His first advent but remains for His return (Luke 4:18–20).

> free to do good because they know that *God will right all wrongs in the end*. . . . The sure realization that God will vindicate us frees us to love others and do good to them and even to pray that God will bless them (v. 14) and bring them to repentance.[264]

This is directly after the example of Jesus. Notice how Jesus responded to His enemies. He is our example in suffering. Peter told us in a directly parallel passage:

> For to this you have been called, because Christ also suffered for you, leaving you an example, so that you might follow in his steps. He committed no sin, neither was *deceit* [hypocrisy] found in his mouth. When he was reviled, he did not revile in return; when he suffered, he did not threaten, but *continued entrusting himself to him who judges justly.* (1 Pet. 2:21–23; italics added)

Just like us, "Jesus could refrain from cursing his adversaries because he entrusted himself to God, 'who judges righteously.'"[265] So, we release the matter of justice into the hands of the only just Judge. We trust Him with the responsibility to justly judge our case.

Prayer: Our Chief Weapon

Blessing others, as opposed to cursing them, is the calling of the Christian in response to enemies.[266] In this, we follow the example and instruction of the Lord Jesus Himself. He told us explicitly, "Love your enemies and pray for those who persecute you" (Matt. 5:44). He practiced what He preached. From the cross, He prayed for His executioners, "Father, forgive them, for they don't know what they are doing" (Luke 23:34).

---

264. Thomas R. Schreiner, *Baker Exegetical Commentary on the New Testament, Vol. 6, Romans* (Grand Rapids, MI: Baker Academic, 1998), 673, 675–676.

265. Schreiner, *Baker Exegetical Commentary*, 675.

266. This duty to bless does not negate all we have said previously. Blessing does not mean "don't hold them accountable" or "just get along."

Prayer for our enemies is our chief weapon both against them in their sin and against our own heart's desire for vengeance.

Prayer guards our hearts against drifting into bitterness and revenge. It helps to maintain an openness in our hearts toward our enemies, an openness that stands ready to transact forgiveness with them immediately upon their repentance. Stephen, the first martyr of the Christian church following Jesus, exemplified this same pattern (Acts 7:60). Hodge stated, "It is not enough to avoid imprecating evil upon our enemies; we must sincerely desire and pray for their welfare."[267]

> *O Lord, we know that you are able, by Your sovereign Spirit, to convert and transform us as we yield ourselves to You. You know the pain we have been caused by our enemies. You care about each tear we have shed as a result of their opposition. Yet, Lord, you tell us to pray for them, for their ultimate good. So, just as you prayed from the cross, Lord Jesus, we pray for those who have sinned against us. We ask in Your grace and in Your mercy, You would grant to them the gift of repentance that they might truly turn toward You and find in You salvation for their souls. Do them ultimate good, we pray, as only You are able to do. We do not seek their destruction, but rather their restoration to wholeness. Amen.*

Overcoming Evil with Good

Paul summed this all up under the phrase "overcome evil with good." He illustrated the principle by quoting from the Proverbs, "If your enemy is hungry, feed him, and if he is thirsty, give him a drink; for in so doing you will heap burning coals on his head" (25:21–22). Doing good to our enemies in practical ways (e.g., food and drink) is said to be a way of "heaping hot coals on their heads."

What is the meaning of "heaping hot coals"? Many of the early fathers, including Origen, Augustine, and Pelagius, taught that this was a way of

---

267. Hodge, *Commentary on Romans*, 403.

making our enemy ashamed as a means of bringing them to repentance. However, there is nothing in the passage that suggests "heaping hot coals" will bring an enemy to repentance. Repentance is not even mentioned. Also, to use shame as a means of manipulating people into a change of heart is not in keeping with God's methodology. God isn't passive–aggressive. Coals of fire throughout the Bible are used to symbolize God's judgment (the topic being discussed in the passage).[268] It could be what Paul intended to teach was by responding to the evil with good (nonretaliation), we actually make our enemy guiltier.[269]

We overcome evil with good when we do not allow evil to overcome us, to pull us down into bitterness of spirit. We are allowing evil to overcome us when we find ourselves preoccupied with visions of immanent justice or planning subtle ways to return evil for evil. We overcome evil by recognizing it's not our job to overcome our enemies. They belong to God. Through prayer for them, we give them and our concerns back to the Lord. We overcome evil, making it of little or no effect, by wishing our enemies well, praying for their eventual repentance and restoration to a right relationship with God and others. This passage rightly warns us to give the matter over to God, to seek the welfare of our enemy, and to be reconciled if the other is willing and honest.

Conclusion

The writer of Proverbs wisely instructed, "Keep (guard) your hearts with all vigilance, for from it flow the springs of life" (4:23). When conflicts cannot be resolved, which is often the case this side of the consummation of all things, our chief concern is guarding our hearts. Instead of chronic anxiety, Peter wrote, "cast (*ballo*) all our anxieties on Him, because He cares for us" (1 Pet. 5:7). Paul agreed. He said to move away from anxiety about unresolvable conflicts through the practice of prayer. Paul advised, "in everything, by prayer and supplication with thanksgiving, let

268. Cf. 2 Sam. 22:9, 13; Ps. 18:8, 12

269. Cf. James 5:6.

your requests be made know to God. And the peace of God [shalom?] which surpasses all understanding, will guard our hearts and minds in Christ Jesus" (Phil. 4:6–7). This shalom will guard our hearts and minds. This current experience directly connected to the ultimate shalom, where all things are made right, guards and keeps our hearts. Our hearts and minds are kept and guarded in our relationship, our union, with Christ. Prayer connects us to Him in a way like nothing else can.

Therefore, we pray. We pray for our enemies. We pray without ceasing. We pray in faith. We pray in the Spirit. We pray, "Your kingdom come, Your will be done on earth as it is in heaven" (Matt. 6:10). These prayers of the saints, which have been adding up for centuries, are collected in golden bowls and poured out like incense before the presence of the Lord. There is a day when the cumulative prayers of the saints will once and for all be answered. The Day is coming when all things will be put right. The answer to our cry, "How long?" is taken up by Jesus Himself. He encourages us, "Behold, I am coming quickly, and My reward is with Me, to give to every one according to His work" (Rev. 22:12). The Final Answer to conflict is Jesus Himself!

Learning about Prayer

Dave and Carol have learned so much about prayer these past few years since the incident with Bill and Jane. They used to go to God with rather mundane requests for health, provision, or traveling mercies. They used to pray at mealtimes thanking Him for their daily bread. The situation with Bill and Jane and the things they learned as a result of that pain have transformed their prayer times together as a couple. At first, it seemed weird to think of their former best friends as enemies. But as they prayed for Bill and Jane on an ongoing basis, something seemed to change inside them and between them. They felt their hearts being transformed. They felt a new softness and concern for their former friends and pleaded with God to intervene in their lives to bring health and blessing.

Conclusion:
The End of Conflict, Life under the Son

> I believe . . . in Jesus Christ, His [God the Father's] only begotten Son, our Lord, Who was conceived by the Holy Ghost, born of the Virgin Mary, suffered under Pontius Pilate; was crucified, dead and buried. He descended into hell. The third day, He rose again from the dead. He ascended into heaven, and sits at the right hand of God the Father Almighty. *From thence, He shall come to judge the quick and the dead.*[270]

There is a day coming when this book will be irrelevant and useless! This book has focused on the present reality of conflict among us that is part and parcel of life "under the sun." The blessed hope is inextricably tied to the glorious reappearing of the Son of Man on the clouds of heaven. When He comes, everything will be brought to completion. As the old chorus says, "Oh, what a wonderful day that will be!"[271] Life was always meant to be lived under the mediation of the Son. One day that will be fully realized. Look at John's description in Revelation:

> Then I saw a new heaven and a new earth, for the first heaven and the first earth had passed away, and the sea was no more. And I saw the holy city, New Jerusalem, coming down out of heaven from God, prepared as a bride adorned for her husband. And I heard a loud voice

270. Apostle's Creed, *Trinity Hymnal* (Suwanee, GA: Great Commissions Publications, 1990), 845 (italics added).

271. Dale Williams, "Jesus Is Coming Again."

from the throne saying, "Behold, the dwelling place of God is with man. *He will dwell with them, and they will be his people, and God himself will be with them as their God. He will wipe away every tear from their eyes, and death shall be no more, neither shall there be mourning, nor crying, nor pain anymore, for the former things have passed away. . . .*

And I saw no temple in the city, for *its temple is the Lord God the Almighty and the Lamb. And the city has no need of sun or moon to shine on it, for the glory of God gives it light, and its lamp is the Lamb.* By its light will the nations walk, and the kings of the earth will bring their glory into it, and its gates will never be shut by day—and there will be no night there. They will bring into it the glory and the honor of the nations. But nothing unclean will ever enter it, nor anyone who does what is detestable or false, but only those who are written in the Lamb's book of life. (Rev. 21:1–4, 22–27; italics added)

Notice the vision of the New Jerusalem that John saw. In the re-creation of all things, we will experience unbroken relationship with God, the same kind of relationship Adam and Eve experienced, "naked and without shame." There is no more pain, no more tears, for full and complete healing has come to our brokenness. There we drink freely of the spring of life and enjoy a perfect relationship with the Godhead and one another. The wicked are no more; justice has been exacted. *There is, therefore, no conflict there.* Old categories that divided us are only a distant memory. There is neither Jew nor Gentile but one new man in Christ there. God Himself is our dwelling place. Christ, the God–man, is at the center of the New Jerusalem as its light. He is the Son who illuminates and expels all darkness. Nothing unclean enters there; conflict is a thing of the past. Nothing detestable. Nothing false. Only pure holiness, love and truth, otherwise known as *full shalom*, the way things ought to be.

It is this vision of the future that energizes us in the present. This glorious future, of which we are certain, according to the promise of God, awaits us at the completion of our mission on earth well done.

> The new heaven and the new earth is the final vision, the end toward which the journey of reconciliation leads. On the journey we can catch only glimpses of this end, but the hope of a new heaven and a new earth is what sustains us on the journey.[272]

Shadows of Shalom in the Now

This future hope is certain! This will be the reality. While we wait for what is to come, the people of God are like spies sent ahead of the invading army. We embody otherworldly kingdom values in this present life in the world.

> The world to come has a beachhead in this one. The church is that beachhead. Believers are kingdom people, to use Jesus' kingdom idiom. They constitute an eschatological community living according to the values of the world to come.[273]

Our ultimate hope is in the restoration, the re-creation, of the heavens and the earth following the glorious return of Jesus Christ. He will make all things new. He will create a kingdom in which righteousness and shalom dwell. Evil and conflict will be finally destroyed. For all eternity, we will dwell with Him. This is the deep longing of our hearts. We yearn for things to be restored to the way they ought to be. This will not come to pass fully until the Lord Jesus Himself ushers it in. Until that Day, we occupy!

The Nature of the Kingdom

This New Jerusalem is the final fullness of the kingdom come. We long for the day when "our faith will be sight, when the clouds be rolled back as a scroll."[274] Jesus, in His first advent, taught us to pray in anticipation of that Day, "Your kingdom come." This is the kingdom to which we belong. We are citizens of another world.

---

272. Katongole and Rice, *Reconciling All Things*, 65.

273. Cole, *God, the Peacemaker*, 204.

274. Horatio Spafford, "It is Well with My Soul."

We, who were once far off and strangers to the covenants of Israel, have been brought near by the blood of Christ. We have been adopted into the very family of God. God is now our Father. Jesus is our elder brother and our husband. The Holy Spirit unites us to Christ and secures our place in the Family of God. As part of our new Family, we are to model God's Family values. As children of God, we are reflect His character, even "in the midst of a crooked and twisted generation" (Phil. 2:15). We are to "walk as children of light" taking "no part in the unfruitful works of darkness" but instead we are to "expose them" (Eph. 5:8b, 11). We are to reflect God our Father's character, in all aspects, as we interact with a world filled with conflicts.

We are children of God. Therefore, we are children of holiness, children of justice, children of love, children of shalom (not just inner peace). If God perfectly embodies all of these divine attributes, we are to seek to be made into His likeness by the transforming work of His Spirit in us. Over time, God is making us more and more to resemble Himself. We can begin to think His thoughts, to feel what He feels, to go where He goes, and to do what He does. Like Father, like sons and daughters.

Life in the Trinity

The Eastern fathers took this one step further. Based on the teaching of Scripture, they emphasized the goal of the Christian life as not only imitating God but participating in the life of God. They often referred to this as *theosis* or deification, which explains why we Western Christians avoid the topic altogether. The potential for misunderstanding is great. Though most of the fathers distinguished between a unity of substance and a unity of fellowship, the heretical potential for merging humanity and deity has always lurked in the background.

The unity of substance, the ontological oneness, shared among the members of the Trinity is untransferable and unsharable. However, the unity of fellowship and relationship also shared in the Trinity is the very relational life into which it is Their aim to bring us. This is what both Paul and Peter referred to when they respectively spoke of "being conformed to the image of Christ" (Rom. 8:29) and being "partakers of the divine nature" (2 Pet. 1:3–4).

> The Fathers expressed this scarlet thread using the Greek word *theosis*, a word that is so easy to misunderstand that we today probably should not use it, but nevertheless, a word that, properly understood, conveys to us a profound truth—the fact that *human life is intimately connected to the life of God*. . . . God created us to share in this relationship and gave us a share in the communion of the Trinity at creation. This is the primary thing we lost through the fall.[275]

God makes us holy. He justifies us through the blood of Christ's atoning sacrifice. He not only imputes righteousness to us but also transforms us more and more into the likeness of His own dear Son by His Spirit. He forgives us all our sins. He adopts us as mature children able to inherit the kingdom He has prepared for us. He does all these things, so we can share unbroken and perfect relationship with Him. This is His goal in all things, *to dwell with us apart from the effects of the fall.* He is making all things new, including us, always in relation to our union with Christ. Union, more than unity, is the language of Scripture. God's purposes in our lives are always in Christ. Abiding in Him is the source of our lives. Life is in Him and we draw from Him like branches on a vine. He is our sustenance and our strength.

> Neither the righteousness of justification nor the righteousness of sanctification is ours in the sense that we could possess it on our own. In both cases, righteousness belongs to Christ, the righteous one, and we participate in that righteousness as we are initially united to him (justification), and we reflect and grow in that righteousness as we continue to remain in him. All aspects of the Christian life, from beginning to end, revolve around our union with the Son and our reflection of his relationship to his Father.[276]

275. Fairbairn, *Life in the Trinity*, 232.

276. Fairbairn, *Life in the Trinity*, 207.

Life in the Trinity is what we were designed to live.

A life of glorifying God and of enjoying Him forever is our destiny. It is the chief end of man. Even now, this life, which has begun, is changing the person we are:

> In Christian spiritual transformation, the self that embarks on the journey is not the self that arrives. The self that begins the journey is the self of our own creation, the self we thought ourselves to be. This is the self that dies on the journey. The self that arrives is the self that was loved into existence by Divine Love. This is the person we were destined from eternity to become—the I that is hidden in the "I AM."[277]

We are members of a new Family, the Trinity. We look forward to our ultimate Family reunion to come.

How Shall We Then Live?

Conflict is part of our present existence. It is to be expected. Though we do not like conflict itself, we can learn to look for opportunities within conflict situations to represent the interests and values of the coming kingdom. We can interact with those who conflict with us in a way that reflects our new Family values. In conclusion, here is a suggested set of goals and values for believers to pursue as they wait for the reality to come. In these ways, we will seek to live life in the Trinity (which, for now, includes the presence of conflict):

- **We will continue to pursue personal holiness in our lives.** This is the key to the prevention of conflict among us. In the power of the Holy Spirit, pursuing holiness and resisting temptation to sin, we will strive to live so we do not create ongoing conflicts.[278]
- **When we sin, we will be quick to own our sin and to take appropriate action when we have offended others.** When we sin,

277. Benner, *Being Yourself.* 110.

278. This is the antidote to antinomianism. Renewing our desire to live holy lives before God and one another is the essence of the solution. If all professing believers returned to this biblical standard, conflict as we know it would cease to exist.

instead of covering our tracks and hiding, we will come to the light, confess our sins to God and those we have sinned against. We will sincerely repent of our sinful patterns, seek forgiveness from those we have offended, offer honest apologies, be willing to make those we have hurt whole through restitution, and in every way, seek transformation in our lives at the heart level.

- **We will live at peace with others as much as it is in our power to do so.** We will be peacemakers within the limitations of this life. We will be willing to do all we can do to bring reconciliation to situations involving us. We will do our part and be responsible to manage our side of conflicts as stewards of God.
- **We will recognize our limits and roles as stewards of conflict situations.** We are, at best, stewards of conflict. We cannot resolve all conflicts because the true resolution of conflict involves ownership and repentance of sin on the part of others. We understand the limitations of our responsibility to be informed by the phrases "as much as is possible" and "as much as it depends on you" (Rom. 12:18).
- **When others sin against us in minor ways, we will forbear offenses and overlook them, erring on the side of grace.** We will avoid being overly offended at minor or unintentional offenses. We will not be easily irritated or easily drawn into conflict. We will seek to see others through the lens of grace we have experienced from God.
- **When others sin against us in more serious ways, we will follow biblical direction and seek to bring awareness to them of the offenses they have committed.** We understand our responsibility to others in the body of Christ to do all we can to help restore them to usefulness. We will follow the directions of Matthew 18, Galatians 6, and other pertinent passages as we bring loving confrontation to them.

- **We will be willing to forgive others and be reconciled to them as they repent and seek our forgiveness.** We will not withhold forgiveness from those who repent, confess their sins, and request our forgiveness. We will grant forgiveness to them freely, just as God in Christ also forgave us, bearing the cost of the offense in ourselves.
- **In situations where reconciliation is not possible, we will guard our hearts against the desire for vengeance by praying for those who have wronged us.** We will recognize the possibility of bitterness creeping into our hearts and will pray for our enemies as Jesus commanded and modeled for us.
- **We will release those who refuse to pursue reconciliation into the jurisdiction of God, the only just Judge.** Recognizing that God alone is Judge and for us to judge others is to play God, we will release those who will not be reconciled into God's hands, preferably that He might grant them repentance, but ultimately trusting in His perfect love and justice to do what is right concerning them.
- **We will place our hopes for ultimate shalom, which includes perfect love and justice, in the coming Person of Jesus Christ and recognize our limitations in the present.** Instead of looking for shalom through human means, we will accept our place and circumstances at this point in history prior to the return of Christ. We will refrain from attempting to usher in ultimate shalom, though as citizens of the kingdom to come, we will pursue shalom within its current limitations in every situation in which we have a part to play.

Lord, help us to live as sons and daughters of the living God, to rightfully walk in a way that reflects our relationship and likeness to You.
Amen.

The Reunion

Dave and Carol continued to pray for Bill and Jane the rest of their married life. As a result, they experienced greater maturity as individuals and grew closer together as a couple. They hadn't spoken to Bill and Jane, however, since the meetings with the peacemaking team. Dave and Carol enjoyed a long married life together. It had been at least twenty-five years since the incident with Bill and Jane. They celebrated their fiftieth wedding anniversary together on a trip to the holy land. Just as they pulled up to the western wall in Jerusalem, there was a loud explosion. Dave looked for Carol but couldn't find her through the smoke and chaos. He grabbed his head. It was bleeding heavily. He heard sirens. Then everything went blank.

The next thing he knew, he was in a beautiful place. Carol was there with him and others from their families whom they hadn't seen in years. The first thing he noticed was he didn't have any pain. Everyone looked joyful. He felt as if he didn't have a care in the world, a feeling he had never felt before. Then, Dave saw Him. He had wounds on His hands and feet. And those eyes, so filled with love more than any he had ever seen. He knew instantly Who He was. He fell into His embrace and released years of pent up tears from a life of pain and suffering. The Lord wiped them all away as He held Dave in his arms.

Dave wiped the remaining dew from his eyes. His vision was a bit blurry, but as his eyes dried he began to see more clearly. "Was that . . . ?" "Is that . . . ?" he asked the Lord. "Yes, Dave, those are your old friends, Bill and Jane. I heard the prayers you and Carol prayed for them and I answered them. They've been here for a while waiting to see you." Bill approached Dave. Jane approached Carol.

Bill couldn't get the words out. In his heart he had planned the speech so many times, he could do it from memory. But Dave didn't let him say it. Dave embraced his long-lost friend. The two wept tears of joy. Jane and Carol held each other. The Lord rejoiced. It was good to be in the New Jerusalem.

Appendix A:
An Analysis of Therapeutic Forgiveness

The topic of forgiveness is of widespread interest both within the evangelical church and among society today. Books, television programs, and other media sources tout the healing power of unconditional forgiveness. This is the silver bullet that brings supposed relief for believers and nonbelievers alike from the deleterious effects of past injustices committed against them. But has the church exchanged its birthright for a lie? This appendix seeks to examine that very possibility.

Therapeutic Forgiveness Defined

Therapeutic forgiveness, though not always clearly identified as such in psychological literature, is a concept connected with many well-known contemporary psychological figures. Forgiveness as a field of study began in earnest in the nineties and has continued to the present. Foremost among the advocates of forgiveness therapy is Robert Enright, the founder of the International Forgiveness Institute and professor at the University of Wisconsin, Madison. Enright and Fitzgibbons offered the following definition of forgiveness:

> People, upon rationally determining that they have been unfairly treated, forgive when they *willfully abandon resentment and related responses* (to which they have a right), and endeavor to respond to the wrongdoer based on the *moral principle of beneficence*, which may include com-

> passion, unconditional worth, generosity, and moral love (to which the wrongdoer, by nature of the hurtful act or acts, has no right).[279]

In subsequent articles, Enright et al. arrived at what has become the consensus definition in the realm of forgiveness therapy and research.[280]

> Forgiveness has been defined as the willful giving up of resentment in the face of another's (or others') considerable injustice and responding with beneficence to the offender even though the offender has no right to the forgiver's moral goodness. . . . Forgiveness is an act freely chosen by the forgiver.[281]

Therapeutic forgiveness is often confused with forgiveness, in general, or biblical forgiveness, in particular. It is important that a thoughtful discussion of the salient points of therapeutic forgiveness precede any attempt to validate or invalidate its claims. Though the concept under consideration is multifaceted and complex, there are several key concepts that can be used to organize a consideration of this understanding of forgiveness.

THERAPEUTIC FORGIVENESS IS AN INTRAPERSONAL PROCESS.

As Lewis Smedes put it, "forgiveness is a private activity in the mind." Forgiveness, in a therapeutic sense, is often meant to encompass the reduction of painful feelings, thoughts, and behaviors and to increase positive and prosocial feelings, thoughts, and behaviors within the individual.[282]

---

279. Robert D. Enright and Richard P. Fitzgibbons, *Helping Clients Forgive: An Empirical Guide for Resolving Anger and Restoring Hope* (Washington DC: American Psychological Association, 2000), 24.

280. The psychological community, for the most part embracing therapeutic forgiveness, also includes some dissenters. Susan Forward with Craig Buck, for example, completely disagree with the premise that forgiveness is the key to healing past wounds. See *Toxic Parents: Overcoming Their Hurtful Legacy and Reclaiming Your Life*. Others also conclude that some skepticism of the new forgiveness interventions is warranted.

281. Thomas W. Baskin and Robert D. Enright, "Intervention Studies on Forgiveness: A Meta-Analysis," *Journal of Counseling and Development* 82 (Winter 2004): 80.

282. Nathaniel G. Wade, Chad V. Johnson, and Julia E. Meyer, "Understanding Concerns about Interventions to Promote Forgiveness: A Review of the Literature," *Psychotherapy: Theory, Research, Practice, Training* 45, no. 1 (2008): 89.

This *intrapersonal healing* is the goal of much forgiveness therapy. Through the practice of forgiveness, clients are able to "resolve bitterness, sadness, and fear and even move to a place of acceptance and peace without the additional complication of resolving a relationship with a hurtful person."[283]

THERAPEUTIC FORGIVENESS IS BASED ON THE GOODNESS OF HUMANITY.

Forgiveness is a virtue. Forgiving those who offend us, with or without their confession and repentance, is a means of our transcendence. We show ourselves to be virtuous by our ability to unilaterally forgive another. Second, our forgiveness of others is predicated in part on our ability to see them as better than their offenses. There is an *inherent optimism about human nature* implied in therapeutic literature. Smedes showed this bias as he described the view Christians should take up toward those who have offended them. He suggested that "they are not only people who hurt us; this is not the deepest truth about them."[284] Earlier in his introduction he proposed that people are unfair and hurt each other deeply "despite their best intentions."[285] The complicity and culpability of those who offend are extinguished in favor of a view that sees offenses as arising by mistake.

THERAPEUTIC FORGIVENESS IS PRACTICED FOR THE GOOD OF THE FORGIVER.

As Lewis Smedes articulated, "we need to forgive the unrepentant *for our own sake*."[286] There are myriad reasons stated by advocates of therapeutic forgiveness for the offended to forgive the offender. Enright listed at least six such reasons as follows: to quiet angry feelings, to change thoughts, to improve relations with the offender, to act out of love for God (obedience to Him), to act morally, and to improve physical health.[287] These reasons to forgive primarily involve the good of the forgiver. The

283. Wade et al., "Understanding Concerns," 92.

284. Lewis B. Smedes, *Forgive and Forget: Healing the Hurts We Don't Deserve* (New York: Harper and Row, 1984), 27.

285. Smedes, *Forgive and Forget,* xii.

286. Smedes, *Forgive and Forget,* 69.

287. Robert Enright, *Forgiveness Is a Choice: A Step-By-Step Process for Resolving Anger and Restoring Hope* (Washington, DC: American Psychological Association, 2001).

mental, spiritual, and physical health of the one who forgives is greatly improved.[288]

Therapeutic forgiveness is unconditional.

Smedes addressed the issue of forgiving the unrepentant. He suggested, "Realism, it seems to me, nudges us toward forgiving people who hurt us whether or not they repent for doing it. . . . we need to forgive the unrepentant for our sake."[289] Smedes' argument is pragmatic, we should forgive others unconditionally because we must admit there is no certainty of the other's repentance, and unless we release the debt, we are kept connected to them indefinitely. For one popular advocate of forgiveness therapy, the necessity of unconditionality is tied to our finiteness as creatures. Worthington commented, "Because God knows people's hearts, God can condition forgiveness on people's repentance. *Non-omniscient humans are called to forgive unconditionally*."[290]

Human forgiveness is substantially different from divine forgiveness.

All of the aforementioned experts are in agreement that there is, in fact, a substantial disagreement and difference between human (horizontal) and divine (vertical) forgiveness. This inherent difference is what allows an author like Worthington to distinguish between the two, thus making the analogy between them incongruous.

Biblical Forgiveness Defined

In fairness, any time we undertake to represent the biblical view of any topic, we must first pause to consider that we are at best representing our view of the topic insofar as we see it revealed in Scripture. The following is a fallible attempt to represent pertinent biblical data that seems at

288.See Worthington Jr. et al., *Journal of Behavioral Medicine* 30 (2007): 291–302.

289. Smedes, *Forgive and Forget*, 69.

290. Everett Worthington, "Just Forgiving: How the Psychology and Theology of Forgiveness and Justice Inter-relate," *Journal of Psychology and Christianity* (2006): 160.

points to contradict the therapeutic concept of forgiveness. There is much disagreement among the various branches of the Christian community as to the nature of forgiveness. Substantial consensus, as appears to be the case in the therapeutic community, does not exist in Christendom. Nonetheless, the following aspects of forgiveness as presented in Scripture seem to define a different process than that of the current therapeutic community. Biblical forgiveness seems to embody a number of pertinent traits.

Biblical forgiveness is an interpersonal process.

Biblical forgiveness is a process that benefits first the offender, and then the entire community of saints and the culture at large. As such, it represents the means by which fallen humanity can dwell in any degree of redemptive harmony with God and one another. Far from being merely an intrapersonal process, *forgiveness is a relational, an interpersonal concept.* L. Gregory Jones said it well,

> When forgiveness is seen in primarily individualistic and privatistic terms, we lose sight of its central role in establishing a way of life—not only with our 'inner' selves but also in our relations with others.[291]

Biblical forgiveness is based on the work of Christ for sinners.

The atoning work of Christ is the basis of all forgiveness both between sinners and a holy God and between sinful individuals and groups. Smedes and others ignored the culpability of humanity and the need for repentance as a means of grace. All forgiveness is directly and indirectly connected to the propitiatory sacrifice of the Son of God who bore the penalty all of our sins justly deserve.

291. L. Gregory Jones, *Embodying Forgiveness: A Theological Analysis* (Grand Rapids, MI: Eerdmans Publishing Co., 1995), 39.

Biblical forgiveness is for the glory of God and the good of others.

Biblical forgiveness is related to the biblical understanding of sin. The Scripture portrays us all as needy undeserving sinners. From a biblical perspective, we all, both offender and offended, are in need of the mercy of forgiveness. Forgiveness is not primarily intended, biblically speaking, for the offended but rather for the Creator and for the offender. It is for the restorative good of the offender and the glory of God.

Biblical forgiveness is conditional as a part of the process of restoration and reconciliation.

Not all Christian perspectives agree on this point. However, many thoughtful exegetes would concur that biblical forgiveness between individuals is a conditional transaction. This conclusion has been well supported in a recent work by Chris Brauns, who demonstrated that the historic teaching of the church reflects an understanding of conditional rather than unconditional forgiveness.[292] In summary then, the concepts of therapeutic and biblical forgiveness can be compared as illustrated in Table 3 below.

Table 3. A Comparison of Therapeutic and Biblical Forgiveness

THERAPEUTIC FORGIVENESS	BIBLICAL FORGIVENESS
Intrapersonal Process	Interpersonal Process
Based on the Goodness of Humanity	Based on the Work of Christ
For the Sake of the Offended	For the Glory of God / Good of Others
Unconditional	Conditional (Part of Restorative Process)

292. Chris Brauns, *Unpacking Forgiveness: Biblical Answers for Complex Questions and Deep Wounds* (Wheaton, IL: Crossway Books, 2008).

Therapeutic Forgiveness Examined

As L. Gregory Jones lamented, "It seems as though Christian forgiveness is too costly for many people; consequently, they seek a cheap, therapeutic forgiveness in its place."[293] This is not to say therapeutic forgiveness literature is void of any valid contribution, but rather the concept as currently defined in psychological literature is at many points difficult to reconcile with biblical data. The foundation of therapeutic forgiveness, being the inherent goodness of humanity and the personal well-being and emotional adjustment of the offended, is inconsistent with biblical revelation. We forgive because we have been forgiven and as we have been forgiven. God forgives us as sinners because we are in need of forgiveness. His forgiveness restores us to a right relationship with Him. He benefits as the forgiver but indirectly. So it is with our forgiveness of others. The one who stands in need of forgiveness is the primary target of its practice.

Therapeutic forgiveness can be shown to differ substantially from forgiveness as described in Scripture. It is, nonetheless, the dominant thinking among most professing believers today. The biblical paradigm of forgiveness seems absurd to many in light of our modern enlightened perspective. Forgiveness is such a significant and central aspect of the subject of Christian conciliation and Christian theology that without giving some serious and critical scrutiny to this new therapeutic view, we may find ourselves drifting hopelessly away from the anchor of biblical truth altogether.

293. Jones, *Embodying Forgiveness*, 36.

Appendix B: Conditional Forgiveness Quotations

Jay E. Adams

It is clear that forgiveness—promising another never to bring up his offense again to use it against him—is conditioned on the offender's willingness to confess it as sin and to seek forgiveness. *You are not obligated to forgive an unrepentant sinner*, but you are obligated to try to bring him to repentance. . . . Such forgiveness is modeled after God's forgiveness, which is unmistakably conditioned on faith and repentance.[294]

Richard Baxter

A brother as a brother, *is not to be so forgiven*, as to be restored to our estimation and affection, and usage of him as a brother, either in spiritual account, or intimate special love and familiarity, *as long as he is impenitent in his gross offenses*; and that is, till he turn again and say, I repent.[295]

294. Jay E. Adams, *From Forgiven to Forgiving: Learning to Forgive One Another God's Way* (Amityville, NY: 1994), 37 (italics added).

295. Richard Baxter, *A Christian Directory* (Morgan, PA: Soli Deo Gloria Publications, 1996) as taken from the 1846 edition printed in London by George Virtue, 788 (italics added).

Dietrich Bonhoeffer

Cheap grace is the preaching of *forgiveness without requiring repentance.*[296]

Chris Brauns

Make no mistake—God does not forgive all. God's forgiveness is conditional . . . And forgiveness is not only conditional for God. It should be conditional in our relationships, too. . . . *complete forgiveness can only take place when there is repentance.*[297]

The Bible always presents forgiveness as something that happens between two parties. Contrary to the conventional understanding, I believe the notion of automatic forgiveness itself fosters bitterness. We are created with a standard of justice written on our hearts. When we forgive someone who is not repentant, we are acting in a way that is unjust.[298]

Ardel Caneday

We debase the cross of Christ by petty refusal to forgive the sins of those who repent, but we also debase and cheapen the death of Christ by unprincipled granting of forgiveness to individuals who remain unrepentant for sins they have committed against us. We prize the cross and live out the gospel when we bestow forgiveness of sins only to those who confess and repent and when we do not diminish the grace of forgiveness by granting it to the unrepentant but instead beckon them to repent lest they perish. We uphold the power and glory of the cross by graciously and indiscriminately offering but not bestowing forgiveness of sins to all who sin against us but who remain unrepentant.[299]

---

296. Dietrich Bonhoeffer, *The Cost of Discipleship*, trans. R. H. Fuller and Irmgard Booth (New York: Macmillan, 1963), 47 (italics added).

297. Brauns, *Unpacking Forgiveness,* 21 (italics added).

298. Brauns, *Unpacking Forgiveness,* 147.

299. Ardel Canedy, *Must Christians Always Forgive? A Biblical Primer and Grammar on Forgiveness of Sins* (Mount Hermon, CA: Center for Cultural Leadership, 2011), 18.

Tim Challies

According to the Bible, our forgiveness of one another is to follow God's model of forgiveness. . . . We are to forgive as God forgives or in the same manner as He forgives. . . . It is beyond any reasonable doubt that God's forgiveness is conditional. God is not a Universalist who chooses to forgive all men for their offense against Him. Nor does He offer forgiveness without expectation or condition. Rather, God forgives only those who turn to Him in repentance and who put their trust in Him. We affirm that God's offer of forgiveness is universal, in that He extends it to all humanity. But the reality of forgiveness is only for those who accept the conditions of faith and repentance. . . . Nowhere in the Bible do I find that God holds us to a higher standard of forgiveness than He does. If God's forgiveness is conditional, and if we are to model Him, our forgiveness will also be conditional. . . . in the fullest sense, *forgiveness requires repentance.*[300]

J. Ligon Duncan

This is a question that many Christians have never thought through. I think that Christians who have themselves harbored unjustified bitternesses and have been unforgiving in places and in ways that they should have been forgiving, often when they are confronted with and gripped by the radical teaching of Christ on forgiveness, out of sorrow for their own sin, read Jesus' teaching on forgiveness in such a way that they understand it to mean that forgiveness is an automatic obligation in every circumstance, irrespective of the repentance of the other party. And, again, I think that that is a mistake.

I believe that *forgiveness always has in view reconciliation*, and reconciliation is always two-sided. So if there is not a repentance corresponding to a forgiveness, then very often there is an impossibility of reconciliation. I think that whatever we think about forgiveness, forgiveness is a compo-

300. Tim Challies, "Is Forgiveness Conditional or Unconditional?" accessed February 15, 2008, http://www.challies.com/articles/is-forgiveness-conditional-or-unconditional (italics added).

nent to what is a larger picture, and the larger picture is reconciliation. And reconciliation is necessarily two-sided. Consequently, I think it is important for us to talk about both forgiveness and readiness to forgive. There may be circumstances where a reconciliation is impossible, but a readiness to reconcile can still be present with a believer.

Consequently, I would want to make that distinction when I was counseling a believer who was in a circumstance where there was not a present possibility of reconciliation of the relationship. *Instead of telling them that they need to forgive or they will become bitter, I think I would rather say that you need to be ready to forgive and not to be captured by your bitterness.*[301]

Ken Ellis, RBC Ministries

If our Lord wanted us always to unilaterally forgive those who harm us, then why did He say in His teaching, "Rebuke [lovingly confront] him, and if he repents forgive him" (Luke 17:1–4)? . . . it is clear that Jesus' teaching here is consistent with other scriptures (Matt. 18:15–17). . . . According to the Bible, God's own example is to forgive us when we acknowledge our wrongs and express our trust in His Son. . . . In both cases [salvation in Luke 18:13–14 and forgiveness in 1 John 1:9], *God's forgiveness is conditional, dependent on the acknowledgement of wrongdoing by the sinning individual.*[302]

Gary Inrig

We are to forgive repentant offenders as fully and freely as possible. But *we are not simply to forgive, forget, and move on when people refuse to repent.* For the sake of both the offender and the offended, we are to pursue truth and a process of restoration.[303]

---

301. Brauns, *Unpacking Forgiveness*, 208 (italics added).

302. Ken Ellis, "Avoiding the Dangers of Superficial Forgiveness," online booklet (RBC Ministries, 2004), 20–22, accessed April 4, 2013, http://web001.rbc.org/pdf/discovery-series/avoiding-the-dangers-of-superficial-forgiveness.pdf (italics added).

303. Gary Inrig, *Forgiveness: Discover the Power and Reality of Authentic Christian Forgiveness* (Grand Rapids, MI: Discovery House Publishers, 2005), 156 (italics added).

Kairos Document

No reconciliation, no forgiveness, and no negotiations are possible without repentance. The biblical teaching on reconciliation and forgiveness makes it quite clear that nobody can be forgiven and reconciled with God unless he or she repents of their sins. *Nor are we expected to forgive the unrepentant sinner.* . . . It would be totally unchristian to plead for reconciliation and peace before the present injustices have been removed. Any such plea plays into the hands of the oppressor by trying to persuade those of us who are oppressed to accept our oppression and to be reconciled to the intolerable crimes that are committed against us. That is not Christian reconciliation; it is sin. It is asking us to become accomplices in our own oppression, to become servants of the devil.[304]

John MacArthur, Jr.

Sometimes forgiveness (in matters that are not small) must be conditional. . . . There are times when it is necessary to confront an offender. In such cases, *unconditional forgiveness (overlooking and forbearance) is not an option.* These generally involve more serious sins—not petty or picayune complaints, but soul-threatening sins or transgressions that endanger the fellowship of the saints.[305]

John Murray

Forgiveness is a definite act performed by us on the fulfillment of certain conditions. . . . *Forgiveness is something actively administered on the repentance of the person who is to be forgiven.* We greatly impoverish ourselves and impair the relations that we should sustain to our brethren when we fail to appreciate what is involved in forgiveness.[306]

---

304. Newberger, *Face of Conflict*, 242 (italics added). The Kairos Document, signed in 1985 by 156 signatories from 20 different South African denominations is a Christian, biblical, and theological comment on the political crisis in South Africa.

305. MacArthur, *Freedom and Power of Forgiveness*, 128 (italics added).

306. John Murray, "A Lesson on Forgiveness," in *The Collected Writings of John Murray* (Carlisle, PA: The Banner of Truth Trust, 2007), 3:191 (italics added).

Kenneth Newberger

There is widespread agreement on the biblical teaching that God's forgiveness is conditional upon a sinner's repentance. . . . whereas his love is unconditional, His forgiveness is not. . . . Divine forgiveness is not automatic. . . . What is true of God is also true of us. *An individual can be a loving person and yet withhold forgiveness from a person who is unrepentant.*[307] (italics added)

Unconditional forgiveness to unrepentant murderers, rapists, and swindlers is contrary to and stands in direct opposition to the very character of God. Does God forgive the unrepentant? No! Should we attempt to "out-love" God by forgiving those He is unwilling to forgive? Absurd! We are to forgive as God forgives, which is based on repentance. . . . True forgiveness does not simply involve the offended party unilaterally forgiving and forgetting. *True forgiveness first must be preceded by the offending party's remembering and repenting.*[308] (italics added)

David Pawson

Forgiveness is therefore a free gift. However, that does not mean that there is nothing we have to do to have it. At the very least, there a need to ask for it and receive it. Unfortunately, there are other misunderstandings, including two big ones—that forgiveness is unlimited and unconditional. These tend to cheapen what has been so costly. . . . Unfortunately, many fail to distinguish between deserving and receiving forgiveness. There is nothing we can do to deserve or earn merit and thus make a contribution to our "worthiness" to be forgiven. However, it is a fundamental mistake to think that there are no necessary conditions. . . . *First, before a person can be forgiven, they need to repent. . . . Second, after a person has been forgiven, they need to forgive.*[309]

---

307. Newberger, *Face of Conflict*, 233-236.

308. Newberger, *Face of Conflict*, 238-239.

309. Pawson, *Once Saved, Always Saved?*, 24–25 (italics added).

John Piper

One last observation remains: forgiveness of an unrepentant person doesn't look the same as forgiveness of a repentant person. In fact, *I am not sure that in the Bible the term forgiveness is ever applied to an unrepentant person.* Jesus said in Luke 17:3–4 "Be on your guard! If your brother sins, rebuke him; and if he repents, forgive him. And if he sins against you seven times a day, and returns to you seven times, saying, 'I repent,' forgive him." So there's a sense in which full forgiveness is only possible in response to repentance.

But even when a person does not repent (cf. Matt. 18:17) we are commanded to love our enemy and pray for those who persecute us and do good to those who hate us (Luke 6:27). The difference is that *when a person who wronged us does not repent with contrition and confession and conversion (turning from sin to righteousness), he cuts off the full work of forgiveness.* We can still lay down our ill will; we can hand over our anger to God; we can seek to do him good; but we cannot carry through reconciliation or intimacy.[310]

Dennis Prager

Though I am a Jew, I believe that a vibrant Christianity is essential if America's moral decline is to be reversed. . . . I am appalled and frightened by this feel-good doctrine of automatic forgiveness. This doctrine undermines the moral foundations of American civilization because it advances the amoral notion that no matter how much you hurt other people, millions of your fellow citizens will immediately forgive you. This doctrine destroys Christianity's central moral tenets about forgiveness—that *forgiveness, even by God, is contingent on the sinner repenting, and that it can only be given to the sinner by the one against whom he sinned. . . .* Some people have a more sophisticated defense of the forgive-everyone-

310. Grace Covenant Church's website, accessed April 13, 2013, http://www.gracecovonline.com/blog/post/quotes-on-forgiveness-as-conditional-or-unconditional:-justin-taylor-and-john-piper (italics added).

everything doctrine: Victims should be encouraged to forgive all evil done to them because doing so is psychologically healthy [*therapeutic forgiveness*]. It brings "closure." This, too, is selfishness masquerading as idealism: "Though you do not deserve to be forgiven, and though you may not be sorry. I forgive you because I want to feel better." The rise of the theology of automatic "forgiveness" is only one more sign of the decline of traditional religiosity and morality. . . . If young Christians have inherited more values from the '60s culture than from their religion, where can we look for help?[311]

Ken Sande

Ideally forgiveness should follow repentance. . . . When an offense is too serious to overlook and the offender has not yet repented, you may need to approach forgiveness as a two-stage process. The first stage requires *having an attitude of forgiveness* [formerly called *positional forgiveness*], and the second, *granting forgiveness* [formerly called *transactional forgiveness*]. Having an attitude of forgiveness is unconditional and is a commitment you make to God. . . . By his grace you seek to maintain a loving and merciful attitude toward someone who has offended you. . . . *Granting forgiveness is conditional on the repentance of the offender and takes place between you and that person.* . . . When there has been a serious offense, it would not be appropriate to [make the promises of forgiveness] until the offender has repented.[312]

Andrew Sandlin

One of the great myths of our time is the virtue of "unconditional forgiveness." We hear Christians again and again demanding that if other believers do not forgive in all situations, they are not being "Christ-like." Indeed, many Christians are under the impression the Bible teaches that God himself forgives in every situation, and therefore of we are to be godly

311. Dennis Prager, "The Sin of Forgiveness," *The Wall Street Journal* (December 15, 1997) accessed April 13, 2013, www.murdervictims.com/Forgiveness.htm (italics added).

312. Sande, *The Peacemaker*, 210–211 (italics added).

Christians, we too must not allow any conditions whatever to enter into our forgiveness of others. The fact that the most cursory reading of the Bible refutes this notion has not cautioned its perpetrators.[313]

John Stott

We are to rebuke a brother if he sins against us; *we are to forgive him if he repents—and only if he repents.* We must beware of cheapening forgiveness. . . . God's forgiveness of us and our forgiving of one another . . . both are conditional upon repentance. If a brother who has sinned against us refuses to repent, we should not forgive him. Does this startle you? It is what Jesus taught. . . . If we can restore to full and intimate fellowship with ourselves a sinning and unrepentant brother, we reveal not the depth of our love but its shallowness, for we are doing what is not for his highest good.[314]

Justin Taylor

"Love your enemies" is something that we should do at all times and in all places. It is modeled after God's love for his enemies, whom he loves even when they are "unjust" and "evil" (Luke 6:35). At the same time, our forgiveness of others is likewise modeled upon God's forgiveness of sinners, whom he forgives conditioned upon their repentance. *God does not forgive apart from repentance; neither should we.* In major offenses, we are not to forgive the unrepentant.

In the event of a tragedy that involves the loss of human life brought about by wanton human sin, it is therefore wrong for Christians to call upon immediate forgiveness in the absence of repentance. Such a call both cheapens and misunderstands the biblical doctrine of forgiveness.[315]

---

313. P. Andrew Sandlin, preface to *Must Christians Always Forgive? A Biblical Primer and Grammar on Forgiveness of Sins*, by Ardel Canedy (Mount Hermon, CA: Center for Cultural Leadership, 2011).

314. Newberger, *Face of Conflict*, 240 (italics added).

315. Grace Covenant Church's website, accessed April 13, 2013, http://www.gracecovonline.com/blog/post/quotes-on-forgiveness-as-conditional-or-unconditional:-justin-taylor-and-john-piper (italics added).

About the Author

Andy Johnson has been passionately focused on the issue of conflict for over fourteen years. Having experienced significant conflict in church and extended family relationships, he is cognizant of the pain and challenges that accompany this difficult subject. He brings his analytical mind to this topic and seeks to clear away many of the common cobwebs in the thinking of modern evangelicals.

Andy is a professional consultant and coach, a trainer, a licensed mental health counselor, a pastor, and a former architect and business owner. He heads up Restoration Consulting with a focus aimed specifically at churches and other ministry organizations as part of his work helping them develop health and prevent conflict. He holds a Bachelor of Architecture degree from Cal Poly, San Luis Obispo, and a Master of Science degree from Northwest Nazarene University.

Andy is married to his high school sweetheart, Sherri. Together they have been blessed with three wonderful daughters (and one son-in-law). They live in southwest Idaho.

Restoration Consulting

Conflict destroys the fabric of families, churches and other organizations. For this reason, the prevention and resolution of conflict is one of the main areas of focus for Restoration Consulting. Restoration provides explicitly Christian consulting services that are directly related to the presence of conflict in a fallen world. We provide consultation, coaching, and other health-related services to the following groups and organizations:

- *Local churches (pastors, other ministry staff, boards, lay leaders)*
- *Denominations (regional overseers, executive leadership)*
- *Parachurch organizations (missionaries, staff members, volunteers)*
- *Families (extended family systems, couples, parents, and adult children)*

Working with these differing groups, we provide services that include:

- *Conflict coaching and mediation*
- *Conflict prevention training and team development*
- *Executive coaching and leadership training*
- *Talent and organizational health assessments*
- *Workshops, seminars, and speaking engagements*

At Restoration, we are passionate about helping Kingdom-minded organizations become more effective in fulfilling their mission. An intentional focus on individual and team health leads to an increase in overall impact.

Conflict is inevitable. Perhaps you're currently in the midst of a conflict situation. Or, maybe you're not currently but you have been previously and you would like to build in protection from future conflict situations in your organization. If you would like to inquire about services we provide, please contact us or see our website for further information.

www.restoration-consulting.com